Becoming The Radiant Woman

Reclaiming the Woman You Were Always Meant to Be

Celeste Case-Ruchala

DOUBLE EDGE
publishing
TM

Becoming the Radiant Woman
Reclaiming the Woman You Were Always Meant to Be
☺2025 by Celeste Case-Ruchala

Paperback ISBN: 978-1-969204-01-2
Ebook ISBN: 978-1-969204-03-6
Editor and formatting: Ashley Hagan
Cover Design: Tammy Largin
Publisher: Double Edge 7 Publishing, Franklin, Tennessee

DISCLAIMER: This book is not written as therapy or clinical advice. I am not a psychologist, psychiatrist, or licensed therapist. These pages hold stories, reflections, and practices from my own journey of becoming. They are not rules, but invitations. They are not prescriptions, but possibilities. If you find yourself in need of deeper support, I encourage you to reach out to trusted mental health professionals. My hope is that the stories and tools within these pages open your eyes to the power of shared healing—that through the lives of others, you may find new ways to shape your own.

DOUBLE EDGE
publishing

Praise for *Becoming the Radiant Woman*

"To the woman who needs this book:

You don't need another checklist for how to be stronger, prettier, or more productive; you need a reminder of who you already are. *Becoming the Radiant Woman* is that reminder. Celeste doesn't hand you a glossy version of empowerment; she shares her heart through storytelling so real it brought me to tears (especially the Ironman story).

This book gave me the courage to question the masks I've been wearing and the strength to begin listening to my own voice again. It will challenge you, comfort you, and call you home to yourself. If you've ever felt like you were "too much" or "not enough," you'll see yourself in these pages; you'll finish them knowing you were always more than enough.

Read this book. Let it be the turning point where you stop settling and start shining."

—Meghan Davis

"I was completely drawn in on the first statement of the introduction —Powerful. It made me say, "YES!!! Me! Yes!" The authentic and vulnerable introduction brought me to tears and hit me like a ton of bricks, and I couldn't wait to read more.

After the tears, I said to myself, "I want to give her the biggest hug." Celeste Case-Ruchala is amazing, and her vulnerability makes me feel it's ok to talk about my experiences. Thank you, Celeste, for being real and blazing the trail so we can follow behind!"

—Jenna Andrews

"Celeste's book blends soulful storytelling with usable tools. The move from hyper-independence to welcoming support is powerful, and her R.A.D.I.A.N.C.E. framework keeps it actionable. Her warm, gentle voice invites you into her life where lived moments become tools you can use."

—Lindsey Ackerman

"Without question, the Introduction will stay with me forever. It broke me open a little. I think every woman who's ever felt limited or unseen would find a piece of herself there. It reminded me of my younger self, the one who quietly dreamed of more but didn't know how to get there. Even now, as I try to rebuild and restart my career, those words echo in me. They gave me hope that growth isn't something we miss, it's something we can always return to."

—Lakshmi Sravya

To the women who carry everyone else's weight and wonder if they'll ever feel alive again.
This is for you.
May it be a spark, a reminder, a lantern on your way home to yourself.

TABLE OF CONTENTS

FOREWORD

by Criss Madrigal

THERE COMES A POINT in every woman's life when the silence becomes unbearable. When the smile you've worn for so long feels more like armor than joy. When the script you've followed—dutiful daughter, devoted partner, successful professional, ever-present caregiver—suddenly collapses under its own weight.

I know this intimately, because I lived it.

I spent twenty years in the corporate world doing all the things "success" was supposed to look like. At the same time, I became a mother of three children in less than two years, including twins with complex medical needs. I wore the mask of the strong, capable woman—career-driven, dependable, the one who could hold it all together.

And for a while, I did. Until my body could no longer hold the weight of the armor I had worn for years.

At forty, I no longer recognized the woman in the mirror. I stared at a body with an empty soul. A woman desperately wanting to be rescued from the prison she created for herself. Then I developed an autoimmune condition that forced me to stop running on autopilot. I had abandoned myself so completely that my body finally screamed what my voice had been too afraid to say: this is not sustainable.

And that is why *Becoming the Radiant Woman* is not just another book; it's a lifeline.

There are some books you read and others you feel. This one is one you'll feel deep in your heart. Every word resonated deep in my core. Every sentence anchored in my truth. I felt seen, and so will you.

Like Celeste, I spent years in the world of Human Resources and corporate leadership, always achieving, always performing, always making sure I was doing all the "right" things. On paper, everything looked great. But on the inside, I felt something was missing. I was living by roles and expectations, not by my essence. And in that journey, I lost pieces of myself.

That's why I felt this book so deeply. Celeste gives language to what so many women feel but struggle to say. She puts words to the quiet ache of self-abandonment, the constant striving for approval, the endless performance of confidence while feeling insecure inside. And then, she offers a way back home.

This book will connect with every woman. You will feel seen because the magic Celeste shares so eloquently describes the woman of today—the one carrying so much, giving so much, and often leaving herself last. She writes for the woman who has been everything to everyone and is finally ready to be something for herself.

I know her words are true because I've lived them. I know the exhaustion of mom guilt, the guilt of saying no, the fear of speaking my truth. I also know the freedom of reclaiming my voice, honoring my body, and choosing to live in alignment. Today, in the work I do, I help women do the same. So, when I say that every chapter of this book is medicine, I mean it.

Every reflection and contemplation holds the power to take you through your own journey of remembrance. A journey that's long been waiting for you.

This book has the power to transform your life. Not in a superficial way, but in a soul-deep, lasting way. Read it knowing you will not be the same woman who picked it up. In fact, you'll walk away a radiant woman—one who sees her value, her worth, and her brilliance. Because life will hand you the biggest mirror, and for the first time, you'll be able to see who you really are.

And let me tell you—what you'll see is breathtaking.

Why does this matter now? Because we are in a season where women are craving to find themselves, to be seen for who they really are. You cannot keep waiting for permission to take up space, to trust yourself, to live fully alive. The old rules of success and approval are crumbling.

We are entering a new era. The era of liberation, of individuality, of empowerment, not from ego but from self-recognition. From your anchored truth, not societal beliefs. From your true remembrance, not from superficial narratives. The world needs more women who are radiant, aligned, magnetic, and unapologetically themselves. That woman is YOU!

This book holds the permission slip to trust yourself fully and take up space. As you read, take your time. Let the words anchor in your truth. Let them stir what's been asleep. Awaken your inner goddess. Let the words remind you of the parts of yourself you've forgotten or tucked away for far too long. Because every story, every reflection, every invitation in these pages isn't just about Celeste—it's about you.

I felt seen in this book and so will you. And when you finish, you'll be grateful because you'll see yourself more clearly than you ever have before.

This is your mirror. This is your moment. And this—this is your becoming.

With love and remembrance,

Criss Madrigal

Founder—Soul Aligned Network, Life Alchemist, Alignment Coach

THE INVITATION

The Moment You Decide, "I Can't Keep Living Like This!"

AS PER USUAL, I'm doing all the things. Raised by two professor parents with doctorates and achievements lining the walls, excellence wasn't optional. It was the baseline. And 36 years later, I'm still carrying it all.

I'm writing this book. Working full-time in a role that chose me more than I chose it—managing consultants, implementing tech systems, and juggling client expectations—all far removed from the degrees I once worked so hard to earn. I travel when customers need support even when my heart longs to be elsewhere.

I'm coaching women through their becoming—guiding them from the quiet ache of "Is this all there is?" to the versions of themselves they almost forgot was possible. I'm creating social media content and podcasts that remind them they're not broken, just hidden beneath years of expectation and noise.

I'm training for a marathon, quietly chasing down a Boston-qualifying pace with miles stacked on miles. Most days, I'm swimming, lifting, tired but staying focused. I'm showing up for my friendships and nurturing my relationships with intention. I'm managing a household, walking my dog, cooking decent meals, stretching when I can, and collapsing when I can't.

And the truth? Some days, I'm thriving. But, other days, I am barely holding it together with threads. Not because I'm failing.

But because I am carrying everything—and no one taught me how to put anything down.

My breaking point didn't look dramatic. It never does, not at first. It was a massage. A necessary part of my marathon training and taking care of my body. Just. A. Massage.

But it was *awful*. Light, ineffective, frustratingly disconnected from what my body was screaming for. This woman must've weighed ten pounds soaking wet, and I desperately needed a sumo wrestler. Someone who could read the tension in my body like Braille and work it out with force and fire.

She asked if the pressure was okay. I said, *"You can go harder."* She tried, I think … but I said it again. Still, nothing changed. It was like being in a slow-motion argument with the universe where you're screaming inside but nothing's changing.

I felt my throat close up. I wanted to leap off the table, grab my clothes, and just walk out. I wanted to shout, "If this were Thai food, I'd need an eleven. I need to feel the relief in my muscles … yesterday."

But instead? I laid there. Quiet. Silent. Shrinking. And then … I cried. Not loud. Not messy. Just quietly. Hoping she wouldn't notice. Tears slowly drying up by the towel on the face rest, nose dripping through the hole in the table. A silent, sharp ache that seeped through my chest and got stuck in my bones.

But what really broke me wasn't the massage—it was the bitter echo of silence, the one I'd been taught to hold in my mouth like a secret. It was every moment from childhood until today when I chose to swallow my voice instead of speak. When I felt deep down that something wasn't okay, but I still kept my mouth shut. When I cried instead of speaking because that's what always came out first.

Because I didn't want to be rude or to cause anyone else discomfort. Or to be too much. I didn't want to be *that woman*.

But this time, the tears didn't bring relief. They felt like a betrayal. To the woman lying on the table chasing down miles to Boston. To my future self. To the woman I'm dreaming of becoming. Because the woman I want to be? *She speaks.*

She uses her voice even when it shakes. Even when it's awkward. Even when she's scared. Even when it might make someone uncomfortable. She doesn't contort herself to fit into someone else's comfort zone. Not anymore.

She says, "No. That's not okay."

She says, "Actually, I need something different."

She says, "This is who I am now."

This is the moment I realized tears aren't enough anymore. They can't be my only release valve. I don't want to cry every time I try to advocate for myself. I want to stand in my truth and speak up when something hurts. I want to take up space without apology and be authentically me. To show up without a mask.

And maybe you're there, too. Maybe you've had your own version of that massage table. Maybe it was a meeting where you stayed quiet when you wanted to speak up. A conversation where you softened your truth instead of saying what you meant. A dinner where you felt forced to linger when you wanted to leave. A thousand little moments where you betrayed yourself in the name of being palatable.

This book is for that version of you.

The one who feels like she's doing everything in life correctly and still feels like something's missing. The one who is tired of being the strong one. The one who is done being quiet. The one who wants to stop just holding it together and start to *actually thrive*. The one who is ready to come home to herself.

This is a reclamation.

A return to your most authentic self. A breaking of the old rules. A new way of living, rooted in presence, truth, and your own radiant power. You're not here to fit in. You're here to *become*.

This book is your invitation.

So, if you're holding yourself together with grit and grace and a little bit of rage—you're in the right place. We begin here. With the moment you said:

Enough.

INTRODUCTION
The Reclamation of You

THERE COMES A MOMENT in every woman's life when she realizes she's been living in the shadows—shadows cast by the world's expectations, by roles she never consciously chose, by the version of herself she thought she had to be. A moment when she realizes the harsh truth of the lie that has been fed to her through years of conditioning from Disney movies and pop culture, by social media, relationships, work, friends, and family.

This book is not going to be about transforming into someone new; it's not here to teach you how to be stronger, braver, or better.

It's about reclaiming the woman you've always been—the radiant, authentic self who was never truly lost, only buried under layers of expectation. The world may have taught you to hide her, to quiet her, to play small. But this is your invitation to uncover her again—to brush off your truth and stand in the light of your own becoming.

This is not reinvention. It is a *return*.

A return to the woman you were truly meant to be.

For me, that moment of realization happened two weeks before my wedding. And certainly not in the way you'd think. It wasn't the day I walked away from the altar. It wasn't in a dramatic breakdown or some fiery declaration of self-liberation. It was a quiet, almost forgettable Tuesday—the kind of day you wouldn't expect to hold a turning point. I was at a tech conference in Las Vegas walking the

Strip with a colleague after ten hours of back-to-back sessions. It was 100 degrees at 9 p.m., and I was still dressed in my professional best—hair perfect, blazer on, makeup intact—doing what I always did: showing up polished, even while I was slowly unraveling inside.

We were just chatting—about work, life, nothing of consequence —when he suddenly turned to me and asked, "Can I ask you something?"

I nodded, assuming it would be some more light small talk, not anything of consequence. *Definitely* nothing life changing.

Instead, he asked, "Have you ever truly felt seen?"

And I broke. Right there in the middle of the sidewalk on the Las Vegas Strip, something inside of me shattered. I burst into tears— not the graceful, misty kind. The raw, uncontrollable kind that blindsides you when you've been holding it together for far too long. That question cut through every layer I had carefully built around myself. It cracked open the façade I had spent years perfecting—the one where I was successful, put together, and easy to love. That one question shattered my perfect illusion. It made me realize that I had spent my entire life molding myself into someone I didn't recognize —someone who didn't even know if she had ever really been seen. Who had never allowed anyone close enough to ask her that very real question. I had worn the mask for so long, it was molded to me. By the time I looked into the mirror, I wasn't sure where it ended or who I was without it.

How many of you know that feeling?

If you were to look around at your life—the job, the relationships, the routine—did you build it all on autopilot? Or even worse, by the world's suggestion? Did you trust that your scripted life was a more beautiful version than the original masterpiece but instead found it to be a forgery? A nice, neat package that looks good on paper, allowing people to see "success" but not the person who actually built it? The life where you're exhausted from performing, pleasing, and perfecting. The life where you keep telling yourself: Just a little longer. Just hold it together. Just one more day of pretending this is enough. Tomorrow will be better.

That moment on the sidewalk forced me to question everything —not just my engagement, but my entire *identity*. It stopped me in my tracks. Made me face the mirror I'd been avoiding my entire life because I was afraid to see the woman I'd hidden, the one I never really allowed to be seen. And in that stillness, I realized: *I didn't even know her. I had never even tried.* The truth? I had spent my whole life looking into the mirror but never actually seeing myself. I never stopped long enough to ask, "Who are you? What do you dream of? What lights you up?" *I* never said, "I love you. You're amazing. You don't have to earn your worth." I never even acknowledged her.

Who was I, really? Why had I spent years shrinking my voice, staying small, saying *yes* when I wanted to scream *no*? Why did I believe that having a man and getting married would finally make my life make sense—that it would be the moment my life could truly begin? I was too concerned with the outside world. *What did they think of me? Was I enough? Was I putting on the right face, the right personality, the right clothing, using the right words that would make them like me?* Even if it was all a mask.

I had a wedding dress hanging in my closet. A date circled on the calendar. A life I was *supposed to* step into. One that the world had conditioned me to crave ever since I first watched *Cinderella*. But something had cracked open inside of me, and I couldn't ignore it anymore.

I couldn't unknow what I now knew.

I spent years whispering to myself: *Tomorrow you'll do better. Tomorrow you won't be such a mess. Tomorrow you'll stop failing.* Spent years believing I was one day away from becoming the woman I was *supposed* to be—without ever asking if that version was someone I even wanted to become.

And surprisingly, no one ever stopped to ask me who I really was, either. Not my friends. Not my family. Not even my fiancé. They were all shocked when I said I wasn't sure I wanted to get married. *But he's so nice,* they said. *Why would you walk away from something so good?* But they didn't feel the same ache in my chest that I did. They didn't know how alone I felt in a life full of people I thought understood me. What I didn't realize was that if I never let myself understand who I was at *my core*, I could never expect anyone else to be able to get close enough to truly know me. If I couldn't go deep into my own understanding first, I couldn't share my internal wonder and beauty with anyone else.

The world had taught me how to perform. How to be agreeable, palatable, easy to love. To shrink from discomfort instead of naming it or to smile through what hurt. To be small when something bothered me. To tell myself I should be grateful—even when I was miserable.And maybe you've done the same. Maybe you've convinced yourself this is just how life is. That you can't trust your instincts. That you should quiet the voice inside that says there is more. That your voice is too much. Or not enough. That you should just keep going even when every part of you wants to stop.

Let me tell you something I wish someone had told me back then:

You don't have to keep living this way!

But no one told me that.

Instead, I always received the well-meaning lines.

"You'll be fine."

"You'll get over it."

"That's just how it is."

Or worse, the silence. The invisible weight that told me to stay in my lane. Be agreeable. Be grateful. *Smile.* Don't ruin a good thing. I was a woman, and somewhere along the way, the world had taught me what that meant: Women weren't meant for *greatness*. We were meant to make it work. To grin and bear it. To be strong. To hold it all together, no matter what it cost us.

Even when I spoke up—when I told the people I trusted the most, *"I'm not sure"*—they looked at me like I was broken. *"But he treats you well, he's a good man. Why would you walk away from that?"*

What they were really saying was: *Settle.* Accept this version of love. This version of life. Because it's good *enough*.

But they didn't feel the silent collapse that started in my gut—the quiet unraveling that happens when you ignore your own intuition.

No one looked at me and asked, *"What do you want?"*
No one said, *"What would make you feel alive?"*

No one told me I could choose something else.

So I went through with it. I smiled through the ceremony ... with a little less joy. Posed for the photos ... without wanting to be seen. Danced ... without authenticity. Drank ... maybe more than I should have. Laughed ... uncomfortably and in shame.

The guests left at a reasonable hour, but the bridesmaids and groomsmen lingered. We sat outside in our backyard laughing, eating snacks, finishing off the whiskey. Stretching the night. Trying to hold on to something that felt memorable. I still loved these people. I was still trying to be in the moment. Trying to make it mean something. But eventually, they drifted off to bed. The door clicked shut. The house fell quiet. And I slipped away.

I just wanted to wash the day off me—the weight, the hairspray, the pressure.

I stripped out of the dress, leaving it crumpled on the floor. And not in the normal, post-wedding fashion. I stepped into the shower. I don't even remember turning it on. I was still wearing the fake lashes the makeup artist glued on earlier that day. I don't know where they ended up. I never found them.

Somehow, I found myself on the floor sitting in the cold water, knees pulled in, head in my hands. My makeup was streaked. My bare skin was freezing against the tile. I don't even know how long I sat there before I realized I was sobbing. Not dainty little tears. Ugly, gasping sobs. Mascara in my mouth. Chest heaving. Body shaking. Full. On. Panic.

At some point, he came in. Tried to help. But I couldn't speak. I couldn't explain. There was nothing he could do. His voice faded into the background. And it was just me and my singular thought, "How did I get here?"

Me and a silence that had waited years to break.

Somewhere beneath the heartbreak and the noise and the numbness, I heard it—that small, steady voice:

This can't be it. This can't be what life truly is.

And in that moment, the mask I'd worn for years—the one I thought was my normal face—just started to dissolve.

It wasn't the movie scene I'd always imagined. Not the dramatic awakening with perfect lighting and music swelling in the background. It was something quieter. Truer. The kind of knowing that lives in your bones. The kind that every woman recognizes when she finally stops running and tells the truth: *I was meant for more.*

More truth. More authenticity. More curiosity, wonder, joy, expression, color, freedom, love. More room to breathe, stretch, and be. More *lifelike.*

Even there, on the floor of the shower, wrecked and raw—*I knew.*

I knew my life could be more than what I had settled for.

Definitely more than the version of me I had tried to shape myself into. Absolutely more than the life I was told I was supposed to want. I had to find the life that had been waiting beneath it all—the path I had never allowed myself to even *consider*.

That night didn't just break me down. It broke me *open*.

And even though I didn't know exactly who I was yet, I knew one thing for sure:

I couldn't keep pretending to be someone I wasn't.

I had to let go of the woman I almost became. And that grief? It gutted me.

But it also set me free.

Because here's the truth: That night wasn't a transformation. It wasn't a reinvention. Or a glow-up. It was a return. A reclamation. Not to a perfect version of myself. Not to someone new, but a quiet, holy homecoming to the woman I was always meant to be. A call to step out of the darkness of the world's shadow and into the light of my true self.

And in that light, I stopped seeing myself as something to fix. I started seeing myself as someone to love. And I learned to offer myself the grace no one else had ever given me.

Every time I passed a mirror, I had a choice. To judge or to embrace. So I started whispering the words I didn't fully believe yet: *I love you. I trust you. You've got this.* And slowly, those whispers became the truth. Until one day, I didn't need to remind myself anymore. I just knew.

So if you've ever felt lost in your own life, if you've ever looked into the mirror and not recognized the woman staring back, I want you to know something: You're not alone. You're not broken. You're not too far gone.

You are already her. You have always been her. She's just been silenced by years of expectations, pressure, and pretending.

And now it's time to find your way back home. Back to the you who's always been waiting deep inside. The one who's ready now. Ready to rise. Ready to remember.

And I'm going to walk with you through it. Not with a map but with a compass. Not with answers but with questions.

This is not the end of something. This is the beginning. The moment everything quietly shifts. Because, yes—I was the woman who went through the ceremony. I was the woman who curled up in the shower grieving the life she almost chose. But I was also the woman who stood up afterward, wiped mascara from her cheeks, looked at herself in the mirror, and said, *not anymore*.

And from that moment on—I stopped asking permission to be me and started coming home to myself.

SECTION ONE:
RECLAIMING YOUR FEMININE POWER

Breaking Free from Expectations and Rediscovering Your True Essence

THERE'S A MOMENT most of us have but rarely talk about. It happens when the door closes behind you after a long day. When the makeup comes off, the bra gets tossed, and your phone finally goes quiet.

It's just you. Alone. No performance. No pleasing. No pretending. And in that space ... something stirs.

Who are you when no one is watching?

When you return home, remove your mask, and sit with yourself —shedding your public skin.

This is where we begin.

Before we can talk about confidence, self-love, intuition, or power, we must first address your *identity*. If you don't know who you are at your core, nothing in your life will feel fully aligned. You'll chase goals that don't fulfill you, follow paths that don't feel like your own, and wonder why—even when you do everything *right*—something still feels *off*.

What *is* identity, really?

It's not just your name, your job, or the roles you play. It's not the adjectives people use to describe you or the labels you've collected along the way. Identity is the *essence* of you. It's what remains when life strips everything else away. It's your values, your desires, your natural rhythms when no one else is watching. It's the fire in your gut when you know something is right and the quiet truth in your bones when something absolutely isn't.

When you don't know who you are, life starts to feel like a guessing game. I've played that game since I was little. I was the "good girl." The "smart one." I knew how to perform. How to say the right thing, smile at the right time, avoid disappointing anyone. But you can't be fully present when you're busy editing yourself. When you live like that, everything is muted. The joy. The connection. Even the pain. It's like living in a grayscale. Always adjusting. Always trying to be what the moment needs.

When you do know who you are—when you stop performing and start being—everything shifts. Decisions become clearer. Relationships deepen. You stop searching for validation because you already have it. And suddenly, life doesn't just get easier, it gets brighter. Full of color. Full of feeling. Full of you.

So, how do you start figuring it out?

You get quiet and you listen with your heart. You discover:

- What excites you and makes you feel alive?

- What drains you and feels like performance instead of just being you?

As you peel back these layers of yourself, something starts to rise beneath the surface. Something radiant, intuitive, and magnetic. It's not just identity—it's power.

Feminine power.

Feminine power isn't about the fact that women can and *should* be able to do it all—it's about *how* we do it. It's the ability to be soft or delicate without being small, to be strong and forceful without being hardened, to move with grace but stand with unwavering presence.

It is fluidity and fire, intuition and willpower, wisdom and playfulness. It is the ability to hold contradictions within ourselves— to be delicate and wild, nurturing and untamed, open-hearted and fiercely protective.

Feminine power looks different for each of us. But at its core, it is always the same—it is *authenticity*. To fully step into your feminine power is to step into your radiance—the truest expression of your essence. Radiance isn't something you strive for; it's what naturally rises when you stop performing and you start being.

Radiance Is ...

- Being fully alive, not just surviving
- An inner glow rooted in self-acceptance and presence
- Feeling at home in your body, your truth, and your energy
- Showing up as yourself, not someone shaped by approval
- Moving through life with ease, not force
- Taking up space simply by existing
- Trusting your intuition without gripping for control

3

- Letting your energy speak before your words ever do
- Attracting what's meant for you through alignment
- A frequency of authenticity, confidence, and quiet power

Radiance Is Not …

- Perfection, polish, or being "put together" all the time
- People-pleasing or earning your worth through performance
- Shrinking yourself to stay likable
- Needing constant validation to feel valuable
- Hustling to keep up or constantly fixing yourself
- Control disguised as confidence
- Exhaustion mistaken for strength
- Seeking permission to be yourself
- Being the best at everything
- Chasing love, success, or attention to feel whole

When you reclaim your feminine power, you don't just exist—you *radiate*. You become magnetic, not because you are trying to be, but because authenticity is the most attractive force in the world. When you live in that truth, everything else—relationships, opportunities, confidence, fulfillment—begins to align. You find yourself in a world of opportunity and abundance instead of scarcity.

So if you're ready to remember who you are, take a breath and let's begin.

CHAPTER 1: LIVING OUTSIDE OF TITLES

Embracing Your Authentic Self Beyond Labels and Expectations

OUR TITLES HELP US introduce ourselves to the world. Mother. Friend. Partner. Athlete. Author. They offer clarity and structure and are a shorthand that helps others understand pieces of who we are and where we belong. Titles create a sense of connection. But as useful as they are, they're just a glimpse. Not the whole story.

When we lead with titles, we present the pieces of ourselves that fit neatly into a conversation, but we risk leaving out the depth, the contradictions, and the complexities that make us who we truly are.

Titles, while useful, can be limiting.

They can box us in, making us feel like we have to live up to an expectation that comes with that label. They can become a crutch, a default answer to the question, "Who are you?" The second I say, "I'm an athlete," the person across from me starts filling in the blanks with their version of what that means based on their own experiences and beliefs of that specific title. Perhaps they recall their high school quarterback who peaked at seventeen. Maybe they picture their favorite elite Olympian they watch on TV. Maybe they remember being picked last in gym class and assume I'm intense or intimidating. Maybe they've never felt strong in their body and think, "I could never be her."

None of them know what I mean when I say it. They don't know about the five AM alarms accompanied by three-hour runs, the recovery days that feel like failure, the moments I've spent crying mid-run and then finding myself again one mile later. They don't know the mental game, the rituals I've lived, or my own resilience. It doesn't capture my style, my energy, my beliefs, or my choices. Even when I try to expand it—they still filter those words through their lens of what it means to them.

"I'm a disciplined athlete."
"I'm a joyful runner."
"I'm a dedicated triathlete."

They slot me into categories I never asked to belong to because titles are shaped by others' perceptions.

But *identity*? That's shaped by lived experience, by truth, by nuance. And that's what we're trying to uncover by digging deeper. Our challenge here is to move beyond titles—to see them as part of our identity but not the entirety of it.

It's about recognizing that while our roles and relationships shape us, they do not define us completely.

You are not just a daughter, just a partner, or just an athlete. You are the way you think, the way you feel, the way you experience the world. You are the things that excite you, the things that challenge you, and the things that make you feel alive. This is where the real conversation begins. Because to truly explore identity, we have to ask: Who am I outside of what I do for others? Who am I when the titles are stripped away?

After my fateful day at the altar, I asked my closest friends and family to describe me so I could understand who I was to the world. The answers I received surprised me. Words were given back to me like *relentless, curious, driven, intense*. Some of them felt true. Some of them felt like looking in a mirror for the first time and noticing things I'd never seen before. But what struck me most was how much of my identity had been shaped by the roles I played—how much of who I thought I was had been tied to external definitions. I could easily wear the mask in the outside world because I didn't know deep down what actually *shaped* me into *me*.

BEYOND THE MIRROR: IDENTITY WITHOUT THE MASK

When I thought about those descriptive words from my friends and how I felt about their choices, I recognized that those words were surface-level. Kind, but vague. Thoughtful, but not personal. They told me how I showed up but not who I was underneath it all. And that's when it hit me—maybe I'd only ever *shown* people the surface. Maybe I'd only ever offered versions of myself that were easy to digest. And if I had, how could they possibly reflect anything deeper back to me?

That was the moment I started peeling back the layers—not just of how others saw me, but of how I had been performing my own identity.

I started asking harder questions: What do I actually want? Who am I when I'm not living to meet someone else's expectations? How do I build a life that reflects *who I am*, not just *what I do*?

I found myself faced with this very decision on the floor of that fateful cold shower on my wedding night. Stripped of the noise, stripped of the plans and promises, I finally got to ask myself: What is my life—*my real life*—authentically going to be? Without the label of fiancée or wife. That script was no longer mine to follow, and that role was no longer mine to perform. For the first time, I could imagine a life beyond that title. I could begin again—not by knowing all the answers, but by noticing what felt true in my body and what didn't. When a label or role surfaced, I was began to ask: *Is this really me? Or is this what I've been taught to believe I must be?* If it didn't resonate, I gave myself permission to redefine it. To expand it. To give it new meaning.

Because I am more than any title can capture. I am a dynamic, living, breathing soul—forever unfolding. And that night, I realized I didn't have to figure it all out at once. I just had to begin by getting curious: Who is Celeste? What does she love? What lights her up? What does she wake up dreaming of doing? That's how I reclaimed my life—not by chasing new titles, but by coming home to who I've always been deep down.

Looking beyond the titles to the real essence of you is where the *real magic* happens. This is where you step into the deepest truth of who you are. It's time to get vulnerable, to set aside the roles you've taken on and explore the *essence* of you in all your multi-faceted glory. Who are you at your core? What makes you *you* in the truest, deepest sense?

Let's begin by stepping below the surface of identity. What brings you fulfillment, joy, and a sense of purpose? These are not just labels that are attached to you, but the qualities, passions, and values that form the very foundation of who you are. We're about to dig. *Deep.*

Start by grabbing a notebook or opening a blank document—no judgment, no rush. Just write down anything that comes to mind when you think of the words, *"Who am I?"*

Don't overthink it. Just let it flow.

Are you a daughter, a sister, a partner? An artist, a teacher, a creator? Do you identify with the roles that society places on you like leader, entrepreneur, or caregiver? As you list them out, let the words spill freely.

This isn't just about listing your roles or titles; it's about capturing the full scope of your identity. Who are you on a soul level when everything else drops away, before you started to be defined by the outside world. Who are you without your job, your relationships, or your material things? What do you feel when you wake up in the morning? What did you dream about when you were young before you entered the world of adulthood and all its expectations? What fills you with energy and purpose?

Now, let's get honest. As you write, think about the following questions:

- What lights me up from within? What activities or passions make me feel alive?

- What do I naturally gravitate toward when I'm given free time?

- What experiences have shaped me and made me feel authentically myself?

- How do I see the world, and how do I want to impact it?

- What makes me feel truly fulfilled—not just in the sense of accomplishment, but in the deep satisfaction of being true to myself?

- How do I define success?

These are the things that are *core* to your identity, the parts of you that are timeless and not easily defined by the roles you play.

They are the things that make you tick: your passions, your values, your *essence*. So, take a moment to capture all of it—your titles, your roles, and the deeper spirit of who you are.

And now, look at what you've written. You'll notice that there are two distinct types of things.

Titles and Roles

These are the things you do—the hats you wear, the roles you fill, the expectations you meet (i.e. mother, teacher, accountant, marathoner, etc.)

Core Identity

These are the things that define your essence—your values, passions, and the truths that reside deep within you (i.e. determined, creative, artistic, etc.)

As you look at your list, notice how many of these are simply titles, things that are expected of you by society or by the people around you. These are often external forces shaping your identity, and while they are part of your story, they do not capture the full picture of who you are down deep. They can change, evolve, or even fade away over time.

Your core identity, however, is unchanging. It's what defines you at your deepest level. It is what stays with you regardless of your job, your relationship status, or what others expect from you. And this is where you learn to step into the heart of who you truly are.

Now, let's take this exploration even further. Here's where we move from reflection to action. It's time to invite the people closest to you into the conversation. This is your challenge. Reach out to your closest friends and family and ask them to describe you in 10 words. You can text them something like this:

"Hey, I'm doing a deep dive to better understand who I am at my core. Could you take a moment and describe me in 10 words or less? No need to overthink it, just what comes to mind when you think of me. Thanks so much!"

This exercise isn't just about asking people to list your roles; it's about how they truly see you. When you ask them to describe you, be open to the possibility that their responses may surprise you. Once you get these responses, take a moment to reflect. What stands out to you? Did they focus more on your titles—mother, worker, caregiver? Or did they touch on your core identity—the things that make you uniquely you, like your sense of humor, creativity, or the way you bring light into a room? Are these perceptions aligned? Do you feel that the labels you've adopted truly represent who you are, or are they restricting you? Do you feel free to express the full spectrum of yourself, or are you confined by roles and expectations?

This is a beautiful opportunity to look at how you define yourself versus how others define you. Take a few moments to reflect upon those questions. In the end, this process is about defining yourself on your own terms separate from society's expectations, labels, and titles. You are so much more than just a mother, a teacher, or a leader. You are a combination of your values, your passions, and your essence. And now, the most important questions: How do you begin to step into that essence more fully? How do you begin to express who you are beyond the titles you've been given? Or, if you haven't already, how do you fully begin to see, understand, and embrace your true identity? This is where you start the journey of being truly seen—not just by others but by yourself.

Here's the kicker: there's always going to be a gap between how you see yourself and present yourself while you're alone versus how the world sees you as you share yourself in the world. The goal, however, is to eventually close that gap. The closer you can get these two versions of yourself—the inner you and the outer you— the more authentic and aligned you will feel. When you live with integrity between who you truly are at your core and how you show up in the world, you create a powerful sense of fulfillment. Of authenticity. Everything you do, all of your actions, words, and decisions, will feel more aligned and meaningful. This alignment is not just important for your own sense of self, it also affects how others see you. When you are fully yourself, not hiding behind expectations or societal labels, you will feel seen—by yourself and by the world around you. There will be no fear of judgment because you're not living in opposition to who you are. You've accepted who you are at your core, and you choose to show up fully and confidently, without apology. You will feel more at peace with yourself and more empowered in your actions. You will be more unshakable in your truth and feel more present in your decisions and movements. That's when the real magic of living authentically takes shape.

The rest of this book will show you how to close that space—the quiet distance between your inner truth and your outer life—until they become one.

Breaking the Script

It's funny. From a young age, I thought that there was this unspoken guidebook for life—a roadmap that was supposed to lead me from one milestone to the next. I just have to get good grades, go to college, find a job, get married, have kids, climb the career ladder, then retire, and I'll finally be happy. This formula seemed to be the unspoken rule of adulthood. I expected that by simply following this script, I would achieve a sense of stability, success, and fulfillment. But the reality was far different.

When I hit eighteen and stepped out into the world, I quickly realized—there is no rulebook. There's no map handed to me, and I was left to navigate the complexities of my adulthood on my own. I remember sitting in my tiny off-campus apartment, fresh out of undergrad, on hold with the car insurance company. I was Googling what a deductible even was while trying not to cry. I had no idea what I was doing. No one had taught me how to do any of this. Not how to read a lease. Not how to write a resumé. Not how to trust my gut when something felt off.

I figured adulthood would just … click. At some point, I'd feel ready. But I didn't. I was just doing my best to look like I had it all together while quietly unraveling under the weight of all the things I was "supposed" to know. Every step I took was an unpacking process, and it didn't end at age eighteen. It continued throughout my life. And every time I went through something new, I always got told by society that there was a right way to do it, a right timeline to follow. But these moments continue to show me that there is no one-size-fits-all guide for adulthood—that each new chapter of life requires us to unpack and define it for ourselves.

Yet, society continues to reinforce this invisible script. Everyone seems to have an idea of what we *should be* doing. The questions and commentary are constant: *"Why are you single?" "When are you going to settle down?" "You should be making this much money by now." "Great, a promotion! What's next in your career?" "When are you giving me grandchildren?"* These societal expectations come at us relentlessly, each one pushing us toward someone else's idealized version of success—marriage, children, career advancement, social milestones. And if we're not careful, we can feel like we're falling behind, like we're somehow not measuring up to the script that's been imposed on us. The script we never auditioned for, never signed for on the dotted line.

But here's the thing—who wrote this script anyway? Why do we feel this drive to follow it? And, more importantly, why are we so afraid to challenge it? These scripts aren't ours. They're societal constructs absorbed from parents, teachers, media, and even well-meaning friends and strangers—people who were raised by these very *same* scripts. Even television shows and movies fuel these expectations, portraying an idealized version of life, shaping us into believing that we should want the same things. The problem is, we're all constantly absorbing these messages without realizing it. What if that version of success doesn't resonate with us? What if our fulfillment comes from something entirely different? What if we're just too scared to speak up? To rip up the script and dump it in the recycling bin?

What if success looks different for you? What if fulfillment comes from building a life on your own terms rather than ticking off boxes on someone else's timeline? It's time to challenge the script we've been handed and ask: *What do I truly want?*

FREE FROM COMPARISON

I want to make a note that one of the biggest obstacles to truly embracing this freedom is the distorted reality we are presented with on social media. Social media often shows us an idealized version of other people's lives—highlight reels that are carefully curated to show only the best moments. These snapshots can create the illusion that everyone else has it figured out, that their lives are somehow more beautiful or successful than ours.

In our scrolling, we might find ourselves questioning why we haven't reached certain milestones or why our life doesn't look like theirs. The truth is, we're not seeing their whole picture, either. Social media doesn't show us the full story of someone else's life— their struggles, their setbacks, or their behind-the-scenes challenges. It's easy to get caught up in comparing our messy, real lives to a polished and filtered version of someone else's.

The more we buy into this mirage of perfectly-curated lives on social media, the more we distort our own reality, measuring our worth against an unrealistic standard and forgetting that our life is already beautiful as it is.

Every day we wake up is an invitation to live in alignment with what we truly want, not what others want for us.

Our journey is uniquely ours, and was never meant to mirror anyone else's. And while we don't need to abandon social media, we do need to remember we're only seeing one side of the story. The more we step away from comparison and embrace grace for where we are, the more we begin to define success by our own values and not by someone else's highlight reel.

Instead of using someone else's version of success as our gauge, we begin to measure our growth against who we were yesterday, and whether our actions, thoughts, and choices are aligned with our core values. Our journey isn't about approval from others; it's about how we show up for ourselves each day. The small steps and decisions we make towards the life that feels truly aligned and right in our gut. It's about honoring where we are and staying connected to our authentic self.

UNBECOMING TO BECOME

What matters most is not what society says you *should* want but what feels aligned with your essence, your true values, and what brings *you* joy. This is where the real freedom lies: in defining success and fulfillment for yourself based on what actually resonates with you, *not what's expected of you.* So, how do we start to unpack this for ourselves?

I asked myself that very question on the edge of my brand new chapter—on the precipice of my first bold choice. Everyone said, *"Your problems will follow you."* I smiled and nodded, but deep down I didn't believe them. I thought I could outrun myself. I took the chance and moved from Phoenix thousands of miles away to my new home in Washington. I was chasing something I couldn't quite name, but I knew the altar I walked away from had been my first right choice, and I felt confident. But I didn't understand. Not really. Not until I unpacked the same restlessness, the same questions, the same ache inside a new set of walls.

I was alone. I was unanchored. And for the first time in a long time, I was quiet enough to hear my own thoughts. Who was I without the roles I'd worn so tightly around me? Without the finish lines to chase? Did I even love Ironman anymore? Did I still want that Boston qualifier—or was that a version of me I had outgrown? If I knew I didn't want to be married, what else did or didn't I want? So I slowed down. I walked in the woods. I tried salsa dancing. I practiced aikido. I dipped my toe into everything that looked different than the life I had built before. I let myself explore, not for achievement but for aliveness. And it was messy. It was uncomfortable. Sometimes, it was wrenchingly painful. When you step outside the familiar story, the inner critic doesn't just whisper— it screams. It begs you to return to the safety of what you know, even if you know it no longer fits.

But this is the threshold. This is where the real transformation begins—not in the becoming, but in the unbecoming. In peeling away every *should*, every *must*, every borrowed belief, and asking: *What if I get to decide?*

It is terrifying to look into the mirror and see the version of you that's been hiding beneath the layers for the first time. But discomfort is not a stop sign—it's an invitation. It's the moment you choose to stay safely misaligned or risk everything to uncover the life that's truly yours.

That's the beginning of real self-love. Not comfort. Not perfection. But truth. So, you may be asking, "Celeste, how do I do this work of breaking free?" Great question—it starts with questioning ... well ... *everything*.

We need to reflect first on how we've been living, why we've been chasing things that don't fulfill us, and what truly matters to us. If you find yourself stuck in the cycle of external validation, take a moment to pause and ask: *"Am I living in alignment with my true self?"* What would my life look like if I stopped seeking approval from others and started living for *me*? And more importantly, what would my life look like in five years or ten years if I don't?

This work isn't going to be easy. It's not a one-time fix; it's an ongoing journey. It's going to be painful. You're going to want to stop, to go back and seek the comforts of your old life. You will need to move forward with grace for yourself to be able to resist that urge to give up and turn back on your dreams. So just remember: every little step you take to strip away the external layers and define success on your own terms is a step toward reclaiming your true identity. Once you intentionally make that shift, the world opens up in a way that's abundant and full of possibility instead of restrictive and limiting. You will finally begin to feel seen, not just by others but by yourself. You'll start to live with authenticity and purpose, free from the burden of expectations that were never yours to carry.

CREATING A LIFE OF ALIGNMENT

It took me two years to get here, but once I began living in alignment with my core values, I began to craft my mornings with devotion—not discipline. I started waking up at five A.M., not because it was impressive or productive, but because I wanted to. It felt like I was giving myself a head start on joy. I'd journal, stretch, sip my coffee in silence, study French, move my body, and fill those early hours with things that made me feel deeply connected to myself. And that connection carried me through the day. It made everything else more grounded, more at ease. I created an evening ritual, too—tea, a book, twinkle lights, stillness. These weren't routines designed to impress anyone. They were moments that made me feel at home in my own life. And that's what it was, really. For the first time, I felt at home inside of myself.

I started looking at my calendar differently. If something didn't align with my energy or my values, I let it go. Saying *no* got easier. Not because I had something *better* to do, but because I had clarity on what actually nourished me. I wasn't just existing anymore. I was living. With intention. With joy. And as I lived more fully, a new kind of abundance started showing up—not in material things, but in possibility. My life no longer felt rigid or linear. It felt wide open. Expansive. Full of color and choice. I had created my own rhythm. My own peace. My own way forward. That's what it means to be in alignment with yourself. That's what it means to redefine success.

As I peeled back the layers of who I was *supposed* to be, I started to feel this quiet but undeniable shift. The anxiety began to loosen its grip—not because life got easier, but because I stopped living on someone else's timeline. I stopped chasing the version of success I thought I *should* want, and instead I started choosing what I actually wanted—right here, in this present moment.

That's when the peace came. I wasn't living for the next achievement. I wasn't waiting for external validation to tell me I was enough. I was building something from within. Something rooted. Something alive. The more we let go of societal expectations and external approval, the more we can cultivate our own peace. Our journey becomes one of curiosity, expansion, and constant self-discovery, instead of criticism, judgement and dissonance.

Just like the universe, our journey never stops expanding. Every moment is an opportunity to learn more, discover more, and grow in ways we didn't know were possible. What was once unfamiliar becomes a part of our story, and we start to ask, "What's next?" That's the beauty of this process—it's endless, full of discovery, growth, and transformation. In doing this, we create a life of true freedom. A life where success is not about external approval or comparison; it's about creating something that is uniquely ours. A life where we can step into our full potential, expand without limits, and celebrate the infinite possibility of what's next.

REFLECTIONS FOR THE ROAD AHEAD

As you begin your journey, here are a few questions to reflect on as you work to break free from external expectations and uncover your true self:

What expectations have I absorbed from others?
Reflect on the beliefs, opinions, and advice you've been given by family, friends, society, and even social media. What are the messages and expectations that have shaped your ideas of success and fulfillment?

What are the *shoulds* and *musts* that I feel pressured to follow?
Identify the things you feel obligated to do or achieve based on these unspoken external expectations. Are these your own desires, or have they been dictated by others?

What stories am I telling myself about who I should be?
What narratives have you internalized and embodied that are keeping you stuck? How are these stories affecting the choices you make? Write them down and challenge their validity. If they aren't true, how can you change them?

How would my life look if no one else's opinion mattered?
Imagine a life where external opinions and societal pressures have no bearing on your decisions. What would your choices be? What would you prioritize if you were free to define success and fulfillment on your own terms? How would you begin and end each day? What would be most important to you?

What does success really mean to me?
Think beyond the conventional markers of success like money, status, or titles. What would success look like if you created your

own definition? What do you truly want to feel and experience in your life? What would make it feel truly yours, truly lived?

What are my core values?

Dig deep and ask yourself: What values resonate with me at my core? These are the principles and beliefs that guide your decisions, actions, and purpose. Are you living in alignment with these values? Where are the areas that feel dissonant to these?

What is my purpose?

Reflect on what drives you at the deepest level. What brings you joy, fulfillment, and a sense of meaning? How can you honor this purpose as you move forward in your life? What shifts do you need to make in your life so you are living more in line with this purpose?

Am I living in alignment with my true self?

After identifying your values and purpose, take an honest look at your current life. Are your actions, relationships, and career aligned with who you truly are, or are you living to meet others' expectations?

What am I willing to release to move forward?

What are the habits, beliefs, or relationships that no longer serve you? What is holding you back from living authentically, and what are you willing to let go of in order to embrace your true self?

How would I feel if I stopped seeking approval from others?

Consider how it would feel to stop trying to meet everyone else's expectations. What would your life look like if you felt fully confident in your own decisions and purpose, without needing others' validation? What possibilities and opportunities would open up if you lived as your authentic self?

CHAPTER 2: THE DANCE OF POWER
The Early Conditioning

WHAT IF THE VERY traits we've been taught to suppress—our softness, intuition, ability to flow—are actually our greatest strengths?

From the time we were little girls, we were given quiet instructions on how to shrink ourselves. Be soft, but not too soft. Be nice, but don't get walked over. Be smart, but not intimidating. Be pretty, but not distracting. Be sensitive, but not overly emotional. Be assertive, but not bossy. Don't take up too much space. Don't ask for too much. We apologize for our emotions, second-guess our instincts, and swallow our words before they ever leave our lips. We've molded ourselves into what is expected, hoping that if we are pleasing enough, if we are palatable enough, we will be loved.

I was taught all of this beginning in the halls of public school. Not through a lesson plan, but by the sideways glances and the silences that followed when I dared to raise my hand in class. I was a swimmer. A clarinetist. I wore glasses before they were cool. I had acne and awkwardness in equal spades and a deep sensitivity I didn't yet know how to carry. I was bullied—not always overtly, but in the subtle way that kids do when they sense someone is *different*. I was considered too bookish, too awkward, too outside from the world that favored the flashy, cool, effortlessly popular kids. I spent so long trying to prove I was enough in a world that rewarded someone for being the loudest. But what I've learned since then is this: power doesn't always roar. Sometimes, it radiates. Every moment I felt "too much" or "not enough" was actually a moment that was guiding me back to the truth of my feminine power.

WHAT FEMININE ENERGY REALLY IS

What if the world has misunderstood feminine energy all along? What if the very things we've been taught to suppress are not weaknesses but the deepest well of our power? Feminine energy is not passive or fragile. It is creation, magnetism, and deep knowing. It's the ocean: powerful enough to carve stone, fluid enough to adapt to its surroundings.

To understand feminine energy, we must also understand masculine energy—because one cannot exist without the other. There is no battle between the two. They are not opposing forces but complementary ones. They are the inhale and the exhale, the ebb and the flow, the structure and the surrender. We all carry both, regardless of our gender. But in a world that glorifies pushing over allowing, logic over intuition, and structure over flow, feminine energy has often been silenced.

Women have been taught to believe that to be strong, we must lean fully into our own masculine energy. To be respected, we must lead like men, move like men, command like men. And yet, we have also been told the opposite—that to be desirable, we must be small. We must be soft, but not breakable. We must be confident, but not intimidating. We must be independent, but never unapproachable. So we learn to shape-shift. We weaken ourselves when our strength threatens others. We shrink when we are told we are too much. We harden ourselves when we fear being seen as weak. And in the process, we lose sight of who we are.

True power is not about choosing one or the other. It is about learning the dance between the two. There is a time to lead and a time to follow. A time to assert and a time to listen. A time to soften, not because we are weak, but because we are wise enough to know when softness is the most powerful choice. The key is knowing when and how to embody each energy in a way that feels authentic rather than forced.

True feminine power is not about making yourself smaller. It is not about stepping back so others can shine. It is not about contorting yourself into what is expected of you. It is about standing fully in who you are. It is knowing that your softness is not weakness. That your emotions are not liabilities. That your ability to flow, to feel, to be is not something to apologize for.

True feminine power is not in proving yourself. It is in knowing yourself.

And from that place, you move—not in fear, not in reaction, but in absolute clarity. This is not about fitting into an outdated mold of femininity. It is about redefining power on your own terms. It is about standing in your fullness without apology. And it all begins with remembering that power is deep within.

The Ironman Lesson: Fire and Flow

When I was training for my first Ironman, I was all fire. I was in my masculine energy—driven, focused, relentless. It was me versus the mileage: 2.4 miles in the water, 112 miles on the bike, and a full marathon at the end. I operated in full output mode—discipline, structure, and force. I measured success in how far I could push. If I was tired, I pushed harder. If I hit a wall, I found a way to climb over it. I wore my exhaustion like a badge of honor. There wasn't room for softness, slowness, or surrender—only progress. I thought discipline was the only way through.

But somewhere in the middle of all the six-hour bike rides and two-hour runs off the bike, I started breaking down. My body was tired, my mind was foggy, and I felt brittle. I had built the schedule, but I hadn't built the support. I hadn't yet understood that to go the distance, I needed more than drive—I needed restoration.

What no one tells you in the beginning is how much of endurance training is actually recovery. Not just the foam-rolling and stretching, but the food, the sleep, the salt, the hydration, the long hours of just being with your body, listening to it. It's in the mornings where you choose to slow down, to stretch for an hour instead of rushing out the door. It's in the hammock with your first sip of coffee, letting your nervous system exhale before the miles start ticking.

And maybe the most surprising thing? That vulnerability didn't always come from within. It came from the world showing up for me when I didn't even realize I needed it. The Ironman isn't just a test of strength—it's a marathon of emotion. There were moments where I wanted to cry, not just from the pain, but from the absurd beauty of it all. You're pushing harder than you ever have, and then out of nowhere, someone on the sidelines is holding a ridiculous sign that says, "Smile if you peed in your wetsuit!" or "Remember, you paid for this!" or "Have you tried therapy?" And somehow, those signs crack you open. You forget to be hard on yourself for a second. You smile. Sometimes you even laugh. And it feels like grace. Not because the pain disappears—but because for a moment, you remember you're human. You remember you chose this. That you can hold power and softness at the same time. That there's room for joy even in the grind.

Feminine energy was in every one of those moments. The cheer stations. The stranger yelling, "You've got a great smile!" The way the race reminded me to be kind to myself—not because I felt strong, but because I was being seen. That's the part we don't talk about enough in endurance—the quiet, invisible nourishment that helps you keep going. Not just fuel, but encouragement. Not just training, but presence.

And that—that—was the feminine energy returning. Not passivity. Not giving up. But surrender. Not weakness. But deep strength. The kind that allows for joy *and* sustainability. The kind that whispers, "You're not a machine. You're a human. And your power is amplified when you're nourished."

I didn't abandon the structure or the discipline—

I just let something softer in. A kind of inner knowing.

A permission to rest.

A commitment to actually enjoy the journey.

My Ironman events became not just a race but a lesson in duality. I learned how to push, and I learned how to receive. I learned how to stretch and strengthen. To listen and act. To hold both structure and surrender in the same hand. That's the dance—the power of both. The masculine in me knew how to push, to plan, to show up no matter what. But the feminine? She taught me how to receive, to soften without losing strength, to rest without losing momentum. That's where true endurance lives: in the balance. That's the feminine, not as weakness, but as the wisdom to know when less is more.

THE ENERGETIC BALANCE: MASCULINE MEETS FEMININE

Feminine energy is not a role to play, a look to achieve, or a set of behaviors to adopt. It is not submission, passivity or irrationality. It is a force—one that has shaped civilizations, created life, and held the unseen fabric of existence together. It is a power so vast and undeniable that, for centuries, it has been misunderstood, feared, and suppressed. To understand feminine energy, we must move beyond the surface-level definitions of gender and step into something deeper—the balance of energies that exist within all of us.

Both feminine and masculine energies exist within every person, regardless of gender. They are not opposites in conflict but complements in harmony. Both are necessary. Both are powerful. The key is not choosing one over the other but understanding how to embody each of them with awareness.

Masculine energy is structured, directional, action-oriented. It is the force that builds, protects, and provides. It moves in straight lines, thrives in logic and order, and values achievement and control. It is forward momentum, discipline, and the protector of boundaries.

Feminine energy is fluid, intuitive, receptive, and creative. It is the force that nourishes, transforms, and brings life to ideas, relationships, and emotions. It moves in waves, thrives in connection and deep knowing, and values flow and expansion. It is magnetism, creativity, and the unseen intelligence that weaves things together.

Neither is superior. One without the other is incomplete. Masculine energy without feminine wisdom becomes rigid, disconnected, and forceful. Feminine energy without masculine structure can become directionless, chaotic, and ungrounded. The key to personal power is not in rejecting one or clinging to the other, but in mastering the dance between them.

- Knowing when to act (masculine) and when to trust (feminine).

- Knowing when to set boundaries (m) and when to surrender to what is (f).

- Knowing when to lead (m) and when to magnetize (f).

This dance is everywhere—in relationships, in conversations, in careers, in how we move through the world. The way we show up in our power is not about manipulation but about alignment. It is about understanding the interconnectedness of people, dynamics, and situations. It is about fluidity and presence, not control.

A woman who understands this dance walks into a room and instantly shifts the energy—not because she demands attention, but because she embodies presence. She knows when to soften, when to listen, when to step forward, and when to allow. She moves with an inner knowing, an unshakable confidence in who she is and how she chooses to show up.

THE GOOD GIRL MASK

However, this kind of power—the ability to be both strong and soft, structured and fluid—has been deeply misunderstood. Society has conditioned us to fear it. Feminine energy has always been powerful, and anything powerful that cannot be easily controlled has at some point been labeled as dangerous.

For centuries, society has revered the masculine—structure, logic, action, dominance—while labeling the feminine as frivolous, weak, too emotional, *too much*. And when you're raised in that kind of environment, you learn how to read the room. You learn which parts of you are safe to express and which parts are not. You learn to become palatable. Not because you're weak but because you're wise. Because survival sometimes looks like silence. Sometimes power looks like holding it all in just to keep moving forward.

There's no shame in this. It's a survival skill. And I learned it well.

Let me ask you, have you become a master at putting on a mask? The good girl. The agreeable one. The one who didn't rock the boat even when you knew better. Even when you had ideas that would've changed the room or clarity that would've made things easier. You would swallow your voice to keep the peace. You held back tears in rooms because you knew if you cried, you'd lose credibility. You dimmed your joy, softened your opinions, shaped yourself around what you thought other people needed from you. Yeah ... me, too.

For a long time, I wore a fake wedding ring because I thought it would make me seem more put together. Like I had been "chosen." Like if a man could love me, maybe the world would take me more seriously. Maybe I'd be respected. Maybe people would see me as whole instead of wondering what was missing. I wore it like armor, as absurd as that sounds now. But at the time, it felt like a strategy. It was me adapting. Bending to stay safe. To stay employed. To keep from being dismissed or objectified or questioned.

But over time, I started to realize that true power wasn't about disappearing. It wasn't about blending in so well that I no longer recognized myself. True power wasn't in rebellion for the sake of making noise, either. It was in discernment. In knowing when to speak and when to listen. In knowing when to soften and when to stand unshakably in my truth.

That's the real dance.

Not shrinking. Not shouting. But choosing—consciously—how to show up. Not because someone told me how I should, but because I finally started to listen to the voice within me that had been whispering all along: *You are allowed to take up space.*

And when I started listening to that voice, my world started to change.

PRESENCE OVER PERFORMANCE

Feminine energy is not about rejecting the masculine side; it is about balance. The key is knowing when to lead and when to allow; it's recognizing there are moments to stand firm, speak with clarity, or take decisive action, and there are moments to soften, listen deeply, or trust the unseen forces at play. There are moments to build, structure, and push forward, and there are moments to surrender, let things unfold, and receive what is already in motion.

This is not about manipulation, and it is not about using femininity to get what you want. It is about understanding how to move in alignment with your own energy and the world around you. It is about recognizing when structure is needed and when intuition must take the lead. When to act and when to trust. Feminine energy does not mean abandoning logic. It does not mean always surrendering or always flowing. It means knowing yourself—so deeply that you can move between energies with ease, with wisdom, with intention. And that is power.

The power of feminine energy doesn't force—it attracts. It doesn't control—it influences. It does not need to chase—it magnetizes. This is why it has been feared. Because it is a power that cannot be measured, contained, or always explained. But this power is not something to wield over others. It is something to embody within yourself:

It is intuition - the ability to sense beyond logic, to feel what cannot be spoken.

It is receptivity - an openness that allows for deeper connection, for unseen opportunities to arise.

It is presence - the kind that fills a room without demanding attention.

It is creation - the force that gives life—not just in the literal sense, but in ideas, art, relationships, movements.

Feminine power isn't loud or quiet. It's rooted deep within. It teaches you that you don't have to prove your worth, justify your emotions, or defend your softness. It doesn't shrink to be loved or harden to be respected. It simply is.

At one point in time, we were taught that strength looked a certain way—unwavering, dominant, detached. That to be taken seriously, we had to toughen up, play by rules never made for us, and prove we belonged. And for a while, we did. We learned how to armor up. How to take up space without being "too much." How to exhaust ourselves for the validation others provided without asking ourselves if we were being authentic.

But here's the truth: Real power has nothing to do with force. It's not about pushing harder or speaking louder. Real power is *presence*. It's knowing exactly who you are and moving through the world in a way that demands nothing yet shifts everything. We have to relearn strength because what we were taught was a poor imitation of it. We were handed a version of power stripped of its softness, fluidity, and depth. We were told to chase strength, build it, fight for it. But what if strength was never something to chase? What if it was already yours—just buried beneath the fear of being too much? Relearning strength means remembering that your softness is not weakness—it's wisdom.

True strength is not in how much you can endure. It's in how deeply you trust yourself. How fully you allow yourself to be seen, unapologetically. This kind of strength doesn't chase—it draws. It doesn't force—it flows. It doesn't fight for space—it becomes space. And when you live from that place? Everything opens for you.

FEMININE STRENGTH IN ACTION

Let's talk about what real strength looks like in action—because you've lived it. Think back to the moment you walked away from something that was draining you. A job that took more than it gave. A relationship where love meant shrinking. A friendship that only survived when you played small.

You called staying with something "loyalty." But letting go? That is power.

This is where you get to determine what happens. No dramatic exits. No slammed doors. Just a quiet decision: Your energy is too valuable to keep pouring where it's not returned. It's your time to remember when you stopped chasing—love, success, validation. You've most likely spent years trying to be "enough," believing more effort would finally get you there. But one day, you'll stop. Not because you give up—but because you wake up. You realize: *I already am enough.* You let go. And what once felt far away starts coming toward you. Effortlessly. That's the thing about true power: It doesn't force. It flows.

I've felt it—mid-run, when your mind finally lets go, and your body just moves. You're not muscling through anymore. You're in rhythm. That's not brute strength. That's flow. That's you, remembering your power.

We've been taught that strength means being solid and unmoving, like a mountain. But even mountains crumble. Real strength is in movement, in fluidity, in adaptability. And this isn't just poetic—it's how we survive. It's the woman who walks away from the life she was *told* to want and builds one that nourishes her soul. It's the leader who doesn't push but waits for the right moment to move. It's the mother who raises her child with trust, not control. It's you every time you choose softness over fear and presence over performance.

Because power doesn't come from resistance. It comes from presence. From knowing when to hold and when to let go. When to lead and when to listen. When to move with life instead of fighting against it. The strongest thing you can do is trust yourself enough to flow. Because the moment you stop resisting who you are and start owning it? *That's when you become unstoppable.*

RECLAIMING BELONGING AND WORTH

Relearning strength means realizing you never actually lost your power. It was just buried beneath layers of conditioning, self-doubt, and the desperate need to be chosen. That need? It's what keeps us in cycles of proving, pleasing, and performing. It's what makes us shrink in relationships, dull our edges, and shape-shift into someone more "lovable." It's what holds us hostage in rooms we've outgrown, friendships that drain us, and careers that no longer light us up. Because we're chasing approval instead of alignment.

The moment you abandon yourself to be accepted, you lose your ability to truly belong. The version of you that people are drawn to isn't real—it's a carefully-crafted performance, a mask you wear to keep the peace, win approval, and avoid rejection. But the cost of that acceptance? *It's you.*

And that's why so many people feel lost. And that fear of rejection? That fear of judgment? It runs *deep.*

We worry about what the world will think—what our coworkers, families, even strangers might say. We imagine their opinions like weapons, sharp and unforgiving. But the truth is: no one's judgment has ever been as cruel as the things we say to ourselves.

Think about the voice in your head—the one that tells you you're not enough, or too much, or that you'll fail before you even begin. The one that keeps a record of every mistake and whispers doubt the moment you start to feel brave. Would you keep that voice around if it belonged to a friend? Would you stay close to someone who spoke to you the way you speak to yourself?

I remember a day when I said something in a conversation that felt a little too honest—just a little too much of me. And the moment it left my mouth, I started replaying it. Over and over. *Why did you say that? That was weird. They probably think you're dramatic now. God, you always take it too far.* I smiled and nodded through the rest of the conversation, still present on the outside, but inside I was unraveling. The rest of the day, that voice wouldn't shut up. *You try too hard. You come on too strong. You make people uncomfortable. Why can't you just be more chill?*

I wasn't just worried about what they thought—I was worried about what *I* thought they thought. I was bending myself into shapes to be likable, acceptable, safe. And I let that voice take the lead. I let it shrink me down before anything even happened. But that voice—she's not the truth. She's fear dressed up as protection. She's shame playing teacher. She's the part of me that thinks belonging means hiding.

But what if we stopped listening to that voice?

What if, instead of fearing judgment, we trusted ourselves? What if we stood firm in who we are even when it's uncomfortable, even when no one claps? Because the people who truly matter—the ones who are meant for you, who will stand beside you, who celebrate you rather than tolerate you—they can only find you when you *choose to be seen.*

Authenticity isn't just about being yourself. It's about trusting that being yourself is enough. It's about realizing that the fear of judgment loses its grip when you stop seeking validation from those who were never meant to understand you in the first place. You don't need to be louder to be noticed. You don't need to prove a thing. You just need to own your space—fully, unapologetically, and without asking for permission. Because when you do? The right people will find you.

The Power of Sensitivity

For centuries, women were told that being "too emotional" was a problem. That feelings were something to suppress, to manage, to keep in check so we wouldn't make others uncomfortable. But here's the truth: sensitivity is power. Do you know why? Because it's information. Sensitivity means you notice what others miss. You feel the energy shift in a room before a single word is spoken. You sense when something's off, when someone isn't being honest, when a moment needs more care, more boundaries, more presence. That's not a flaw. That's a gift.

But here's what it's not: it's not flying off the handle every time you feel something. It's not using emotions to manipulate, to justify recklessness, or to demand that the world cater to your every reaction. And it's definitely not confusing drama with depth. True power doesn't come from being the loudest or the most reactive. It comes from being the most intentional.

Emotional Intelligence

Emotional intelligence is your ability to recognize, understand, and manage your emotions while also being aware of and empathetic toward the emotions of others. It's what allows you to respond rather than react, to navigate difficult conversations with grace, and to make decisions that align with your values rather than being ruled by fleeting feelings.

If you can't regulate your emotions, you can't effectively lead your life. Emotional intelligence helps you:

- Make aligned decisions instead of reactive ones.

- Build better relationships by responding with understanding rather than defensiveness.

- Develop resilience by working through challenges instead of avoiding them.

- Cultivate self-trust because you know you can handle your emotions, no matter what life throws at you.

At its core, emotional intelligence is about self-awareness, self-regulation, motivation, empathy, and social skills. It's not about suppressing emotions but about understanding them, using them as data, and responding in a way that aligns with who you truly are. Many people think that emotional strength means not feeling emotions deeply or ignoring them altogether. But true strength comes from emotional mastery, not suppression.

Emotional intelligence isn't just about being kind or compassionate—it's about knowing how to read the world and respond in ways that create real impact. It's the ability to lead, to connect deeply, to influence without force. So instead of suppressing what you feel, refine it. Use it. But not every feeling needs to be shared. Not every reaction deserves an audience.

Think about Princess Diana. She was often in rooms full of power, where every move was watched, every word scrutinized. Her impact wasn't loud, but it was felt. She felt the moment and responded with presence. Whether holding a child with HIV or walking through a minefield, she didn't need to speak loudly to be heard. That's emotional intelligence—not shrinking, not performing, but choosing presence over performance. Power over reaction.

Ask yourself:

- What is this feeling trying to tell me?

- What am I picking up on that others aren't seeing?

- How can I express this in a way that's clear, grounded, and aligned with the outcome I actually want?

That's what power is—not in cutting yourself off from emotion, but in knowing exactly how to wield it. When you do that, you start responding with purpose. You stop drowning in your feelings—you navigate them with grace. You stop apologizing for your depth, your intuition, your clarity, and instead, you lead with them. Because sensitivity at its highest level isn't fragility, *it's mastery.*

RECEIVING AS POWER, NOT WEAKNESS

For so long, we were taught that strength means independence. That asking for help makes us weak. That control equals security. We've been conditioned to believe we must do it all, hold it all, be it all—alone. But true feminine power? It's not about control. It's about connection. And connection requires receiving.

When you begin truly connecting, you stop seeing receiving as a weakness. You start seeing it as intimacy. An invitation to deepen relationships. A quiet acknowledgment that we were never meant to go it alone. Even in the smallest of moments—like someone holding a door open for you.

I used to think everything in relationships had to be perfectly balanced—like there was this invisible scorecard I was responsible for keeping. If someone paid for my coffee, I felt like I owed them next time. If someone offered to help, I rushed to find a way to repay it. I couldn't just receive without feeling like I was in debt.

It wasn't about money—it was about discomfort. I didn't know how to let myself be cared for without earning it. Even simple moments, like someone asking, "Can I help you carry that?" would make me flinch. My instinct was always, *No, I've got it.* Not because I didn't want help, but because I didn't want to need it.

I thought I was being strong, but in hindsight, I wasn't holding boundaries. I was holding walls.

The old way: You resist it. *"I can do it myself. I don't need anyone."*

The new way: You accept it. Not out of need, but out of grace.

Because receiving isn't about dependence—it's about honoring the balance of energy between you and another. You let others give, and in doing so, both of you feel seen, valued, connected. This is the sacred dance between masculine and feminine energy. Not a war. Not a hierarchy. But a balance. A breath. A flow.

Understanding this dance is only the beginning. Once you've learned how to move with both strength and softness, structure and flow—you're ready for the next part. This is where we stop performing and start embodying. Where we let our energy lead the way. Where we receive—not because we need, but because we're ready.

So why do we struggle to receive in relationships? Well, it's not just about opening your doors. It's about emotional labor. Invisible work. How often do you over-give—at work, in friendships, in your family? You carry the load. Say yes when you're tired. Fix what isn't yours to fix. But when someone offers to carry you, you resist. You feel guilty. Undeserving. Like receiving is a weakness.

Here's the truth: When you refuse to receive, you're saying to the world: *I don't need anyone. I can do it alone.* You keep pouring from an empty cup. And in doing so, you deny others the joy of giving. You rob them of the chance to feel needed. You keep the connection at arm's length.

When you allow yourself to receive, you say: *I trust you. I see you. We are in this together.* You replenish your own energy and allow others to do so. You strengthen your relationships. You create space for mutual nourishment. Because the art of receiving isn't a weakness. It's wisdom. It's wholeness. It's power in its most magnetic form. Embracing your feminine energy means opening yourself—not just to love from others, but to yourself. It's about receiving: compliments, support, care—without deflecting, downplaying, or apologizing.

When someone says, *"You look great,"* don't brush it off or point out your flaws or immediately give them a compliment back. Simply say, *"Thank you."* In that moment, you let love land. You affirm your worth. Receiving may seem small, but it's transformative. It says, *I am worthy of goodness.* And that quiet shift in how you accept things deepens every relationship you touch.

Remember that feminine energy doesn't push—it pulls. It doesn't chase attention—it draws it in. In a world that confuses loudness with confidence, feminine power waits, listens, and speaks when it matters. You don't need to force your way into the room. You are the room.

MAGNETIC CONFIDENCE: THE ENERGY YOU EXUDE

I used to be quiet in meetings. People overlooked me—until I finally spoke. And when I did, I'd already connected the dots in my head that no one else saw. My voice landed because it came from clarity, not noise. Feminine power is that: not volume, but impact. Not performance, but presence.

We've been taught to smile, nod, over-deliver—to earn our space. But feminine energy says: You belong without performance. True presence is magnetic. It doesn't need to prove—it simply is. Think of the most magnetic person you know. They don't rush to fill silences. They don't scramble to prove their worth. They don't shrink themselves to make others comfortable. Yet, when they speak, people lean in. That's presence.

Presence isn't just about how you carry yourself. It's the energy you bring into a room without saying a word. It's about owning your space so fully that others can't help but notice—even in silence. Because true power is felt long before it's heard.

Here's the truth: You don't have to choose between being respected and being authentic. Feminine leadership isn't about forcing your way to the top. It's about moving with such alignment that the right opportunities find you. It's knowing that your presence is your power. When you stop performing—when you stop trying to prove yourself and start simply being—that's when people listen. That's when doors open. That's when success stops being something you chase and it starts chasing you.

Feminine energy is magnetic; it's felt before it's seen. It's the energy you radiate before you even speak, the presence you exude in your every step. But here's the thing: You can't fake this energy. It starts with how you perceive yourself.

I used to dismiss my self-worth, dressing in sweatpants, telling myself it didn't matter. But *I* was paying attention. And when I saw my reflection—slouched, blending into the background—I shrank. My energy shrank. It wasn't the sweatpants that were the problem. It was the mindset they represented: a belief that I didn't matter enough to be noticed. But the days I chose differently—the days I stood taller, put in the effort, and shifted my energy—those were the days that felt different. Because when you show up for yourself, others notice. And so do you.

True confidence is born from being at home inside of yourself. It's moving through the world knowing you belong—not because someone else made space for you, but because you claimed it. It means stopping the cycle of shrinking or changing to fit spaces that were never meant for you. You stop waiting for permission to exist as you are. You realize that your presence is enough. Your existence is not an audition.

THE UNLEARNING: A RETURN TO TRUST

And getting there? That takes work. It's a process of unlearning everything that taught you to earn your worth through others' validation. True confidence happens when you stop asking for permission to be yourself and start listening to the part of you that already knows your value.

Reconnecting with your feminine energy is not about learning something new. It's about remembering what has always been inside you. It's a return to trust, to intuition, to authenticity. And it starts with these simple, radical acts of self-trust:

Tuning Into Intuition Through Stillness and Self-Trust

In a world that values speed, stillness is rebellion. Tune into your inner knowing before seeking outside validation. What if you stopped outsourcing your decisions and listened to the voice within?

Allowing Emotions to Flow
Emotions aren't obstacles; they're guides. Let them move through you. Stop apologizing for feeling. Let grief soften you, anger sharpen you, and joy overflow without questioning whether you deserve it.

Embracing Creativity and Play Without Guilt
Feminine energy thrives in creativity and flow. Play is not a luxury; it's a necessity. Allow yourself the freedom to create, to dance, to imagine—without needing it to be productive. Let yourself be immersed in something that makes you feel alive.

YOUR INVITATION BACK TO YOU
Reclaim the space you've always been meant to occupy. When you stop performing and start being—when you embrace your power, your authenticity, and your presence—the world changes. Not because you've forced it, but because you've allowed it to unfold. And in that allowance, everything becomes possible. This journey isn't about becoming something new. It's about remembering who you've always been.

So ask yourself:

- What would shift in your life if you stopped seeing your softness, your flow, your deep knowing as weaknesses but instead saw them as your greatest strengths?

- What parts of yourself have you been holding back for fear of being too much?

- How much of your energy has been spent performing instead of being?

- What would change if you trusted yourself fully—without hesitation, without second-guessing, without waiting for permission?

Feminine energy isn't something to earn. It's something to remember. It's not about being more. It's about being fully you. When you trust that, everything changes—not because you pushed harder, but because you finally stopped resisting your power.

You didn't lose it. You just stopped listening.

And now? You're coming home to it.

That's the shift. That's the power.

That's you.

REFLECTION FOR THE ROAD AHEAD

Every time you feel yourself shrinking to make others comfortable, pause. Breathe. And ask yourself:

- *Am I making myself small to feel safe, or am I stepping into a space that actually demands more of me?* Because safety is a seductive lie—it keeps you hidden, but it never makes you whole. Growth happens when you let yourself be fully seen.

- *Am I silencing myself out of fear, or is this a moment to stand firm and own my voice?* Because every time you swallow your truth, you teach yourself that your voice doesn't matter. And that's the biggest lie of all.

- *Am I dismissing my emotions, or am I recognizing them as insight into something deeper?* Because your emotions are not the enemy. They are a signal, a message, a map. Stop ignoring the very thing that was built to guide you.

To cultivate true feminine power, try this:

Drop the nervous filler words. Speak with pauses, not apologies.

Hold eye contact. Not aggressively, just long enough to show you're fully present.

Own your posture. Shoulders back, chin up—your body tells the world what you believe about yourself before you ever say a word.

Stop explaining, start deciding. Every time you over-explain yourself, you're subconsciously asking for permission.

Instead:

Replace "Does that make sense?" with silence. Let your words land.

Stop justifying your choices to people who haven't earned that access.

Trust that your "No" is a complete sentence.

People can feel when you're performing. Authenticity isn't about being liked—it's about being real. If something excites you, stop downplaying it. Speak about it boldly. If something isn't working for you, stop tolerating it. Speak up. If you're in a space where you feel like you can't be yourself, question whether that space deserves you.

Strength isn't about never bending—it's about knowing when to bend and when to stand firm. To embody this:

Recognize that discomfort isn't a stop sign. It's a threshold. Walk through it.

Let go of what you can't control. It's not yours to hold.

Trust that surrendering is sometimes more powerful than pushing.

Your emotions aren't weaknesses; they're data. Learn to translate them rather than be ruled by them.

When you feel anger, ask: *What boundary is being crossed?*

When you feel sadness, ask: *What needs my attention?*

When you feel discomfort, ask: *What is this trying to teach me?*

Here's the truth: The moment you fully choose yourself, the need to be chosen disappears. Because when you know your worth, you stop outsourcing it. When you stand in your truth, you realize validation is a hunger only self-acceptance can satisfy. When you stop waiting to be picked, you start walking like you belong.

And now? You're taking it all back. Not by fighting. Not by forcing. Not by twisting yourself into someone else's version of "enough." But by deciding—once and for all—that you already are. By walking into every room like you belong there. By standing in your truth even when your voice shakes. By showing up as your whole self, not the watered-down version that makes everyone else comfortable. Because when you are fully yourself, the right people recognize you. The right opportunities find you. The right life meets you—exactly where you stand.

This is your feminine power. It doesn't chase. It doesn't beg. It doesn't shrink. It simply is.

CHAPTER 3: EMBRACING YOUR ESSENCE
Soft and Strong, Wild and Wise

WE'VE BEEN TOLD a lie. A quiet, insidious lie that has shaped the way we see ourselves and our power. The lie that says we must choose. Be strong or be soft. Be wild or be wise. Be nurturing or be ambitious. *But never both.* From the time we were young, we've been nudged into one category or the other—too much or not enough, too emotional or too detached, too assertive or too passive. We learned to shrink parts of ourselves, to quiet the wildness, to soften the edges of our strength, to be digestible. We're taught that power is singular, that strength must be unyielding, that softness is weakness, that wildness is recklessness, and that wisdom is restraint.

But what if real power isn't found in choosing between them? What if it's in the ability to hold both at once? This chapter is about integration, not limitation. It's about reclaiming the fullness of who you are—the fire and the flow, the grace and the grit. You don't have to choose between softness and strength because the real power is in being both. You don't have to dim your playfulness to be wise because wisdom comes from knowing when to let go and when to hold firm. When you stop forcing yourself into a mold and start embracing the contradictions within you, your life begins to realign. You move differently. You lead differently. You love differently. You stop performing and start embodying. And in that space of full presence—where strength meets softness and wildness meets wisdom—you don't just exist. *You radiate.* This is your invitation to step fully into the wholeness of your being. Not just parts of you—the whole, untamed, powerful, intuitive, unstoppable you.

PATIENT AND DRIVEN

I want to tell you a story. Several, actually. Because I know what it feels like to believe I had to be one or the other. I've been soft in moments when softness seemed foolish, and I've been strong when the world told me to yield. I've followed my wild instincts and found wisdom in them. I've stood my ground with unshakable certainty and felt the deepest tenderness in the same breath.

Training for an Ironman is an endeavor that demands everything of you—body, mind, and spirit. The preparation isn't just grueling; it's obsessive. You train, you push, you ignore the warning signs, driven by the singular goal of crossing the finish line. It's 140.6 miles of extreme endurance: 2.4 miles of swimming, 112 miles on the bike, and a full marathon at the end, as if you didn't feel like the rest was already enough. The sheer physicality of it is both exhilarating and exhausting.

In my pursuit of that finish line, I learned an important lesson: being driven alone doesn't always lead to success. There's a fine line between pushing yourself and pushing too hard. And for me, that line was crossed when I tore my posterior tibial tendon, the very tendon that supports the arch of my foot. A silent reminder that my body was screaming for attention—and I hadn't been listening.

The injury was a wake-up call. The doctor's words were blunt: "If you don't take it easy for the next three months, you'll be lucky if you can walk without pain again, let alone run." My heart sank. This wasn't just a setback; it was a halt in the middle of my journey. For someone who had lived and breathed the idea of being driven, it was the hardest pill to swallow. I was forced into a boot and told to rest, a luxury I had never allowed myself. But in that forced stillness, I had no choice but to learn the art of patience. Patience with my body. Patience with the process. Patience with myself. I had no idea how long it would take to heal, no idea if I'd ever return to my original goal. I could only show up every day, slowly. And that was a difficult lesson.

But healing, like endurance, doesn't happen overnight. As I slowly and methodically took the time to heal, something unexpected began to unfold. I realized that healing wasn't just about time; it was about learning how to nurture my body, listen to it, and treat it with the kindness I had neglected before. I sought out learning new ways to run, enrolling in classes that taught me how to land my feet properly, how to move with grace rather than force. Every step felt like a struggle at first. It was humbling to admit that my progress wasn't linear. There were days when I couldn't even run five minutes without pain, when I felt like I was moving backward rather than forward.

But I was committed to my vision, even when the results were invisible. Every single day, I showed up. I was patient enough to let the process unfold and driven enough to keep showing up for myself even when progress felt like a distant dream. Eventually, the pain began to subside. My body started responding. Slowly, I began to run faster, bike longer, and move with more freedom. It wasn't the swift recovery I had imagined, but it was progress. When race day finally arrived, I crossed that finish line. I was exhausted, elated, and triumphant. But the real victory was deeper than the miles I'd covered. It was in the journey itself—the quiet moments of showing up for myself, of being driven despite the slow progress, of learning what it truly meant to be both patient and committed.

I had been told that to finish an Ironman, I had to push harder, go faster, and never stop. What I learned was that the true strength of an Ironman journey doesn't come from sheer force alone. It comes from the integration of both patience and drive—knowing when to press forward and when to hold back, when to push and when to pause. And in the end, the greatest success was not just crossing the finish line; it was learning how to honor the process of healing and growth. Because in that balance, I discovered a new relationship with myself—and a deeper, more sustainable power that I will carry with me far beyond race day. In learning to be patient and driven, I discovered how the rhythm of waiting could propel me forward with even greater strength. And in that same rhythm, I found a moment where commitment to myself became the very thing that set me free. It's not about choosing one over the other, but about embracing both—like the dance of freedom in the heart of commitment.

FREE AND COMMITTED

There's a certain weight we all carry when we feel bound by society's expectations—expectations about who we should be, what we should want, and the paths we should follow. For a long time, I played along, thinking that the way to fulfillment was through the lens of those expectations. For me, it looked like the promise of marriage, of settling into a life that followed a very clear script. The path I had once believed would fulfill me suddenly felt like it was holding me back. I had been seeking a sense of belonging through someone else, through a role, a title, an external commitment, but it had left me feeling empty—like I was about to enter into a life that wasn't truly mine.

In walking away, I wasn't rejecting commitment. Quite the opposite. I was choosing to commit to myself. I was choosing to explore who I was, what mattered to me, and how I wanted to show up in this world. I was saying yes to a life that was mine to design, to one that wasn't dictated by societal norms or external pressures. The freedom I found in that choice wasn't just about independence —it was about embracing the responsibility of my own growth. It wasn't about running away from something; it was about fully committing to a life that honored *me*.

The new life of commitment to myself opened doors I hadn't even known were closed. I began to see the world differently. I could walk into a room full of strangers without fear because I wasn't relying on anyone else to validate me. I wasn't seeking approval or trying to fit a mold. I had already committed to being myself, and in that, I found the most beautiful freedom—freedom to explore, to make mistakes, to delight in new experiences without the weight of someone else's expectations holding me down.

I traveled solo, not out of a need to escape, but as a choice to immerse myself in my own curiosity. I met new people and tried new things, and every experience became a chance to deepen my commitment to the person I was becoming, not the one society told me I should be, but the one I was discovering through my own eyes, on my own terms. I finally understood what it meant to be free—not in the absence of commitment, but because of it.

And through this, I realized that true commitment isn't about locking yourself into something. It's about aligning your actions, your decisions, and your intentions with your authentic self, and in doing so, you find a kind of freedom that's only possible when you stop trying to conform to what others expect of you. From the freedom found in commitment, I moved toward the freedom that's found in truth. As I stood in the space where I could no longer hide behind expectations, I found that my rawness, my realness, was the spark that ignited my true radiance. It was in shedding the layers of who I thought I should be that I uncovered the brilliance of who I truly was.

REAL AND RADIANT

For as long as I can remember, I lived in the shadow of a version of myself that wasn't truly mine. I used to be a people-pleaser, someone who avoided confrontation, feared judgment, and made herself small to fit in. I never corrected people when they mispronounced my name because I didn't want to cause any discomfort. I feared the world's judgment so much that I lost sight of who I truly was. It wasn't about who I was, but about how I thought others perceived me. I kept hiding behind that mask, never daring to let the world see the true me.

But somewhere along the way, I felt a pull—a deep, unshakable desire to stop living in the shadows of someone else's expectations. As I began creating something that was truly meaningful to me—a space for women to connect, share, and grow—I realized I couldn't hide behind that people-pleasing person anymore. I had to step forward and own my truth. I had to let go of the fear that had been holding me back, the fear of what people might think, the fear of rejection. It was time to embrace my real self and let it shine, without pretense, without filters.

I remember the moment I put it out there: announcing to the world on Facebook and Instagram that I was creating something. It wasn't perfect. It wasn't polished. It wasn't the way I imagined it in my head. But it was *me*. I wasn't worried about whether people would approve or not. I didn't care if some might judge me. I didn't care if someone rolled their eyes or mocked me from the sidelines. The act of saying *"This is me, and this is what I'm doing,"* was liberating. It was my declaration of independence from the expectations of others.

Instead of shrinking in fear, I chose to shine. And you know what? Something incredible happened. In stepping into my truth, in showing up as the real me, I felt a radiance I had never known before. I felt a surge of confidence that went beyond anything I had experienced. It was as if the more I allowed myself to be raw and authentic, the more vibrant I became. It wasn't just about overcoming fear; it was about thriving despite it. And in that thriving, I found something even more beautiful—a confidence rooted in my truth.

This new version of myself—the one who embraced vulnerability, creativity, and authenticity—shone brighter than any polished image I could have crafted. She wasn't perfect, but she didn't need to be. She was real, and that was more than enough. She didn't hide. She didn't hold back. She showed up, and in doing so, she radiated.

The truth is, authenticity isn't ugly or messy. It's powerful and beautiful. It's like a phoenix rising from the ashes—an emergence that feels messy at first, but in its rawness, it reveals something extraordinary. The more I allowed myself to be vulnerable and real, the more I recognized the beauty in the process. The more I leaned into my creativity, my dreams, and my values, the more radiant I became—not because I was trying to shine, but because I stopped trying to hide.

And now, I look at myself, and I am amazed at how far I've come. I no longer feel like I have to apologize for who I am or water down my message. I am both real and radiant, and there's nothing more freeing than that. This is the magic of embracing your truth. It's not about being perfect or putting on a façade. It's about being you—fully, unapologetically, and without reservation. And when you do that, you shine in a way that nothing else can replicate.

True Resilience

We live in a world that demands we choose a side or way of being, that tells us we must be either one thing or the other. But why can't we embrace both? You can be gentle and unshakable—the person who offers warmth and softness but doesn't break when things get hard. You can be intuitive and strategic—the person who trusts their gut but also knows how to think five steps ahead. You can be fierce and tender—someone who stands up for what they believe in but leads with love, not aggression.

So ask yourself:

- Where have you been told you had to choose—between softness and strength, between following your instincts and making the "logical" choice?

- What parts of yourself have you been suppressing because they didn't seem to fit?

- What would it look like to embody both—to be strong and soft, wild and wise, all at once?

Because the truth is, you already are. You just have to let yourself be all of you.

Society has long equated strength with rigidity—the unyielding backbone, the immovable stance, the idea that true power means never bending. We see this in how leadership is often portrayed as forceful decisiveness, how success is tied to relentless perseverance, and how emotions, particularly in women, are sometimes mistaken for fragility. But real resilience isn't about being unbreakable. It's about being flexible enough to absorb life's shocks and still stand tall.

Consider the oak and the reed—a fable that has been told for centuries. The oak stands mighty and proud, but in the face of a storm, it resists so fiercely that it eventually snaps. Meanwhile, the reed bends with the wind, yielding just enough to let the force pass through, and in the end, it remains standing. True resilience is not about refusing to yield—it's about knowing when to move with the forces around you so you don't break under the weight of them.

We've internalized the idea that being adaptable means we're weak, that compromise is a sign of surrender, and that if we soften, we will lose ourselves. But some of the strongest people in history—Nelson Mandela, Eleanor Roosevelt, Ruth Bader Ginsburg—knew that power lies in knowing when to stand firm and when to adjust. Ginsburg, for instance, fought tirelessly for gender equality, yet she also knew how to strategically navigate opposition, making incremental changes that eventually reshaped history.

In our own lives, we must ask:

- Where have we mistaken control for strength?

- Where has surrender been more powerful than force?

- How can we be strong in our convictions while also fluid in our approach?

To be truly resilient, we must embrace both firmness and flexibility, holding our ground while knowing when to move with the winds of change.

Recognizing True Wisdom

There's a misconception that wisdom is solemn, that growing older and gaining insight must come with a kind of seriousness. But the most alive people—those who radiate presence and understanding —are often the ones who never stop playing, laughing, or remaining curious. Wisdom and playfulness are not at odds; in fact, they fuel each other.

Routine has a way of settling in quietly, disguising itself as efficiency, as responsibility, as adulthood. We wake up, check our phones, move through the motions of the day, filling every gap with productivity or distraction. When was the last time we simply sat— not to plan, not to analyze, but to wonder? To let a question drift in without immediately seeking an answer? To look at something familiar as if seeing it for the first time? A child asks, "Why?" over and over, not to challenge but to understand. Somewhere along the way, we are taught to stop asking, to accept the way things are, to let routine replace wonder. What if the deepest wisdom lies in never losing that sense of curiosity?

Reintroducing curiosity doesn't mean overhauling our lives; it starts in the smallest moments. Lingering in a conversation just to explore a new perspective, letting ourselves be fascinated by the way light moves through a window, or pausing in a quiet space without rushing to fill it. Wonder isn't something we have to find; it's something we have to allow.

And maybe that's the real question—when did we stop allowing it? When did we decide that stillness had to be justified, that every empty space needed filling? As children, we could lie on the grass for hours, watching clouds shift and reshape, dreaming up stories from the patterns in the sky. But somewhere along the way, we began to believe that time spent in simple presence was time wasted. What if we let ourselves return to that? To sit outside, feeling the warmth of the sun on our skin without needing to name it as "self-care." To listen to the wind move through the trees without needing to label it as "meditation." To exist in a moment simply because it is. Perhaps the deepest wisdom lies in reclaiming these spaces—the ones where joy is quiet but infinite, where wonder is not something we seek but something we remember how to receive.

Play is Life

Take Sister Madonna Buder, better known as the Iron Nun. She began running in her late 40s and went on to complete over 45 Ironman races, becoming the oldest woman ever to finish one at 82. When asked how she keeps going, she says that movement is her prayer, her play, and her connection to the divine. Her story is proof that playfulness is not childish—it's life-giving.

Even in the smallest ways, we can reintroduce wonder into our lives. An older woman in my swim lane the other week finished her workout and, instead of just climbing out of the pool, she started doing handstands in the water. Just because. Watching her, I felt a pull—why don't I let myself do that more? When did we stop playing just for the sake of it?

So how do we cultivate both wisdom and playfulness in daily life?

By staying curious—asking new questions, seeking new perspectives, and never assuming we have all the answers.

By embracing impractical joy—whether that's dancing in the kitchen, learning something just because it fascinates us, or flipping upside down in a pool for no reason at all.

By remembering that growing wiser doesn't mean growing heavier—it can mean growing lighter.

There is a wildness in all of us. It is not recklessness, not chaos—it is something far deeper, something ancient, something that cannot be contained by rules that were never ours to begin with. It is the knowing in our bones, the voice inside us before the world told us how we should be. Wildness was never meant to be easy. It is meant to be true. To be wild is not to be careless; it is to be free. And freedom does not mean abandoning responsibility or setting fire to what you've built. Freedom means belonging to yourself first. It means unlearning the quiet apology woven into your existence. It means expanding back into the full shape of who you are, even when the world would prefer you smaller.

So ask yourself—where have you tamed yourself for the comfort of others? Where have you traded in your instincts for approval? And more importantly—are you ready to take it all back? Because reclaiming your wildness isn't about running away; it's about returning home. Not to a place, but to yourself. To the voice that was always there beneath the noise. To the girl you were before the world told you who to be, before you started editing yourself. Run towards *her*.

Strength Without Rigidity

In our journey toward embracing both the fire and fluidity within us, it's essential to remember that balance does not mean perfection —it means integration. It means finding moments where your inner fire can burn bright, propelling you forward, and where fluidity can guide you with ease, making sure you don't burn out.

True strength lies in resilience—not in force. It's standing firm in your truth without needing to prove it. It's rooted in the quiet certainty of your being, knowing who you are and honoring that, regardless of external opinions or pressures. This strength doesn't shout; it hums. It doesn't force its way through; it creates its own path.

For example, consider the story of Maya Angelou. She was a woman of incredible strength, not because she was loud or domineering, but because she stood firmly in the quiet power of her words. Maya grew up in poverty, faced racism, and endured trauma that left her mute for nearly five years as a child. But in that silence, she listened deeply, absorbing the cadence of language and the power of storytelling. When she finally spoke again, she carried words like sacred tools. Her autobiographical book *I Know Why the Caged Bird Sings* broke new ground in American literature, giving voice to experiences of racism, identity, and womanhood that had long been silenced. She became a celebrated poet, a singer, an actress, and eventually a cultural icon. Presidents invited her to speak. Millions found courage in her poems like "Still I Rise" and "Phenomenal Woman," which became rallying cries for dignity and self-worth. Her strength was not in force but in resonance. She didn't shout to be heard; she spoke with such grounded truth that the world leaned in to listen. That is how she shaped the world: by embodying confidence that didn't need to prove itself; it only needed to express itself.

The Fire of Flow

Flow doesn't mean aimless drifting. It means finding a rhythm between intention and surrender. It means flowing without losing direction—moving forward with grace, even when the path isn't clear. It is honoring your intuition and inner knowing while also staying grounded in your goals and values. This is where the dance of fire and fluidity happens. Think about a river carving through rock. It doesn't force its way through; it moves with the terrain. It adapts to obstacles, but the water always moves forward, relentless in its direction. This is how we move with ease in life—adjusting to what comes but always moving with intention.

Intuition is the spark of the divine within us, our fire, while intention is the steady flame that keeps us on track. To balance these two forces is to honor your gut feelings but also direct them toward a clear purpose. It's knowing when to trust the whispers of your soul and when to act on them with deliberate force.

A beautiful example of this balance is Serena Williams, one of the greatest athletes of all time. Her strength wasn't only in her physical power—though she dominated tennis for over two decades —it was in how she combined intuition with intention. On the court, Serena often described "feeling" her way through a match. She didn't just react to the ball; she anticipated it, reading her opponent's energy and letting her instincts guide her movement. That was her intuition: the spark, the gut sense of what was about to happen. But intuition alone doesn't win twenty-three Grand Slam titles. Serena paired that inner knowing with relentless intention:

hours of practice, strategic precision, mental toughness, and the clear vision of victory that drove her every swing. She trusted her body to tell her when to adjust, and then directed that wisdom into focused, deliberate action. That balance—listening deeply to her gut and then channeling it through intention—is what made her not just a champion but a legend. Her fire wasn't chaotic; it was flow, honed and directed. Throughout her career, she has embodied a fierce determination, but there's a quiet knowing behind her every swing. She doesn't just play the game; she reads it, allowing her intuition to guide her movements but always with a clear vision of victory.

To embody both fire and fluidity is to honor the parts of yourself that are fierce as well as the parts that are soft. It is not about choosing one over the other—it's about integrating both in a way that honors your most authentic self. We cannot force the fire to burn constantly, just as we cannot allow fluidity to carry us aimlessly. But when we embrace both, we create a life that is purposeful, resilient, and filled with grace.

EMBODYING INTEGRATION

You cannot imitate your way into wholeness. You cannot perform freedom, pretend confidence, or force authenticity. Embodiment is not an act—it is a state of being. And the truth is, you will know the difference. *The world will, too.*

Going through the motions is not the same as *living* the truth. You can stand tall without truly believing in your strength. You can whisper words of self-love without actually feeling them. You can loosen your grip without ever trusting the fall. But this path—the path of integration—asks for more. It asks for patience, for presence, for the willingness to sit in the discomfort of undoing before the ease of becoming.

I used to always need something—music, a show, scrolling, a glass of wine—anything to keep me from being fully alone with myself. The silence felt too loud, too honest. I'd tell myself I was just relaxing, just winding down, but really, I was avoiding the stillness. Because in the quiet, there was no one left to perform for. Just me, with all the feelings I hadn't wanted to feel. But at some point, I got tired. Tired of pretending I was okay when I wasn't. Tired of avoiding the very space I needed to heal. So I started doing the brave thing. I put the phone down. Left the TV off. Let the wine sit unopened. And I sat with myself—restless, uncomfortable, unsure. But in that space, something began to transform. I didn't try to become anything. I just stayed. And slowly, the noise inside started to quiet, too. That's when I started remembering who I was.

Because real transformation is not something you can fake your way through. It is something you grow into. And that growth happens in the quiet moments—when you catch yourself softening instead of bracing, when you stop seeking permission to take up space, when strength no longer feels like something you prove but something you are. So ask yourself—where have you been acting rather than being? Where have you mistaken effort for embodiment? And what would it take to feel this truth in your bones rather than just understanding it in your mind?

REFLECTIONS FOR THE ROAD AHEAD

Now, let's turn to some tangible practices that can help you integrate these concepts into your life:

Breathwork: Breathwork is one of the most powerful practices for balancing the body and mind. It is deeply calming yet invigorating. When you feel scattered, use breathwork to regain focus. Breathwork helps to balance the fiery energy of the mind and the fluidity of the body, allowing you to come back to center.

- **Practice:** Try alternating between long, slow exhales to release tension and sharp, controlled inhales to ignite focus. This simple practice can instantly bring you back into balance.

Movement: Movement—whether through yoga, dance, or any form of physical activity—helps us integrate fire and fluidity in the body. Yoga, for example, combines strength (fire) with flow (fluidity). It teaches us how to hold a position with power while allowing breath and body to flow seamlessly through the next.

- **Practice:** Try a simple yoga movement, like a sun salutation. Move from one pose to another, focusing on the sensation of the body shifting between stillness and movement. Feel the strength in each pose, but also the fluidity between them.

Daily Habits for Inner Fire and Ease: This balance is also cultivated in the small, everyday moments. What daily practices can support this dynamic flow between strength and ease?

- **Practice:** Start your day with a moment of stillness, a quiet meditation, or a breathwork practice. Then, as you move through your day, practice being intentional with each task you take on, but don't get so caught up in the results that you forget to enjoy the process. Notice how being present can allow both fire and fluidity to coexist effortlessly.

Embrace the Present Moment: Perhaps one of the most challenging, yet rewarding, practices for this balance is being present. When we're fully present, we can tap into both our strength and fluidity with ease. The practice of mindfulness allows us to tap into the quiet fire of focus while remaining fluid and adaptable to whatever arises.

- **Practice:** Set aside moments during your day to stop and notice the world around you. Feel the ground beneath your feet. Listen to the sounds in your environment. This practice of being present cultivates an inner fire of mindfulness while remaining fluid in your ability to adapt.

Journaling Prompts for Deep Integration

What would it feel like to move through the world with nothing to prove and nowhere to perform?

Where in my life am I still performing instead of fully embodying who I am?

If I deeply trusted myself—my voice, my timing, my truth— how would that trust shape the way I live?

Where have I been quieting my wildness to stay safe, small, or palatable?

In what moments have I chosen control over softness? What was I protecting?

What am I afraid might happen if I let myself be fully seen— unpolished, unfiltered, undone?

What would it mean to feel this truth not just in my mind, but in my bones?

CHAPTER 4: INDEPENDENCE VS. EMPOWERMENT

Why "I Don't Need Anyone" is a Trap

WE'VE ALL HEARD it—or maybe we've even said it ourselves: *"I don't need anyone."* It's worn like a badge of honor, proof that we can handle anything on our own. We've been told that independence is the goal, that relying on others is weak, and that being a strong woman means never needing help. But let's be honest—*how's that working out for us?*

The truth is, hyper-independence isn't always strength. Most of the time, it's just fear in disguise. A defense mechanism built from past disappointments, betrayals, or the belief that no one will catch us if we fall. It's the armor we put on to avoid vulnerability, but in doing so, we shut out love, support, and the deep human connection we actually crave.

This chapter is about breaking that pattern—not by abandoning our self-sufficiency, but by redefining what strength actually looks like. Because true empowerment isn't about doing everything alone. It's about knowing when to stand strong and when to let others stand beside us.

There's a moment—sometimes a single defining one, sometimes a slow accumulation—where we decide: I will never rely on anyone again. Maybe it was a heartbreak so deep it left cracks in your foundation. Maybe it was a betrayal that taught you that trusting the wrong person is dangerous. Or maybe it was growing up in a world that told you strong women don't ask for help. So, we armor up. Bit by bit, we stack the defenses. We convince ourselves that needing nothing and no one is the safest way forward. We build careers without leaning on anyone. We handle life's storms alone, pride swelling every time we make it through another challenge without asking for support. And the world applauds us for it. Look at her—she's doing it all. *But at what cost?*

We glorify the woman who "does it all." The one who juggles a demanding career, personal growth, friendships, and maybe even kids—without ever showing a crack in the surface. She's the one who says, "*I got it,*" even when she's drowning. She's celebrated for her resilience, for never needing anyone, for being so strong. But strength, when used as armor, turns into isolation. Hyper-independence comes at a price—and often, we don't even realize we're paying it until the exhaustion sets in.

Hyper-independence doesn't just appear out of nowhere. It's often born from:

Childhood Conditioning
If you grew up in an environment where asking for help led to disappointment or punishment, you likely learned to rely on yourself.

Betrayal & Broken Trust
If someone you deeply trusted let you down—whether in love, friendship, or family—you may have internalized the belief that no one is truly dependable.

Emotional Exhaustion
When you refuse to lean on others, even for the smallest things, you drain yourself faster than you realize. Hyper-independence feels like power, until one day, you wake up exhausted. Until you realize that the strength you built was never supposed to be a prison. Until you see that, in avoiding dependency, you've also avoided intimacy, ease, and true support. This leads to loneliness and disconnection.

When we push people away long enough, they stop trying. The relationships that could have brought us joy and support fade into the background, leaving us wondering why we feel so alone. There's a fine line between being self-sufficient and being emotionally detached. *Self-sufficiency* says, I know I can take care of myself, but I am open to love, support, and collaboration. *Emotional detachment* says, I don't trust anyone enough to let them close, so I'll do everything myself—even if it hurts me. *The difference?* One is rooted in security. The other is rooted in fear.

FEAR OF VULNERABILITY

Let's be honest—being independent can feel safe. No one can hurt you if you don't let them get close. But that safety also keeps out the depth, warmth, and connection we need to thrive. Somewhere along the way, we started equating strength with isolation. We glorified the lone wolf, the woman who never needed a shoulder to lean on, the one who handled everything herself. But real strength isn't about doing it all alone—it's about knowing when to let people in.

The longer we wear our independence as a shield, the harder it becomes to let love in. When someone tries to help, we flinch. When someone offers care, we reject it. Not because we don't want it, but because we don't know how to receive it. A lifetime of carrying everything alone often leads to resentment—toward the people who don't help (because we never let them) and toward a world that told us we had to be this tough in the first place.

The truth? Hyper-independence isn't empowerment. It's self-protection in disguise. And while it may feel like control, what it actually creates is disconnection. Real power isn't just the ability to stand tall—it's the ability to stand tall and remain open. To know that you could do it all alone, but that you don't have to. To trust yourself deeply while also trusting that the right people can meet you in that strength.

Let's take a minute to redefine strength:

- Strength is knowing when to ask for help without feeling like it diminishes your worth.

- Strength is allowing yourself to receive without guilt.

- Strength is knowing that letting someone in isn't a sign of weakness—it's a sign of wisdom.

Empowerment has been sold to us as independence at all costs. But empowerment isn't about proving that you don't need anyone. It's about knowing that your power is unshaken whether you stand alone or with others by your side. Think of the women you admire— are they truly alone? Or have they built networks of support, community, and connection that make them even stronger?

Let's check out some stories of women who let go of the Lone-Wolf Mentality:

Michelle Obama
In her early years, Michelle was fiercely independent, balancing her law career, motherhood, and public life. But she has spoken openly about how learning to accept help—from mentors, her husband, her close friends—allowed her to grow in ways she never expected. Her strength was never in doing it all alone, but in knowing how to build a powerful ecosystem of support.

Glennon Doyle
In *Untamed*, author and activist Glennon Doyle reflects on how she spent years equating strength with self-sufficiency—silencing her needs, enduring quietly, and wearing her independence like armor. Despite her outward success as a writer and speaker, she

realized that her "togetherness" was a form of hiding. True empowerment, she discovered, wasn't about doing it all alone but about allowing herself to be fully seen—messy, needy, and human—by the people who loved her. That shift from hyper-independence to radical connection became the cornerstone of her work, inspiring millions of women to stop performing resilience and start practicing truth.

Oprah Winfrey
Oprah is one of the most powerful women in the world, and yet she never credits her success to isolation. Instead, she constantly acknowledges the mentors, friendships, and partnerships that helped shape her journey. She embraces both self-sufficiency and collaboration, proving that you don't have to choose between independence and connection.

LEARNING TO INTEGRATE

True empowerment is integration. It's knowing when to lead and when to lean. When to carry your own weight and when to let someone else help. When to stand in your strength and when to allow yourself to be held. Because at the end of the day, a woman *in her power* isn't the one who does it all alone. She's the one who knows she doesn't have to.

Before you can truly receive in a healthy way, you have to know what you actually need. When you aren't deeply connected to yourself, it's easy to seek validation instead of true support. To look for answers outside of yourself rather than developing inner trust. It's also easy to accept things that don't actually align with you simply because they're offered. Being grounded in yourself means knowing who you are before inviting others in—so that when they do show up, you can receive them without trying to shape them into something they're not. You don't need them to complete you, but you welcome what they bring.

This is where the real work begins. It's easy to swing to one extreme—either relying too much on others for direction and validation or shutting people out completely to prove you don't need them. But the magic happens in the middle, in the space where you are both deeply grounded in yourself and open to love, support, and guidance. This isn't about losing your independence. It's about refining it. True independence isn't about doing everything alone—it's about knowing yourself so well that when you receive love, support, or guidance, it's not filling a void, it's expanding you.

RESIST RESISTANCE

For a lot of women, receiving is uncomfortable. We've been taught to be the caretakers, the givers, the ones who handle everything. So when someone offers us something—whether it's help, love, or even a simple act of kindness—we instinctively resist.

How many times have you said:

- "Oh, you don't have to do that!" when someone offers to help?

- "I'll just handle it," even when you're drowning?

- "I'm fine," when you're absolutely not?

Receiving requires softness, and softness can feel vulnerable when you've spent years building walls. But here's the shift: receiving doesn't make you weak, it makes you whole.

Start practicing:

- Saying thank you instead of deflecting when someone offers you something.

- Letting people show up for you without feeling like you owe them something in return.

- Expressing your needs without fear of being a burden.

It's not taking—it's allowing. And allowing is one of the most powerful things you can do.

BOUNDARIES

Boundaries are often misunderstood as walls. But real boundaries don't shut people out—they create the space for deeper, healthier connections.

Boundaries let you say:

- "I trust myself enough to know what is and isn't right for me."

- "I am open to love and support but not at the cost of my well-being."

- "I can give and receive in a way that honors my energy."

This means:

- Learning to say no without guilt. Your time, energy, and emotional well-being are valuable.

- Speaking your truth instead of shrinking to fit what others expect.

- Being intentional about your *yes*—not saying yes out of obligation but because it's truly aligned.

Boundaries are what allow you to stand firmly in your power while still being open to connection. They don't keep love out—they make space for the right kind of love, the kind that fuels you rather than drains you. The goal is not to be independent to the point of isolation or so open that you lose yourself. The goal is to live in balance—rooted in who you are while deeply connected to the world around you.

Isolation

The myth of *"I don't need anyone"* thrives in isolation, and it's a dangerous myth that many women fall into. At first, it feels empowering—like we're proving to ourselves and the world that we can stand on our own two feet. But what happens when we go it alone for too long is we lose touch with something incredibly powerful: *connection.*

In my time living in Phoenix, I had a circle of friends, but it was built on surface-level connections. We'd cycle together, laugh together, and have Sunday dinner together, but when we parted, no one reached out to check on me. There was no *real* bond. No one cared to know how I was doing or what had changed in my life during the week.

Then, I moved to Olympia and discovered that it was important not just to find new friends but to create deep, authentic relationships with people who aligned with my core values. Suddenly, I had a group of people who cared. They didn't just talk about the weather; they sent me text messages just to check in on me during daylight savings time (something we didn't observe in Phoenix), making sure I was doing all right in the darkness. These little gestures told me something profound: they *saw* me, they *valued* me, and they wanted to be part of my journey. This is why going it alone is overrated. Powerful women don't thrive in isolation. We *need* each other. Our growth is nurtured in connection, in true, meaningful relationships that fuel our souls.

So, let's talk about how to cultivate these meaningful friendships and partnerships. Because building a community isn't just about finding people who are similar to you—it's about creating bonds with people who will challenge you, support you, and inspire you.

CREATING CONNECTION

When I started aligning my life with my core values, I sought out communities where I could do more than just "exist"—I sought spaces where I could *grow*. I joined running clubs, went to improv classes, took salsa lessons, and even started subbing in the Symphony. These spaces weren't just hobbies for me; they were opportunities to connect with others who shared my passions. But as I grew, I realized that simply doing these things wasn't enough. I needed something deeper, something that would nourish my inner world. So, I created women's groups. These weren't just casual meetups.

I asked the big questions:

- What lights you up?

- What scares you the most?

- What are your deepest desires, and what do you want to create in this life?

These questions allowed us to connect at a soul level. We could show up with all of our fears, dreams, and uncertainties, and we knew we wouldn't be judged. Instead, we'd be supported, encouraged, and empowered. That's when I realized: this is what *connection* looks like.

LEARNING ABOUT OURSELVES

We've discussed that independence, when misused, becomes a fortress, an armor we wear to protect ourselves from the world's chaos, pain, and disappointments. We've learned that strength is not defined by isolation, but true strength doesn't mean pushing people away and pretending we don't need anyone. In fact, strength grows in the moments of vulnerability, in the quiet spaces where we allow others in, not as saviors, but as partners in this journey. We've unpacked how hyper-independence often hides wounds—broken trust, fears from the past, or that persistent belief that relying on others is somehow a weakness. But we've also learned that self-sufficiency and emotional detachment are not the same thing. We can be self-reliant, deeply grounded in who we are, and still lean on others, still allow ourselves to be seen.

Now, the question is: what have we learned about ourselves through this exploration? Where have we been too afraid to receive? Where have we built walls thinking we were keeping ourselves safe only to find that they've isolated us, kept us stuck, and worn us thin?

My relationship with independence has been complicated. There was a time when I was afraid that if I leaned too much on others, I'd lose myself, lose my power, or become a burden. But the truth is, the more I allowed myself to be seen—vulnerable, open, real—the more I found that my own strength was magnified by the love and support of others. I wasn't weaker for receiving; I was stronger for giving others the chance to lift me up.

So now, as I reflect on this journey, I ask myself: How can I invite more collaboration, connection, and support into my life? How can I stop running solo and open my heart to the wisdom, love, and guidance that's already available to me? What if the very thing we've been afraid to ask for is the thing that helps us evolve? That's where the growth takes root: when we stop holding so tightly to our self-sufficiency and start flowing, allowing others to flow with us. The true power of collaboration lies in trusting, not just the other person, but the process itself.

The next chapter of this journey isn't about standing alone in the spotlight of our independence. It's about weaving our threads together with others, about living in flow, tapping into our intuition, sensuality, and inner knowing—because when we surrender to connection, we step into a power greater than we could have ever achieved alone.

REFLECTIONS FOR THE ROAD AHEAD

Let's talk about the small but meaningful ways to shift from, *"I've got this alone,"* to *"I am supported."* This transition is subtle, but it's informative. It's about consciously shifting from an attitude of self-reliance to one of interdependence. These shifts don't always need to be grand gestures—they can be simple, everyday moments that make all the difference.

Start with small asks.
Instead of pushing through everything alone, ask for help when you need it—even if it's just for something small, like a coffee date or advice. It creates space for deeper connection.

Engage in authentic conversations.
Go beyond the small talk. Ask your friends the big, scary questions. Ask them about their dreams, their fears, their challenges. When you open the door for these types of

conversations, it invites others to share their true selves, and that's where real connection happens.

Create space for people to support you.
It's not just about asking—it's about letting people show up for you without guilt or hesitation. When someone offers you help, simply say, "Thank you," and receive it.

Be intentional about who you invite into your life.
Align yourself with people who are committed to their own growth and who support yours. It's about creating a network of people who encourage each other to rise, not just stay in comfortable, superficial places.

Building a life rooted in collaboration and community means intentionally choosing people who will help you rise, challenge you, and, most importantly, see you for who you truly are. This is the power of connection: it doesn't diminish you—it amplifies you.

CHAPTER 5: LIVING IN FLOW

Tapping Into Your Intuition, Sensuality, and Inner Knowing

WE'VE SPENT so much of our lives believing that effort equals outcome. That if we push hard enough, strategize well enough, anticipate every possible variable, we can shape the world to fit our vision. We pride ourselves on our ability to make things happen—to hustle, to plan, to force things into place. And for a time, it works. But eventually, the exhaustion sets in. The frustration. The burnout.

Because not everything in life is meant to be pushed. Some things are meant to flow.

Water doesn't force its way around a mountain; it follows the natural curves of the land. It doesn't fight the rocks—it moves around them, over them, reshaping the landscape over time without resistance. Flow is not passivity. It's power in its purest, most sustainable form. But the shift from force to flow is uncomfortable at first. When you've built your life around control, surrender feels like a foreign language. You second-guess it. You want to reach for the steering wheel to make sure things are still moving. You mistake effortlessness for carelessness.

I've felt this shift most in my past relationships. The moments when I tried to make something happen—when I analyzed every silence, reached out just to get a response, orchestrated connection instead of simply allowing it to become—I felt drained. It's a grasping kind of energy, a tension that builds in my body and mind.

But when I step back? When I let things unfold without force, without manipulation, without needing an answer right now? That's when I feel the most at peace. That's when I'm not just waiting for something to happen—I'm living in what is.

This shift isn't just about relationships. It's about everything—our careers, our creative pursuits, our personal growth. Force drains. Flow fuels. So, how do we begin to move from one to the other? How do we stop pushing and start allowing?

TRUSTING THE FLOW

It begins with trust. Trust in ourselves, trust in the timing of our lives, and trust that what is meant for us will not require us to force it into being. We've been taught that power looks like action—doing, deciding, initiating. And while those things are important, they are only half of the equation. True power isn't just about what we do; it's also about what we allow ourselves to receive.

Receptivity is often misunderstood. We associate it with passivity, weakness, or dependency. But in reality, the ability to receive—love, support, wisdom, even rest—is a form of strength. Receptivity is not inaction. It is an active state of allowing, of trusting, of knowing that sometimes the most powerful thing we can do is simply be open—to love, to life, to the wisdom that is always trying to reach us. It requires trust. It requires openness. And most of all, it requires an understanding that we are worthy of what we are given.

Think about how difficult it can be to accept a genuine compliment. Someone tells you, "You're incredible at what you do." And instead of simply receiving it, you deflect: "Oh, it was nothing," or "I got lucky." Or when someone offers help, and you instinctively respond, "No, I've got it," even when you're drowning. We do this because we equate receiving with burdening others or with being weak. But what if receiving is actually what allows us to grow?

Imagine a tree. It stands strong, rooted in the earth, reaching toward the sky. It grows, not by forcing itself taller, but by receiving —sunlight, water, nutrients. It takes in what it needs without apology, without questioning whether it deserves it. And in that receptivity, it thrives. The same is true for us. The more we allow ourselves to receive—love, support, insight—the stronger we become. It's in the listening, in the surrender, in the allowing that we cultivate a deeper power.

A woman who can receive love fully without fear of losing herself is powerful. A woman who can accept support without feeling indebted is powerful. A woman who can trust the wisdom that comes through stillness rather than constantly seeking answers through effort is powerful. This doesn't mean we stop taking action. It means we learn the art of discernment—the dance between knowing when to move forward and when to let go.

- **Recognizing When to Act**: If you feel clear, grounded, and inspired—move. If an opportunity arises and everything in you says yes, take it. Action in flow feels aligned, not frantic. It comes from confidence, not fear.

- **Recognizing When to Surrender**: If you feel resistance, forcing, or chasing—pause. If you're grasping for certainty, replaying conversations in your head, or trying to make something happen that isn't unfolding naturally, step back. Surrender doesn't mean giving up; it means creating space for things to come together in their own time.

Here's how this plays out in different areas of life:

- **In Relationships:** There's a difference between reaching out because you genuinely want to connect and reaching out because you want validation. When connection flows naturally, it feels good; when we force it, it drains us.

- **In Creativity:** Inspiration doesn't always come on demand. There's a difference between following an idea that excites you and forcing yourself to create when you feel blocked. Creativity thrives in space, not pressure.

- **In Your Career:** There are moments to push forward, to advocate for yourself, to take a leap. But there are also moments when the best move is to pause, observe, and allow the right opportunities to reveal themselves.

- **In Self-Discovery:** Growth isn't about constantly seeking, fixing, or proving. Sometimes, the biggest shifts happen when we stop trying to figure it all out and let clarity arise in its own time.

SENSE AND SENSUALITY

We often think of sensuality in a narrow way—something tied to romance, seduction, or external beauty. But true sensuality is something much deeper. It is the art of being fully present in your body, attuned to the world through your senses. It is the ability to experience life—not just think about it.

Sensuality is how we feel the world around us. The warmth of the sun on our skin. The grounding sensation of bare feet on the earth. The pleasure of deep, slow breaths filling our lungs. It is how we connect, not just with others, but with ourselves. Yet, so many of us are disconnected from this. We live in our heads—overanalyzing, strategizing, pushing forward. We ignore what our bodies are telling us until we're exhausted, anxious, or burned out. Reclaiming sensuality is about coming home to ourselves, moving from disconnection to embodied confidence.

Think about sensuality as being a gateway to our intuition. Intuition is often described as a gut feeling, a knowing without explanation. But at its core, intuition is body wisdom. It's the signals and sensations we experience before our minds even process what's happening. A tightening in the chest when something isn't right. A sense of lightness when something aligns. The pull toward something or someone before we understand why.

When we are disconnected from our senses, we struggle to trust ourselves. We second-guess decisions. We seek external validation. We rely on logic alone, even when something inside us is saying wait or go for it. Tuning into our sensuality sharpens our instincts. It teaches us to listen—to the subtle shifts in energy, the way our body responds to people and situations, the inner nudges guiding us toward what's right.

How to Reconnect to Feelings

Reconnecting with sensuality isn't about doing more; it's about *feeling* more. Here are some practices to awaken your senses and strengthen your trust in yourself:

Mindful Movement
Move in ways that feel good rather than just productive. Stretch slowly in the morning. Dance in your kitchen. Walk barefoot in the grass. Let your body lead without an agenda.

Touch
Place a hand on your heart when you need reassurance. Wrap yourself in a soft blanket. Indulge in luxurious textures. The simple act of feeling can ground you in the present moment.

Self-Care Rituals
Sensuality thrives in slowness. Create rituals that engage your senses—lighting a candle, applying lotion with intention, savoring a warm drink. Let these moments be a reminder that you are here, in this body, in this life.

Breathwork
Your breath is the fastest way to return to yourself. Take deep, intentional breaths when you feel disconnected. Let them anchor you, reminding you that your body always knows the way home.

Listening to the Body's Cues
Start noticing how your body reacts to situations. Does your breath quicken? Do your shoulders tense? Do you feel expansion or contraction? Your body speaks: learning its language is an act of self-trust.

Sensuality and self-trust go hand in hand. The more present you are in your body, the more you believe in yourself—your instincts, your emotions, your needs. Self-trust is knowing that you don't need all the answers right now. It's feeling the pull of something and allowing yourself to follow it. It's sensing that something is off and honoring that even when there's no logical explanation.

The more you connect with your senses, the more you remember that you are not just a mind, endlessly analyzing life. You are a body *experiencing it*. And when you fully inhabit yourself, you become powerful in a way that doesn't need to be proven—it simply is.

Creativity is not something we do. It is something we allow. It isn't about forcing our will upon the world; it's about surrendering, opening ourselves to what's already in motion and to the current of inspiration that flows through everything. The more we embrace ease, the more we allow creativity to work through us, not because we made it happen, but because we trusted that it would.

MEDITATION

When I first began meditating, it wasn't about becoming enlightened or achieving anything at all. It was simply a quiet offering—ten minutes each morning before the world rushed in. I would sit in the stillness, eyes closed, breath soft. At first, it felt unnatural. My mind, so used to movement and momentum, didn't know what to do with the stillness. Silence was unfamiliar, even uncomfortable. But, with time, something began to shift.

Without trying to make anything happen, I noticed the noise begin to soften over time. The more I let myself just be, the more my mind started to clear, like silt settling in a glass of water. And in the space that opened, something beautiful emerged. Ideas. Clarity. Nudges from somewhere deeper than thought. Not during the meditation itself, but later—while running, swimming, or stirring a pot on the stove. It was as if, by sitting still, I had opened a door. The creativity I had always tried to chase came wandering in, unannounced, during the in-between moments. I felt more able to hear myself. To recognize when something was a full-body yes, and when it wasn't.

This was the beginning of self-trust. Not as a concept, but as a feeling. A knowing. And it came, not through force but through stillness, surrender, and letting life meet me where I was. When we surrender to the flow, we stop chasing perfection. We stop trying to shape everything into what we think it should be. Instead, we let the moment *shape* us, like a sculptor yielding to the natural curve of the stone, trusting that the art is already there waiting to be revealed. We learn to receive inspiration rather than forcing it, and in this receiving, we unlock the door to authenticity.

THE CYCLE OF CREATIVITY

True creativity comes from the core of who we are. When we're not overthinking, not struggling to fit into someone else's mold, we become fully present—curious, wide-eyed, and ready to explore. We question, we notice, we experience. The world becomes a place to play and to wonder, and in that play, creativity blooms. When we embrace flow, we're no longer second-guessing ourselves or shrinking our ideas. We let our wildest, most raw selves come through, because we trust that our authenticity is what the world needs to see.

Creativity isn't a one-time spark. It's a cycle—a dance between trust and action. The more we trust ourselves, the more confident we become. And with every burst of creativity, that confidence expands. We begin to trust our instincts, and from that trust, we create. Our ability to create with our authentic expression strengthens our confidence. That confidence gives us the courage to take bolder risks. And taking those risks deepens our trust, allowing us to create even more.

It's this cycle that builds on itself. The more we let go, the more we step into ourselves, and the more we step into ourselves, the more we create. It is effortless yet powerful. This cycle of trusting, creating, and becoming doesn't happen all at once. It unfolds slowly, often quietly, through practice. Through presence. Through permission.

For me, that permission began when I picked up *The Artist's Way* by Julia Cameron, a book that has guided countless creatives for over thirty years. It's more than a book—it's a journey back to your inner artist, the one who has never asked for permission, the one who speaks in colors, sensations, and gut feelings. Cameron invites us to reconnect with this part of ourselves through two rituals: *Daily Morning Pages* and *Artist Dates*.

The *Morning Pages* are simple but profound—three handwritten pages each morning, a brain dump of whatever is on your mind. For me, they became a sacred space. Every day, no matter what, I showed up to the page. Some days it was messy. Some days it was monotonous. But slowly, I began to notice something: the clutter was clearing. That constant mental chatter—what she calls the "censor," the critic inside—started losing its grip.

And underneath the noise? There was me. My voice. My feelings. My curiosity.

Writing gave me access to my own aliveness. It wasn't about writing something good—it was about writing something true. And from that truth inside me, creation began to stir again.

Then came the *Artist Dates*. Once a week, I would take myself somewhere with no agenda—an antique shop, a bookstore, the beach, a new trail. Just me and the quiet intention to wonder. These dates weren't about productivity; they were about pleasure. About filling the creative well. They reminded me that inspiration isn't manufactured. It's received. And in order to receive, we have to be open—unguarded, imperfect, and wildly curious.

What I learned through *The Artist's Way* was how to create from a place of softness. How to loosen the grip of control and listen more deeply. How to question, observe, and play. How to become a vessel for creativity, not a manager of it.

When it comes to creating, we need to be able to let go of perfectionism in order to invite our boldest ideas to flow. Perfectionism is a prison. It shackles us to expectations, to rules that were never ours to follow. When we let go of this need for everything to be perfect, we create space. Space for spontaneity, space for growth, space for breakthroughs. Without the constant grip of perfection, we find the courage to speak our truth, even when it's raw and messy. We let ideas unfold as they are—flawed, uncertain, and yet full of possibility. We no longer fear failure. Instead, we embrace it as part of the process of creation.

Here are some examples of this shift:

In Relationships

By letting go of the need for everything to look perfect, we allow ourselves to show up authentically—no masks, no pretenses. This opens up the space for deeper, more meaningful connections that would have been stifled by perfectionism. Rather than overthinking every word or action, we can simply be, and in that simplicity, trust grows.

In Creativity

By abandoning the pursuit of flawless execution, we free ourselves to experiment. The first draft doesn't have to be perfect; the art doesn't need to be polished. A messy canvas or a rough sketch becomes the doorway to something entirely new. The imperfections lead us to unexpected ideas that never could've been planned. Sometimes the beauty is in the mistakes —the moments of failure that lead to discoveries we never would've imagined had we been focused only on perfection.

In Career

When we stop controlling every outcome, we become open to opportunities that we never saw coming. A spontaneous idea shared in a meeting may lead to a collaboration you didn't expect, or a project that at first seems risky may unfold into something far more impactful than anticipated. Letting go of rigid expectations opens us up to innovation and possibility.

In Self-Expression

Perfectionism keeps us small—afraid to be seen for who we truly are. When we release that need for everything to be just right, we give ourselves permission to step into our full power. Whether it's dancing without worrying about how we look or writing without judging every sentence, we begin to trust that our raw, unpolished selves are worthy of expression. And in that openness, we are seen—truly seen—for the first time.

By releasing control, we unlock the doors to what we couldn't have predicted. We welcome surprises, we step into discoveries we couldn't have planned for. Ideas that were once hidden behind the veil of perfection emerge—new, bold, and raw. The universe begins to throw at us what we never even knew we needed. And in that moment, we realize: Creativity is not something we chase—it is something we receive. And with every new step into flow, the possibilities are limitless.

LISTENING TO INTUITION

Living in flow isn't about drifting aimlessly—it's about attuning ourselves to the deeper currents of our lives, the ones that move beneath the surface, guiding us toward alignment, toward what feels right. Intuition is that quiet knowing, the whisper before the thought, the nudge before the decision. The more we cultivate it, the more effortlessly we step into the life that was always meant for us.

Intuition isn't about guessing. It's about listening—*really* listening. The more we practice tuning in, the more we recognize the difference between the noise of fear and the clarity of truth. Whether it's listening to our own thoughts, the way our body feels in a moment, or the deeper meaning behind someone's words, mindful listening hones our ability to sense what's real and what's just distraction. The more we do this, the more we become open to receiving. To trusting ourselves. To moving with ease instead of resistance.

Intuition thrives in consistency. The more we cultivate daily rituals, the more attuned we become to the natural rhythm of our bodies, our emotions, and our energy cycles. When we flow with our rhythm instead of against it, life unfolds more effortlessly.

THE BEAUTY OF FLOW

Flow isn't about forcing. It's about allowing. And when you master that, the path ahead unfolds effortlessly, exactly as it was always meant to. Remember that flow is not a destination–it's a way of *being*.

There is a moment—one we often resist—when we realize that all the pushing, the forcing, the overthinking has never truly led us where we long to be. Control is an illusion, and in our grasping, we only tighten the knots. And then, there is another moment. The moment we let go. When we surrender to the flow, life doesn't fall apart—it falls into place. This is not passivity. It is power. Because to trust the flow is to trust *yourself*. To stop gripping so tightly and allow life to move through you, shaping you, guiding you, revealing paths you could never have found through sheer force alone. To step fully into your intuition, your sensuality, your deep, unshakable knowing.

REFLECTIONS FOR THE ROAD AHEAD

Here are some simple practices to strengthen your intuition:

Meditation
Sitting in stillness teaches us to distinguish between mental chatter and deep knowing. The more we listen, the clearer the inner voice becomes.

Journaling
Free-writing without judgment allows subconscious wisdom to surface. The answers we seek often emerge when we let the pen move without restriction.

Morning or evening rituals
Whether it's starting the day with stillness, movement, or intention-setting, or winding down with reflection, these moments act as anchors to our inner world.

Movement in alignment with energy
Some days call for intensity, others for rest. Honoring what the body needs instead of forcing it into rigidity strengthens the connection between body and mind.

Checking in with yourself
Taking a few moments throughout the day to pause, breathe, and ask, *What do I need right now?* sharpens your self-awareness and allows for realignment.

Repetition creates rhythm, and rhythm deepens connection. The more we engage in these practices, the more naturally we slip into flow—without force, without struggle, just movement in harmony with our being. Flow is not a one-size-fits-all experience. What feels aligned for one person may not for another. Learning your rhythm—

the times of day you feel most energized, the environments that inspire you, the signals your intuition sends—is the key to unlocking your fullest potential.

Try these different ways to explore your unique flow:

Track your natural energy patterns
Notice when you feel the most creative, most introspective, most productive. Patterns will emerge, revealing when and how you function at your best. You can try this using a daily energy tracker for a week. Notice what activities bring you joy and energy, and what activities diminish or drain your energy. Once you've filled this out, review it and see where you can replace activities that are more aligned with your flow

Pay attention to soul signs
Intuition speaks through sensations: a sense of lightness, a deep exhale, a subtle pull toward something new. These are your signs of alignment. Pay attention to them and follow them.

Trust what feels expansive
If something makes you feel small, drained, or disconnected, it's likely not meant for you. Learn to let them go. Flow is found in the things that feel open, alive, and right.

CHAPTER 6: EMBODIED CONFIDENCE

The Kind That Doesn't Waver When People Watch

CONFIDENCE IS OFTEN mistaken for volume—the loudest voice in the room, the boldest presence, the unwavering certainty. But real, embodied confidence is quieter. It doesn't demand attention; it draws it in effortlessly. It isn't about proving, performing, or persuading—it's about knowing. A knowing so deep that even when the world questions you, you don't question yourself.

This is the anchor of everything we've explored so far. The final piece of reclaiming your feminine power is not just discovering who you are but standing fully in that truth. Without shrinking. Without seeking permission. Without apology. Because confidence isn't just about how you present yourself to others—it's about how you inhabit yourself. How you move, how you speak, how you take up space, and most importantly, how you feel within your own skin.

There's a kind of confidence that looks good in photos, the kind that walks into a room and makes sure everyone knows it has arrived. It's polished, practiced, put together. It knows how to say the right things, strike the right pose, perform the part. And for a little while, it works. But there's another kind of confidence. The kind that doesn't waver when the lights go down. The kind that still feels whole when no one's clapping, still stands tall when there's no one there to impress. The kind that isn't about being seen—it's about knowing, deep in your bones, who you are. That's embodied confidence. And once you have it, no one can take it from you.

If you've ever chased confidence in the form of external validation, you know how exhausting it is. Maybe you've looked for it in someone's eyes, hoping they'll tell you that you're good enough, pretty enough, smart enough, or worthy enough. Maybe you've built it from numbers—likes, follows, promotions, paychecks—only to realize the goalpost *keeps moving*. Maybe you've felt it surge when someone notices you, compliments you, praises you ... only for it to fade away the moment they stop. External validation feels good, but it's like trying to fill a well with a bucket that has a hole in the bottom. No matter how much you pour in, it never quite stays.

The reason? Validation from the outside world is conditional. It's based on how you perform, what you produce, how well you fit into whatever mold people expect of you. And because those expectations are always shifting, external confidence is always at risk of crumbling. This chapter is about moving beyond the need for external validation, beyond the instinct to soften yourself for the comfort of others, beyond the *performance* of confidence. This is about the kind of confidence that remains steady even under the weight of others' expectations. The kind that doesn't waver when people watch.

Because inner confidence? That's *yours*. It's unshakable. It's the kind of confidence that doesn't need an audience to exist. Think about the moments when you've felt most at peace with yourself— when you've been alone, unfiltered, uncurated, just existing in a way that felt right. That's the version of you that doesn't need to prove anything. That's where real confidence begins.

Take Maya Lin, the visionary artist and architect who designed the Vietnam Veterans Memorial in Washington, DC. She faced intense backlash for her design. People called it too somber, too unconventional, too different. But she stood firm in her vision, knowing that true power comes not from forcing something to fit expectations, but from trusting the quiet certainty of what feels true. She defended her work through the undeniable impact of its presence. Lin stood by her creation even when others doubted her. She let the memorial speak—not through grandeur, but through its quiet depth.

You are not here to be approved of. You are here to stand fully in who you are, no matter who is watching. So when someone criticizes you, when they reject you, when they make you feel small —remember this: their words are just echoes. They are not your truth. You are the one who gets to define who you are. You are the one who gets to choose your worth. The truth is, when you stop depending on external validation to define you, you become unstoppable. You become unshakable. Nothing that anyone says can touch you when you are already whole. *Nothing.* Because you've done the work. You've built your worth from the inside out. And that is something that can never be taken from you.

This is what unwavering self-worth feels like:

Knowing that your value is not up for debate.
Knowing that you are enough just as you are.
And when you are rooted in that truth,
nothing, nothing can shake it.

I remember a time when I could walk into any room and read it like a script. I knew how to smile just enough, laugh at the right moment, wear the outfit that fit the vibe, and say exactly what would make someone feel seen—and in return, I hoped they'd like me. I wasn't lying, not exactly, but I *was* performing. Constantly. I was auditioning for roles in people's lives without ever stopping to ask if I actually wanted the part. It was like being the lead in a show I didn't audition for, but I stayed in character anyway. The mask fit well. It even got applause. But it was exhausting. Because the moment the lights went down, I wasn't sure who I was without the audience.

I've been a swimmer since I was six. That's always been mine. No stage, no pretense. Just me in the water. It didn't matter how I looked. It didn't matter if I was the fastest. It was just mine. That same feeling showed up in long hours of clarinet practice—those moments where I wasn't playing to impress anyone. I wasn't performing; I was existing. Fully immersed in something I loved, not wondering how it sounded to anyone else, because I already knew I loved who I was in that moment. I trusted myself. I didn't need permission to belong there.

That's when I started realizing—real confidence doesn't shout to be noticed. It doesn't need to take up space to prove that it belongs. It's the quiet knowing that even when no one is watching, even when there's no applause, *you still matter*. You still trust yourself. You still like yourself. It wasn't about shutting people out. It wasn't, "I don't care what anyone thinks." It was: *I care what I think more*. I began to hold my own approval as the most important feedback. And suddenly, the exhausting auditions stopped. Not because I was louder, tougher, or more unbothered—but because I no longer needed the part.

Here's where people get stuck: they think confidence means not caring what anyone thinks. They picture someone with an IDGAF attitude, stomping through life, shutting out all feedback, refusing to be affected by anything. But that's not confidence—that's armor. Confidence isn't about detachment; it's about security. It's knowing that you can listen to other people without needing their approval. It's allowing yourself to be influenced by the people who matter without handing them the keys to your self-worth.

So how do you get there?

You start by noticing where you seek approval the most:

- Do you change your opinion the second someone questions it?

- Do you shrink when someone disapproves of you?

- Do you only feel beautiful, talented, or worthy when someone else confirms it?

Once you recognize where you seek approval, practice standing in your truth instead. Start small. Wear the outfit you love even if no one compliments it. Express your thoughts even when they're unpopular. Make choices based on what feels right and not what earns you the most approval. Remind yourself that connection isn't built on applause. It's built on presence, on showing up as your whole self even when that self isn't universally liked. When you realize that the right people will love you not because you're performing for them but because you're *you*, the need for approval starts to loosen its grip.

Here's a question: Are you the same person when you're alone as you are in front of others?

For most people, the answer is no.

There's a version of us that sings in the car, dances in the kitchen, has deep thoughts and silly moments and raw emotions when no one's around. And then there's the version we put on for the world—the curated, refined, socially acceptable version. The wider that gap is between the two versions, the shakier our confidence feels. Because deep down, we know: if our confidence depends on playing a role, then it's fragile. It only lasts as long as we can keep up the act. True confidence happens when that gap gets smaller or disappears altogether, when the way you show up in a crowded room is the same way you show up when it's just you and your thoughts.

Imagine walking into any space and feeling at home—not because the room is welcoming but because you are. No matter where you go, you bring yourself with you, and that's all the permission you need. That's the kind of confidence that doesn't crumble. That's the kind that doesn't waver. That's the kind that lasts.

At the end of the day, the goal isn't to be the loudest in the room or to collect the most praise, rack up the most approval, or prove your worth through someone else's eyes. The goal is to know yourself so deeply that confidence isn't something you put on; it's something you are. And when you have that? The world doesn't change you. You change the world.

OWNING YOUR SPACE

There's a difference between taking up space and owning it. Taking up space can feel like a performance—loud, attention-grabbing, trying to prove something. But owning your space? That's different. That's when your presence is felt before you even speak, not because you're pushing yourself forward, but because you belong there. Owning your space means knowing in your bones that you don't have to earn your right to be in the room. You don't have to apologize for existing. You don't have to shrink to make other people comfortable. You belong the moment you arrive. No one else gets to decide that.

Owning your space isn't about dominance. It's about presence. It's walking into a room and knowing you belong. It's speaking with authority even when your voice shakes. It's carrying yourself in a way that says, "I am here, and I am not sorry for it." It's moving like you have nothing to prove, because you don't. Confidence is about being rooted. And when you learn how to root yourself? The whole world will feel it.

So how do we get there? Let's break it down.

There's a moment in every person's life where they have to speak before they're ready. Maybe you've had one of those moments—the kind where your heart is pounding, your throat is tight, and you're convinced that if you open your mouth, everyone will hear the fear in your voice. But here's the thing: confidence isn't the absence of fear. It's action in the face of it.

I think about moments in my own life when I felt like I had no business speaking with authority. When I walked into a room and thought, *What the hell am I doing here?*—but I opened my mouth anyway. The first time I led a meeting where I was the least experienced person in the room. The first time I told someone I was a writer even though I had nothing published yet. The first time I spoke my truth in a conversation where I knew it wouldn't be popular.

And every time, my voice shook. But I spoke anyway. With every word, I started to become the person I was wanting to be.

Because here's the secret: you don't wait until you feel confident to act confident. You step into it. You trust that even if your voice wavers, even if your hands shake, the words still count. And the more you do it? The less you shake. Confidence isn't about never feeling afraid. It's about knowing you belong despite the fear.

Before you speak, before you introduce yourself, before you do anything, your energy has already entered the room. People pick up on it. They feel it. Think about someone who walks into a space and commands attention because they have a quiet certainty about them. They don't fidget, they don't rush, they don't shrink. They move like they belong. *That's embodied confidence.* And the beautiful thing? You can practice this. You can teach your body to exude confidence before your mind even catches up.

Here's how:

Open posture
Uncross your arms. Relax your shoulders. Stand tall, but not rigid. Confidence is open and at ease.

Eye contact
Not in a weird, unblinking way, but in a way that says I see you, and I'm here.

Ground your voice

Not in a way that forces your voice to be something it's not, but in a way that roots you. A slow, steady tone commands attention more than volume does.

Plant your feet

When we're nervous, we fidget. We shift. We make ourselves smaller. Instead, plant yourself firmly. You're meant to be here. Let your body know it.

Breathe deeply

Shallow breathing makes you seem nervous, hurried, out of sync. Deep, steady breaths tell your body: we're safe, we belong here.

And the biggest thing?

Slow down.

When you rush, you communicate insecurity. When you move and speak with ease, you communicate presence. Because real confidence doesn't need to force anything. It just is.

No Apologies

I used to apologize to inanimate objects. I'd bump into a chair and whisper, "Oh, sorry." I'd side-step out of someone's way and say, "Oops, my bad!" I'd enter a conversation with, "Sorry to bother you, but—" before I even said anything of substance. It took me years to realize: I wasn't apologizing to the chair. I was apologizing for *existing*.

But what if we stopped apologizing?

What if we walked into a room, and instead of shrinking, we expanded? What if we spoke without cushioning our words? What if we took up space with our full presence? What if we stopped apologizing for things that don't require apologies? Because the truth is: You don't need to apologize for having an opinion. You don't need to make yourself smaller to make others comfortable. You don't need to soften your edges to be worthy of belonging. You are worthy. As you are.

A CHALLENGE: For the next 24 hours, notice how often you say "*sorry*" when you don't need to. Instead, try:

- "Excuse me" (when you need to get by someone).

- "Thank you for waiting" (instead of "Sorry, I'm late").

- "I need a moment" (instead of "Sorry, I just—uh …").

And most importantly, notice when you instinctively shrink. When you move to the sidelines, when you quiet yourself, when you step back. And then? Step forward instead.

DAILY PRACTICE FOR EMBODIED CONFIDENCE

There's a moment when you first wake up. A quiet space, before the world begins to push in. Your mind hasn't yet remembered who it thinks you should be, who you should become, or what you should do. You're not your to-do list. You're not your responsibilities. You're just *you*—in all your raw, unfiltered truth.

In this sacred space, walk to the mirror. Don't just glance at your reflection. Look *deeply*. Look into your eyes, the windows to the soul. Don't rush. Don't judge. See the person staring back at you. Not the person who feels like she needs to fix something. Not the person who thinks she's not enough. Just see *her*.

And say this, with every ounce of honesty you can muster: *I love you. What do you need today?*

Yes, it might feel silly at first. You might feel a little foolish, standing there in the soft, groggy light of morning. But trust this: your body knows what it needs, and the more you listen, the more you'll hear. In this moment, you're showing up for yourself in the truest way possible. You're telling yourself: *I see you. I'm here for you. I will support you today, just as you are.*

Because this is where you get clarity. The more you show up, the more you begin to understand what your body, your heart, your soul really need. You start to hear the quiet whispers beneath the noise, the subtle desires that had been buried in the rush of life. This is where confidence is born—not from the world's validation, not from the approval of others—but from the act of showing up for yourself, every single day. So go ahead. Look deeply. Ask the question. And let yourself feel the power of truly seeing yourself, of knowing what you need, and trusting yourself enough to give it to you. Because once you do, you'll realize that no one else's opinion matters as much as your own. You will be enough, just as you are.

Confidence isn't just a state of mind. It is a language your body speaks—loudly, without words. It's in the way you carry yourself when you are at ease, when you feel whole, when you move through the world unburdened by insecurity. But your body speaks in other ways as well. It may shrink when self-doubt creeps in, when you feel exposed or unsure, when the weight of judgment presses on your shoulders. So listen to your body. Pay attention to how it feels in different moments:

- **The Neutral State:** When you're just you in a moment of peace. What does it feel like? Is your body open, relaxed, at ease? Can you breathe freely, or do you hold your breath without realizing it?

- **The Fulfillment State:** That time when you're fully alive, fully present. When you're doing what you love surrounded by people who see you, or maybe when you're alone but whole. How does your body feel here? Is there a lightness in your chest? Do your feet feel rooted, like they belong to the earth?

- **The Triggered State:** When the doubts hit, when the world questions you, when the opinions of others or even your own self-doubt make you pull back. What changes? Do your shoulders tighten? Does your stomach knot? Do you feel small or like you want to hide?

These physical shifts? They're your body speaking to you. When you can recognize them, you can change them. So check in. Take a deep breath. Roll your shoulders back. Stand a little taller. You don't need to wait for confidence to show up in your mind first. You can summon it in your body. When you move with intention, when you ground yourself, when you breathe deeply, your body will tell your mind: *We've got this.*

SILENCE THE OLD YOU

The loudest voice in your life is the one you hear every single day. It is not your best friend, not your family, not even a stranger—it's the voice inside your own head. And let's be honest—it's not always your biggest fan. It whispers doubts when you're on the verge of something great. It says, *What if you fail? What if they don't like you? What if you're not enough?*

But here's the truth: That voice is not you. It's just old patterns. It's an old version of you that doesn't know how to trust your potential. And if you want to change your life, you've got to start by changing that voice.

The harshest critic you will ever face is yourself. If you were to write down every negative thing you say to yourself in a day—every doubt, every insult, every "you're not enough"—and then imagine someone saying those things to you out loud, would you stay in the same room? *Probably not.* And yet, we live inside these thoughts. We let them shape us. We believe them. So here's the question: If you already survive your own criticism every single day, why are you afraid of someone else's?

Nothing anyone says about you will ever be harsher than what you've said to yourself. And yet, you are still standing. You are still here. Which means you are already stronger than you think. So the next time someone doubts you, judges you, underestimates you— remind yourself: *Their opinion does not change my worth.*

Dr. Joe Dispenza is a neuroscientist, author, and speaker who bridges science and spirituality. He's best known for his work on how our thoughts shape our reality, blending neuroscience, epigenetics, and quantum physics with personal transformation. His books, including *Breaking the Habit of Being Yourself* and *Becoming Supernatural,* explore how changing our patterns of thought and behavior can literally rewire the brain and body. Through meditation, visualization, and intentional practice, he teaches that we're capable of moving beyond old habits and self-doubt into new identities and possibilities.

When he describes the shift from self-doubt to confidence, he frames it as a three-stage process:

1. **Thinking** – You imagine confidence.

2. **Doing** – You act as if you already have it.

3. **Being** – You become it.

It sounds simple, but it's powerful. The more consistently you think and act in alignment with confidence, the more your brain believes it's true. Confidence stops being a destination and becomes something you are. And you can create it, right now, with every thought, every movement, every breath.

BE YOU

At the start of this journey, we began by shedding the weight of external expectations. We peeled away the layers that weren't ours —those things we picked up from the world around us, the shoulds, the supposed-to's, the demands of what it means to be a woman, to be a *good* woman. We took a deep breath and let them go, piece by piece. What you've been through, what you've learned, and what you've discovered about yourself is a beautiful unfolding. It's a journey of moving beyond the confines of society's boxes, of stepping out from the shadows of roles that were never yours to begin with. You've seen how we are often conditioned to shape-shift into something other than what we are, how society expects us to fit into neat little categories: the daughter, the mother, the lover, the worker, the friend, the caretaker, the list goes on.

But here, in this moment, you stand outside of all of those roles. You have learned that your power doesn't come from conforming to an ideal. *No.* Your power is in embracing your unique, authentic expression, whatever that looks like. It's in living life on your terms, trusting that every twist, every turn, every leap is part of your grand, perfect design. This is where you learn to live outside of the titles, the roles, and the labels. Where you realize you don't need to be anything other than yourself. You don't need to fit into a mold that someone else created. You are your own mold, your own masterpiece, constantly evolving, constantly flowing with the current of life—unapologetically.

The practices we've explored together—the mirror affirmations, the body awareness, the grounding, the trusting of your own inner wisdom—are all about remembering who you truly are. They are about coming home to yourself after years of being pulled in every direction, after years of silencing your voice, after years of shrinking to make room for others. You're learning to stand tall, to take up space, to speak your truth, and to trust that you are enough—just as you are. You're learning that strength doesn't come from perfection; it comes from authenticity. It comes from being real with yourself, with your fears, with your flaws, and with your wild, beautiful, untamed heart.

Here's your challenge:
Show up in the world exactly as you are.

Not as the woman you think others want you to be. Not as the woman who conforms, who plays small, who bends to fit into someone else's expectations. But as the woman who knows deep in her bones that she is more than enough. Show up as the woman who isn't afraid to embrace her uniqueness, her quirks, her brilliance, and her power.

When you walk into a room, walk in as yourself. When you speak, speak your truth. When you move through life, do so with confidence and grace, knowing that everything you need is already inside of you. And when you feel the fear creeping in—the fear of judgment, the fear of being too much, the fear of standing out—remember: *you are already whole.* You are already powerful. You are already enough. The world needs you to be exactly who you are. There's no one else like you. And that is the most beautiful thing you could ever offer.

So, stand tall. Stand proud. Be unapologetically you. You've reclaimed your power. Now, let the world see it.

REFLECTIONS FOR THE ROAD AHEAD

Some ways to change the voice in your head:

Step One: Catch It
When that voice of doubt speaks up, pause. What is it saying? Can you catch it before it takes over?

Step Two: Question It
Is this actually true? Would you say this to a friend? What would happen if you didn't listen? What if, instead of believing that little voice, you chose to ask: What if I succeed? What if I'm exactly where I'm meant to be right now?

Step Three: Reframe It
Instead of: *I'm not ready for this,* try: *I am more than capable of doing this, even if I'm still learning.* Instead of: *What if I fail?* Try: *What if this is just the beginning of something incredible?* Instead

of: *I don't belong here,* try: *I belong wherever I decide to stand, and this is where I'm meant to be.*

This isn't about denying fear or pretending everything is perfect. It's about choosing to believe that you are worthy of the success you crave. That you have the strength to rewrite the stories that no longer serve you. Because the most powerful belief you can hold onto is this: *I have my own back.*

Sometimes, confidence is a trick of the mind. And sometimes, the fastest way to trick your mind is to use your body. Your body and brain are constantly communicating. So if you want to become more confident, start moving like someone who already is. And when you move with intention, the mind follows.

Here are some techniques that have helped me:

Grounding
Confidence starts from the ground up. Start by anchoring yourself to the earth. Stand with your feet firmly planted beneath you, and imagine roots growing from the soles of your feet and stretching deep into the ground. Feel the solid earth beneath you. You are unshakable. You are grounded.

Movement
Shake off hesitation. Confidence doesn't stand still. It moves, it flows, it dances. So get up, stretch, dance, move in whatever way feels right. Let your body find its rhythm and remind you of your strength.

Breathwork
Reset your nervous system. When doubt creeps in, your breath is your anchor. Slow it down. Inhale deeply through your nose. Hold for a moment. Exhale through your mouth. Breathe until you feel your body soften and your mind quiet.

Trick Your Brain

Dr. Joe Dispenza talks about how our brain can't tell the difference between what's real and what we believe to be real. So if you move like you're confident, your brain will start to believe it. When you feel yourself shrinking, step into a power pose. Shoulders back, chin up. Walk through your day like someone who knows their worth. Soon enough, you'll become that person.

SECTION TWO:

MASTERFUL RELATIONSHIPS & POLARITY

Building Magnetic, Fulfilling Connections Through Self-awareness and Authentic Expression

THIS SECTION IS where we step into the deep, electric pull of connection—the kind that shakes us awake, leaves us breathless, and lights us up from the inside out. We're diving into the magic of real relationships, the kinds that are forged when we drop all the masks and stop pretending to be someone we're not. This is where we shed the roles we've been taught to play and stand fully in the magnetic power of our authentic selves.

Magnetism is about being so fully, unapologetically YOU that the universe has no choice but to lean in and respond to your frequency. When you know your worth, when you know your energy is enough, that's when life responds in kind. Polarity is the spark, the fire that keeps this dance alive. It's the tension between light and dark, push and pull. It's in this space that we find the chemistry that turns connection into something unforgettable.

But here's the thing: connection isn't free-flowing if we don't know how to protect it. Boundaries are the unsung heroes of our relationships. They're the gates we use to let in what serves us and filter out what doesn't.

And then, there's sisterhood. True sisterhood. Not the superficial kind where we pretend to be perfect or hide behind filters, but the kind that cuts to the bone. The kind that celebrates your whole, messy, beautiful, raw self. It's the energy of women who see you— really see you—and meet you where you are. These are the relationships that hold space for your evolution. These are the women who celebrate you for being *you*. These are the friendships that make you feel like you can breathe, like you're not alone in this journey. When you've got that kind of support, anything is possible.

And at the heart of all this is communication. Not the small talk, surface-level conversations that leave you empty and drained, but the deep, soul-stirring dialogue that binds us together. This is where intimacy is built. This is where vulnerability thrives. This is where trust lives.

As we explore the following chapters, you'll learn to embrace this energy that is uniquely yours and apply it with mastery in all your relationships—whether it's romantic, platonic, or professional —allowing them to become the source of true growth and fulfillment.

CHAPTER 7: MAGNETISM IN LOVE & CONNECTION
How to Create Real Chemistry Without Games

MAGNETISM IS the energetic pull we feel toward someone or something when our frequencies resonate. It's not about manipulation or playing games—it's the authentic alignment of energy that makes others notice and pull toward you. Magnetism happens when you are fully grounded in who you are, radiating clarity, worth, and presence.

True magnetism isn't the frantic rush of butterflies in your stomach or the instant jolt of chemistry that makes your heart race. It's not about pulling away to create desire or presenting some version of yourself that isn't quite real. Real attraction—the kind that sticks and builds over time—is a slow burn. It's the presence, energy, and authentic spark that arises when two people show up fully as themselves, not as the people they think they should be. Sometimes it feels like recognition—you sense yourself in another. Other times it feels like awe—you're drawn toward someone whose energy is so alive, it elevates you.

Attraction thrives in the spaces where vulnerability and authenticity are allowed to live. True chemistry isn't something you create by pretending to be someone else. When you hide behind masks or play games to get attention, what you're really creating is uncertainty. And people can feel it. There's a subtle undercurrent of inauthenticity that makes them hesitate, second-guess, and ultimately want to pull away. It's like a wall that forms between you, built from the dissonance between who you are and who you're trying to be.

But what if we stopped pretending? What if we let go of the masks and showed up as the truest, most raw versions of ourselves? What would happen if we simply allowed the chemistry to unfold, without pressure, without expectation, just a steady, authentic flow between two people?

That's the art of attraction. It's the magnetic pull that occurs when two people are not trying to impress each other, but are instead deeply aligned with their own essence, showing up with nothing to prove and nothing to hide. It's about creating space for the connection to grow naturally without forcing anything. And this —this, right here—is the foundation for what we'll dive into next: creating lasting chemistry through real, grounded connection. No pretending. Just being.

THE FLOW OF CHEMISTRY

Chemistry is a dance, not a race. It's a rhythm, a flow that moves at its own pace—sometimes slow, sometimes steady, but never hurried. We live in a world that glorifies instant gratification, the rush of attraction, the spark that ignites without warning. But true chemistry doesn't happen in an instant. It isn't about the fireworks you see in a movie or the electric jolt you feel in your chest. It's something deeper. Something quieter. A steady build, a deepening current, a spark that grows into steady fire. It builds layer by layer, until you realize that what you feel between you has become something so much more than a fleeting moment.

It's easy to get swept up in the instant surge of intensity, to chase after that immediate hit of excitement. But the problem is, when we move too fast, we bypass something more precious—the slow unfolding of a real bond. An instant spark is a fleeting thing, often born from the tension of need or the allure of the unknown. It might feel intoxicating, but it doesn't lay the foundation for something lasting.

For years, that spark was what I chased. I would jump from relationship to relationship, stacking one on top of the other, barely pausing to breathe in between. It was like being on a romantic conveyor belt—first date, then a kiss, then constant texting, then imagining a life together before I even knew their middle name. I mistook attention for connection. I mistook intensity for intimacy. And I mistook butterflies for truth. But the butterflies weren't love—they were anxiety, novelty, shock to the system.

They were my nervous system reacting to someone new, not my soul recognizing someone true.

I didn't know how to be alone. So when the initial spark faded—as it always did when reality replaced fantasy—I'd start scanning for the next one. I wasn't falling in love with people. I was falling in love with the idea of being in love. With filling a space. With being chosen, even if it wasn't right.

There was a time I thought I was craving *him*—Anthony, Robert, Thomas, or whichever name came next—but I was really craving the feeling of being needed, of being wanted. And when that feeling waned, I panicked. I clung. I ran. I moved on. The relationship was never built slowly enough to anchor into anything real. Now, though? I want something different. I'm not looking to force anyone into a space just because I have one available. I've stopped searching for puzzle pieces to fill a shape I haven't fully defined. If someone enters my life, it's because they fit, not because I'm lonely. Not because I'm bored. And certainly not because I can't stand the silence of being with myself.

The deep bond you crave, the one that feels like home, isn't built on that quick rush. It's created when you allow the connection to grow at its own pace without forcing it to fit into a preconceived timeline. It's about creating space for each moment to unfold, each conversation to deepen. It's the beauty of getting to know each other in layers, one slow revelation at a time.

Pacing is everything in love. Just like a song that builds in crescendo, a real connection swells with meaning over time. You don't need to rush to the end of the story. Every moment of getting to know someone—the quiet pauses, the soft laughter, the shared experiences—is part of the magic.

But here's the real secret: you can't create that connection if you don't honor your own space, your own autonomy. As you allow someone else to enter your world, you have to remain grounded in who you are, not in who you think you should be. If you lose yourself in the process of connection, you're no longer creating something real. You're creating a reflection of what you think the other person wants to see. Authentic chemistry only thrives when both people show up fully as themselves, without masks, without pretense, without rushing to become something they're not. It's a balance. A dance. You both step closer, but never at the expense of your own soul. You take your time. You give each other space to breathe. And, over time, you begin to realize that this slow burn is exactly what you've been waiting for—a chemistry that isn't fleeting, but grounded in something real, something sustainable. In the slow burn of real chemistry, you learn that the connection doesn't need to be fast to be powerful. The power is in the patience, in the space, and in the shared moments that stack on top of one another. It's in the knowing that no matter how slowly it unfolds, it's the kind of connection worth waiting for.

THE CONFIDENCE OF BEING REAL

When you show up as your true self, unfiltered and unapologetically, you create a space for others to do the same. You offer the freedom to be seen in your rawest form—flaws, quirks, and imperfections included. And guess what? Those very things are often what others are drawn to. The imperfections that you're afraid to show? They're the same things that make you real, human, and utterly magnetic. Maybe you hate that mole on your cheek, or you try to cover up the little zit that shows up before a date, but it's that very mole, that very blemish, that someone else might find endearing. People want to see the whole picture, not a hologram of perfection. They want to connect with the full spectrum of who you are—the real you, not some idealized version.

It's easy to get trapped in the idea that in order to be loved, we have to be flawless, polished, and perfectly put together. But the truth is, it's the raw, unfiltered moments that create the strongest bonds. People aren't attracted to perfection. They're attracted to authenticity. They want to know the real you. Not the version you think is acceptable, but the one who's comfortable in their own skin —flaws and all. And it's when you embrace those imperfections, those things you wish you could change, that you unlock your true power. Because when you stop hiding, others can finally see you. Not the filtered version, but the whole picture. The beauty that exists in your flaws is what makes you irresistibly human.

And this is where vulnerability comes in. It's the gateway to true emotional connection. You can't form a deep bond if you're not willing to show the deeper parts of yourself. But vulnerability doesn't mean spilling your darkest secrets on the first date. It's a slow unwinding, a delicate dance of revealing bits and pieces over time. It's about sharing the small things first—the favorite color, the childhood memory, the fact that you can't stand pineapple on pizza —and letting the intimacy grow with each little revelation. It's in those moments of shared vulnerability that true connection is forged.

Vulnerability isn't about oversharing or rushing the process. It's about allowing someone into the parts of yourself that you normally keep hidden, trusting that they'll accept you as you are. You can't rush this. It's a process. Just like you wouldn't hand someone your heart and soul on a silver platter the first time you meet, you can't dive into the deepest emotional layers right away. You start small. You show up, little by little, as your truest self. And with each new layer revealed, the connection deepens. It's the slow burn of building trust, of sharing not just the highlights, but the everyday moments, the vulnerabilities, the fears, and the dreams.

I remember one time at the pool, I was in full training mode— goggles on, swimsuit covered in little cats with unicorn horns and rainbows, totally zoned into my swim sets. I wasn't trying to be approachable or attractive; I was just being my intense, hyper-focused, slightly ridiculous self. I am a fast swimmer—ridiculously fast—and between sets, I'd pause at the wall, breathless, staring down at my Garmin, calculating my splits, lost in my own little world. It wasn't graceful or polished—it was obsessive, awkward, and completely me.

Someone I'd never met before approached me at the edge of the pool. I figured it was just to ask if the lane was open, but instead, he started talking—asking what I was training for and what my intervals were. I answered, mid-breath, probably still goggled and dripping, not trying to impress anyone. But he didn't leave. He stayed. Between every set, he'd ask another question, linger, laugh, and make some offhand observation. I remember thinking, "Wait ... you like this version of me?" The competitive, rainbow-cat-suited, laser-focused version that most people might find a little extra or too intense? But that was the magic. I wasn't performing. I wasn't polished. I wasn't trying to be charming. I was just me—flushed, winded, and living my life. And that was what drew him in. Not a filtered version. Not a curated one. Just the raw, unfiltered reality of who I was.

When both people show up in their most authentic form without the pressure of being perfect, something real begins to unfold. This is the foundation of chemistry—the kind of connection that lasts. The kind that's sticky, unshakable, and real. So take a deep breath, let go of the masks, and just be. Because when you do, you'll realize that being yourself is the most magnetic thing you could ever do.

EMBRACING POLARITY

Polarity is the presence of two equal and opposite forces—like yin and yang, masculine and feminine, light and dark. It's the natural tension between contrasts that creates balance, attraction, and movement. Polarity isn't about one side being better than the other; it's about how the existence of both creates wholeness. Without contrast, there is no pull, no dynamic energy.

Polarity is the invisible force that ignites chemistry, stirs passion, and keeps the spark alive in relationships. It's the dance of masculine and feminine energy—not tied to gender, but to the dynamic forces that flow through all of us. At its core, polarity is about balance. It's about the ebb and flow of energy, the give and take. These forces exist in every relationship, and it's when they are aligned that attraction, desire, and passion come alive.

In the first section, we explored the essence of feminine energy —the fluidity, the receptivity, and the depth of connection it fosters. But here, we're shifting gears to look at polarity: how both masculine and feminine energies play their part in creating a magnetic connection. This is where things get exciting. It's not about one energy being better than the other; it's about how they complement each other in the dance of love and connection. When masculine and feminine energies are in balance, they create a tension that fuels attraction. This isn't about fitting into rigid roles or expectations; it's about embracing the natural dynamics that exist between the two.

When polarity is embraced, it makes the space between two people, the distance that creates that delicious tension. It's the push and pull, the subtle dance that allows desire to grow and passion to spark. Without this polarity, there is no magnetism—just a flat, lifeless connection.

Polarity creates space for attraction to build, for desire to intensify, and for passion to flow. It's the art of maintaining a delicate balance. It's a give and take. The masculine energy takes the lead, while the feminine energy responds. One gives direction, the other receives and nurtures. This dynamic creates the spark— the chemistry—that makes love come alive.

Intentionality is the key to sustaining polarity in your relationship. When you understand how polarity works, you can use it to deepen your connection and create lasting chemistry. You don't have to live in a state of constant tension, fighting for dominance or balance. Instead, you can flow with the rhythms of your relationship, knowing that as you grow together, so will the polarity. This doesn't mean you won't face challenges—relationships are never static, and growth isn't linear. There will be moments of disconnection, times when the polarity shifts or feels out of sync. But this is where the beauty lies. When you understand polarity, you can navigate those moments with intention and awareness, using the energy of each person to bring the connection back into balance.

The key is recognizing it's not a static game but an ongoing play where the dynamics shift and change as you both evolve. As you grow together, so will the dance between the masculine and feminine. The relationship that thrives on polarity is one that can grow, adapt, and create lasting chemistry—even through the ebbs and flows of life.

But here's the thing: while polarity is the foundation of attraction and passion, it's easy for it to tip into unhealthy dynamics. We've all been there—caught in the cycle of codependency, where one person is overly reliant on the other, or in anxious attachment, where the need for reassurance can lead to suffocating behavior. Or maybe the opposite happens: avoidant attachment, where one person pulls away to maintain independence, leaving the other feeling abandoned. These dynamics come from an imbalance in polarity; the energy exchange becomes distorted. The masculine becomes too dominant, the feminine too passive, or vice versa.

So, how do we find the healthy space in between? How do we strike that delicate balance where polarity fuels chemistry instead of creating friction? It begins with self-awareness. Recognizing your own energetic tendencies is key. Are you leaning too heavily into the masculine, constantly taking the lead and losing sight of your own needs? Or are you retreating into the feminine, becoming passive and waiting for others to make moves? The connection deepens when both partners honor their own energy and meet in flow.

I learned this the hard way.

For years, I didn't understand how much I was tipping the scales, how much I was living in overdrive, trying to control everything out of fear. I had been in a relationship that was emotionally abusive and deeply destabilizing. At the time, I didn't have the language for narcissism or coercive control—

I just thought I was trying to keep the peace. But the reality was I was being conditioned to respond instantly to every text message or face severe emotional backlash. If I didn't reply within minutes, I risked being locked out of the apartment, being screamed at, called names I wouldn't repeat even to my worst enemy. There were nights I was on the kitchen floor, sobbing, being told I was unlovable, that I should be grateful someone like him would stay with me because no one else ever would.

That dynamic rewired my nervous system. It made me anxious, hyper-vigilant, constantly monitoring my behavior to avoid punishment. I lived in a state of emotional survival, not connection. I lost trust in my own instincts because I was always walking on eggshells trying to prevent the next explosion. The tipping point came in a parking lot after a late-night rehearsal. I had just received another text from him—sharp, demanding, the kind that made my stomach flip. One of my friends, who barely knew me at the time but saw the panic in my face, snatched my phone from my hands. I remember chasing her around the parking lot for half an hour, begging—pleading—for her to give it back.

"Why do you need your phone that badly?" she asked, dead serious, holding it high like she was guarding a secret.

"Because if I don't respond, I'll be yelled at," I shouted.

"Say that again," she said.

I paused. "If I don't respond, I'll be yelled at."

Hearing myself say it out loud broke something open. It was the first time I realized just how deep I'd been pulled into something so toxic and how much I was operating out of fear, not love. Even after the relationship ended, I didn't yet know how to live differently. In future connections, I tried to do everything right—to show I cared, to stay connected, to never be forgotten. But what I was actually doing was gripping too tightly. If I sensed any emotional distance, I'd send a message, make a plan, bring up the future—not out of joy but out of fear. I didn't recognize it then, but what I was really saying was: *Please don't forget me. Please prove I still matter. Please don't disappear.*

In my mind, I thought I was being proactive, but I was over-functioning. I was dominating the space. I was filling every silence before it could echo. And in doing that, I unknowingly cut off any chance for the other person to show up for me.

I didn't leave room to be missed. To be pursued. To be chosen.

Eventually, someone I was dating told me—gently, but truthfully—"You're suffocating me. I never get the chance to miss you." That moment was painful but sacred. It woke me up. He later shared that he had begun to resent me—not for who I was but because I never gave him space to step into his own role in the relationship. I was always the one initiating, planning, guiding. I thought I was creating connection, but I was actually controlling it. That conversation changed everything.

I started to ask myself: *What am I really reaching for when I nudge someone? What am I afraid will happen if I don't text first? What feeling am I hoping they'll give me?*

And slowly, I started giving those things to myself. The reassurance. The attention. The sense of being chosen. I began to see that my over-functioning wasn't a sign of strength—it was a response to past hurt.

In trying to be seen, I had been erasing myself.

This was the beginning of learning how to soften. How to trust. How to let my feminine energy—the part of me that receives, feels, flows —have space again. I started to understand the sacred balance between giving and receiving, leading and surrendering. Between holding space and taking space.

That was the beginning of learning how to dance with both energies—feminine and masculine—in a healthier way. How to trust the natural rhythm of connection. How to pull back, not to manipulate, but to trust that *space* is a necessary part of intimacy. (If you're struggling with this, too, head to my website to take the quiz to find out if you're Over-functioning in Relationships.)

NEEDINESS OR MAGNETISM?

There's a fine line between neediness and magnetism. One repels, the other attracts. One stems from a place of lack, the other from a place of fullness. Understanding this distinction is the key to maintaining chemistry without losing yourself in the process.

Neediness isn't just about wanting love—it's about grasping for it, about trying to hold onto something so tightly that you squeeze the life out of it. It comes from fear: fear of being alone, fear of losing someone, fear of not being enough. And the thing about fear is that it's loud. It distorts our energy. It turns attraction into desperation. And desperation? It isn't magnetic. You can feel it. That pull that says, I need you to make me feel whole. That energy that subtly begs, *Please choose me.* Even when it's unspoken, it lingers in the air. It disrupts the natural flow of attraction. Because real chemistry isn't created through effort—it's a byproduct of alignment.

Magnetism, on the other hand, is effortless. It's standing so deeply in your own truth that you naturally draw people toward you. It's the energy of someone who doesn't need connection but deeply values it. It's the quiet confidence of someone who is rooted in themselves, someone who knows they are worthy of love but doesn't chase it. True magnetism doesn't beg to be seen; it simply exists, and in doing so, it invites others in.

So, how do you stay grounded in your own power without suffocating the connection? How do you keep the chemistry alive while maintaining your autonomy? It starts with recognizing the source of neediness when it arises. When you feel that urge to grasp, to cling, to make something happen—pause. Ask yourself: What am I actually craving? Is it love? Validation? Security? Are you seeking reassurance from another person that you haven't yet given yourself? Understanding the root of the feeling allows you to address it without acting from a place of desperation.

The secret is to remember that love is an enhancement, not a solution. It's not meant to complete you—it's meant to complement you. When you anchor yourself in your own worth, you naturally shift from chasing love to attracting it. You stop trying to mold yourself into what you think someone else wants, and instead, you allow your true self to shine. And that—more than anything—is what creates the deepest attraction.

True magnetism flourishes in a life already rooted in abundance. When your days are filled with purpose, passion, and presence—when you're actively building a life you love—you stop seeking someone to fill a void and instead become someone others want to join. Love becomes a conscious choice, not a desperate need. You're not auditioning to be chosen; you're discerning. You're not waiting to be fulfilled; you're already full. That fullness creates space for genuine chemistry because the connection is no longer about survival or scarcity—it's about expansion. You're inviting someone into a world that's already vibrant, already magnetic, already alive. And in doing so, you remain grounded in your power while creating a relationship that feels like an addition, not a lifeline.

This is also where polarity plays its role. Polarity thrives on space, on the ebb and flow between two energies. When one person collapses into neediness, that space disappears. The push and pull of attraction flattens. So, how do you stay magnetic without becoming needy? By leaning into trust. Trusting yourself. Trusting the connection. Trusting that you don't have to force what is meant for you.

Learning how to attract without chasing means embodying the energy of *I am whole as I am*. It's understanding that you don't have to overextend, over-give, or over-explain to be chosen. Real chemistry doesn't require effort—it requires presence. It requires being so deeply aligned with yourself that the right people can't help but be drawn in.

As we explored in the last section, polarity isn't about control—it's about balance. It's about maintaining that natural rhythm of attraction without tipping into over-reliance. And now, we're taking that even deeper. How do you sustain this magnetism over time? How do you keep the energy flowing, keep the attraction alive, without falling into patterns of neediness or distance? That's what we'll uncover next. Because the true art of magnetism isn't just about creating attraction—it's about sustaining it.

CREATING BOUNDARIES

Attraction isn't something you grip tightly with both hands; it's something you allow to breathe. It's in the pauses, the moments apart, the knowing that you do not need to be intertwined at all times to be deeply connected. This is where boundaries become the quiet protectors of chemistry. Not walls to keep someone out, but structures that allow the energy between you to move freely, without suffocation.

How do you know where boundaries are needed?

Start with your body. Notice how you feel in different moments. Does a situation leave you feeling drained, anxious, or disconnected from yourself? Do you find yourself saying yes when you want to say no? Do you crave space but fear that taking it will make you seem distant? Boundaries begin in the spaces where you feel tension

—where you begin to shrink, mold, or override your own needs for the sake of keeping the peace.

Boundaries are not about keeping love out—they're about keeping you intact within it. Real magnetism is sustained through the ability to say yes to yourself as often as you say yes to someone else. It's in honoring your needs, your time, your solitude—not as a rejection of the other person, but as an affirmation of who you are. Attraction fades when we lose ourselves, when we mold too quickly, when we collapse into each other without leaving space to breathe. Boundaries are what keep you whole, and wholeness is what keeps you magnetic.

The mistake people often make is believing that closeness is measured in time spent together. That more time equals more intimacy. But intimacy isn't built in proximity; it's built in presence, in attention, in the moments when you are fully with each other, not just physically near. There is something intoxicating about someone who moves through life with purpose, someone who has a world of their own, someone who invites you in rather than needing you to complete them. This is why boundaries nurture attraction. Because they say: *I am here, I am present, and I am still my own.*

Creating space for individuality while building connection is an art. It's knowing when to fold into each other and when to step back, not in withdrawal but in reverence. It's the balance between self-dating and partnership, between knowing yourself deeply and sharing that depth with someone else. Love is not meant to erase you—it's meant to amplify you.

And here's the beauty: Boundaries do not push love away; they allow it to grow organically. Love breathes in the space between *I want you* and *I do not need to own you*. Attraction thrives in the rhythm of togetherness and apartness, in the trust that comes from knowing you are not abandoning each other, only allowing the energy to move as it is meant to. Trusting the process, trusting yourself, trusting that love does not need to be controlled to stay.

Some connections ignite quickly and fade just as fast. Others grow slow and steady, deepening with time. Both have their purpose. But the ones meant for you—the ones that truly align—will never require you to chase, to convince, or to abandon yourself. So let it unfold. Let attraction be a meeting, not a pursuit. Let connection be a dance, not a game. Keep the burn steady, not by clinging, but by continuing to stand in the full force of who you are. And most of all—trust. Trust that the love meant for you will always find you. And trust yourself enough to walk away from anything that asks you to be less than who you are.

Trust that real connection won't crumble when you stand firm.

REFLECTIONS FOR THE ROAD AHEAD

What boundaries are you setting?

Time & Space
Allowing yourself and your relationship room to breathe. You don't have to be available at every moment to be connected.

Emotional Energy
Not overextending, not carrying the entire weight of the relationship, not pouring endlessly without receiving.

Physical & Mental

Recognizing when you need rest, solitude, or to follow your own rhythms rather than merging completely into another.

Personal Values & Desires

Honoring what feels right to you, not just what keeps someone else happy.

How do you actually set them?

Speak your truth early and often.

Boundaries are most effective when they are clear from the start. It's easier to maintain space than to reclaim it.

Use "I" statements.

Instead of, "You're suffocating me," say, "I need some time alone to recharge." Instead of, "You never respect my time," say, "I feel best when I have space for my routines." If expressing a boundary makes someone pull away or react with frustration, it's a sign of deeper misalignment, not a failure on your part.

CHAPTER 8: BOUNDARIES THAT LIBERATE

The Power of Saying No with Grace and Confidence

SAYING NO SHOULD be simple. It's just a word, right? For most of us, it feels like an act of war. Setting boundaries often triggers a flood of discomfort—guilt, anxiety, self-doubt. It can feel like rejecting someone, letting them down, or even abandoning them. Why is it so damn hard?

Let's break it down:

1. **People-Pleasing: The Fear of Disappointing Others**
   From a young age, we are conditioned to believe that being "nice" means saying *yes*. We're taught that prioritizing others —helping, agreeing, accommodating—is the key to being liked and accepted. But the problem is, when we make everyone else comfortable at our own expense, we become uncomfortable. People-pleasing isn't kindness—it's self-abandonment in disguise. It's saying, *Your comfort matters more than my truth.* And when we operate from this place, we end up exhausted, resentful, and disconnected from our own needs.

   I remember one night when I said yes to a dinner invite I didn't actually want to attend. It had been a long week—one of those weeks where everything feels a bit too loud, a bit too much. What I really needed was a quiet evening to myself, maybe a hot bath and a journal session, or just the luxury of silence. But the text came in:

   "You should come! It'll be fun." And before I even thought about how I felt, my fingers typed out, *"Sure, I'll be there!"* I showed up—physically, at least. Emotionally, mentally,

energetically? I was tapped out. I smiled on cue and nodded along to conversations, but my mind was far away, running through the list of things I was neglecting by being there. I felt scattered, guilty, resentful—and not because anyone had done anything wrong. It was because I had abandoned myself. *Again*. I wasn't doing anyone a favor by being half-present. I wasn't being kind; I was being compliant. And when I left that night, instead of feeling connected or appreciated, I just felt empty. That's when it really hit me: saying yes to someone else while saying no to myself wasn't noble—it was self-betrayal dressed up as politeness.

2. **Fear of Rejection: The Need to Be Liked**
   Saying no risks pushing people away. We don't want to be seen as difficult, selfish, or cold. And underneath that? A deeper fear: *What if they stop liking me? What if they leave?* Let's reframe this—what kind of relationships are we maintaining if they require us to betray ourselves? If saying no ends a friendship, it was never a friendship—it was a transaction.

   Try this example on for size. You go on a first date. It's ... fine. Nothing terrible, but nothing sparking, either. You know deep down you don't want to go on a second one. But then comes the follow-up text: "I had a great time. Want to hang out again?" And immediately, your stomach knots. Not because you're unsure of your answer but because you're afraid of the response your *no* might provoke. You hesitate—not because your decision is unclear but because you don't want to be the "bad guy." You don't want to hurt someone's feelings, or worse, deal with them lashing out, trying to change your mind, or calling you cold. In the past, you might've ghosted. Or delayed. Or sent a soft, vague text meant to keep things polite but unclear. And every time, you dreaded reading the reply. You'd wait hours, sometimes a whole day, afraid of what might be waiting for you in that little text bubble.

But here's the truth: the fear wasn't really about them. It was about you not wanting to feel guilty for honoring your boundary. You were so afraid of being misunderstood or disliked that you abandoned your own clarity to protect someone else's comfort. But when you finally realize that a healthy connection doesn't require self-abandonment—that being liked isn't worth being drained—you begin to own your *no*. And suddenly, you're not afraid of the text back. Because your peace isn't up for negotiation.

3. **Guilt: The Feeling That Saying No is Wrong**
   Many of us have internalized the belief that putting ourselves first is selfish. That good people help, accommodate, and sacrifice. But boundaries aren't about rejecting others—they're about honoring ourselves. Self-care is not selfish. It's not indulgent. It's a requirement. And setting boundaries isn't an act of harm; it's an act of integrity.

   Check out this example: A friend texts asking for help moving this weekend. You look at your calendar—it's your only day off after a packed week. You were planning to finally sleep in, catch up on rest, maybe take yourself on a slow morning walk or do absolutely nothing at all. You type out a polite but clear reply: "I wish I could, but I'm not available this weekend." Their response comes fast: "Must be nice to have free time." And just like that, guilt punches you in the gut. You stare at your phone, heart rate up, thoughts racing. Maybe I should go ... maybe I'm being selfish ... maybe I can rearrange a few things. You consider backpedaling—not because you want to help but because you're afraid of being seen as inconsiderate. The need to be "good," to be liked, to not disappoint—it all rushes in.

   But here's the truth: you don't owe anyone an explanation for protecting your time, your energy, or your well-being. Setting a boundary isn't an act of harm. It's an act of integrity. You didn't say no out of cruelty. You said no because you are finally learning that your needs matter, too. That you don't

131

have to earn rest. That it's not selfish to choose yourself. And here's the other truth: someone who genuinely values you won't try to guilt you for having boundaries. They'll respect them. And in doing so, they'll create space for a relationship rooted in mutual care, not silent obligation.

BRIDGES NOT BARRIERS

It's not the act of saying no that's hard—it's the aftermath. Because deep down, *we want to be liked*. We want people to respect us. And we don't want to feel bad for doing something that is, ultimately, good for us. But here's the thing: The right people will respect you more when you're honest. The people who can't handle your no? They were never meant to stay.

What if we stopped seeing boundaries as walls and started seeing them as guidelines for a healthier life? Setting boundaries is about creating the conditions where you can show up as your best self. It's about saying, *"I matter, too. My energy is valuable. I respect myself enough to be clear about what I will and won't allow."* Boundaries are not barriers; they are bridges to deeper, more authentic relationships. They don't create disconnection—they create clarity. And clarity is the foundation of trust.

Boundaries are a form of self-respect in action. You can say all day that you love yourself, but if you consistently allow people to overstep, ignore, or take advantage of your time and energy, your actions tell a different story. When you consistently allow things that drain, disrespect, or deplete you, you're sending a message—not just to others, but to yourself—about what you believe you deserve. When we fail to set boundaries, we invite people to treat us however they like. And the hard truth? If you don't stand up for your own needs, no one else will.

As we move into this chapter, let's remember: Saying no is not an act of rejection. It's an act of self-respect. And the more you practice it, the more you'll realize—you don't need everyone to like you. You just need to like yourself.

Self-check:

- Do you say yes to things you don't want to do just to keep the peace?

- Do you let people interrupt your time, drain your energy, or demand more than you're willing to give?

- Do you tell yourself "it's not a big deal," when actually it is a big deal?

The effects of failing to set boundaries can show up in the following ways:

- **Resentment:** When you constantly overextend yourself—always saying yes when you want to say no—you create an unspoken agreement: *I will always give, and you will always take.* This doesn't just lead to exhaustion—it leads to resentment, burnout and more. When you give more than you receive, you start to feel undervalued. You might not express it, but it builds up. And over time, it poisons the relationship.

- **Burnout:** When you stretch yourself too thin—whether in work, friendships, or family obligations—you eventually hit a wall. Your energy depletes, your patience wears thin, and even things you once enjoyed start feeling like burdens.

- **Unbalanced relationships:** If one person is always the giver and the other is always the taker, the relationship isn't healthy—it's transactional. A true connection requires mutual respect and effort.

The more you practice saying no—without guilt, without over-explaining—the more you step into your own power. And when you do, you'll notice something incredible: The people who belong in your life will adjust. The ones who only benefited from your lack of boundaries will fall away. And either way, you're standing in your worth.

Let me tell you a story. I used to have this friend who only ever reached out when she needed something—help with a project, advice, emotional support, favors, you name it. At first, I didn't think much of it. I like being someone people can rely on. I like being supportive. But over time, I noticed something: the connection was always one-way. I was pouring in, and nothing was coming back. She never checked in just to see how I was doing. Never celebrated my wins. Never offered support in return. And slowly, I started to feel it—resentment. That gnawing, hollow feeling that says, *This doesn't feel good anymore.* I felt undervalued, invisible even. But instead of setting a boundary, I kept giving. I kept showing up. And in doing so, I silently taught her that this was okay—that I would always give, and she could always take.

Eventually, I hit a wall. I remember sending a message that said something like, "I care about you, but I'm feeling really depleted in this friendship. I don't feel like there's mutual effort or reciprocity. And that's something I need." It was hard. My hands shook a little as I wrote it. But it was honest. And it was necessary. Because here's the thing: if you never set boundaries, you train people to keep taking—and worse, you train yourself to believe that being depleted is normal. That you're supposed to accept crumbs and be grateful. But you're not. You deserve relationships that feel balanced and honoring—not transactional.

DOORS NOT WALLS

That moment taught me something big. There's a difference between walls and boundaries. Walls come from fear and pain; they shut the world out. Boundaries come from self-awareness and self-worth; they open the door to real connection, built on respect. Walls say, *I won't let anyone in.* Boundaries say, *I will let in only those who respect me.* And sometimes, the most loving thing you can say is: *This dynamic doesn't work for me anymore.*

Here's an example: Let's say you've been hurt in past relationships. A wall would mean shutting people out entirely, avoiding intimacy, and assuming everyone will hurt you. A boundary, on the other hand, would mean setting clear expectations —communicating what you need in a relationship and refusing to accept anything less. Boundaries aren't about keeping people away —they're about creating a space where the right people can connect with you in a way that feels healthy and balanced. And when you start enforcing them, something powerful happens: The people who truly value you will step up. The ones who only benefited from your lack of boundaries will step away. And either way, you win.

Every time you say no with clarity and confidence, you reinforce your self-respect and invite deeper, healthier relationships into your life. On the flip side, every yes you give is a withdrawal from your energy bank. When you spend that energy on things that don't serve you, you end up depleted, resentful, and misaligned with what you actually want.

Think about it:

- Saying yes to plans you don't want to attend just to avoid disappointing someone.

135

- Saying yes to extra work when you're already stretched thin just because you don't want to seem unhelpful.

- Saying yes to emotional labor—listening, supporting, fixing—when you have nothing left to give.

Every unnecessary yes is a no to something that actually matters—your rest, your growth, your priorities. Saying no isn't just an act of self-preservation—it's an act of honesty. When you set clear boundaries, you prevent misunderstandings, unmet expectations, and relationships built on obligation rather than genuine connection. You teach others how to respect your time and priorities. And those who value you will adjust—not push back.

One of the biggest struggles with saying no is feeling like you need to soften it with excuses:

- "I would, but I'm just so busy right now … "

- "I can't make it, but maybe next time!" (when you don't actually want there to be a next time)

- "I'd love to, but I have this other thing …"

These justifications don't strengthen your boundaries—they weaken them. They leave room for negotiation, pushback, and guilt. The truth is, you don't owe anyone an explanation for protecting your time and energy. *No* **is a complete sentence.**

SETTING BOUNDARIES

Now that we've established the power of saying no, let's get practical. Setting boundaries is about understanding what truly matters to you and having the tools to communicate it effectively. Here's how to set boundaries that protect your energy, ensure mutual respect, and keep your relationships balanced—without guilt or over-explaining.

Step 1: Identify Your Non-Negotiables

Before you can set boundaries, you need to get crystal clear on what you will and won't accept in your life. Boundaries aren't one-size-fits-all—they're deeply personal.

- Take inventory of your time and energy. If needed, try time mapping—track your activities for a few days and note:

    + What excites and energizes you?

    + What leaves you feeling drained, irritated, or resentful?

    + What obligations do you take on out of guilt rather than desire?

- Ask yourself: What are my absolute non-negotiables? These could be:

    + Not responding to work messages after a certain hour.

    + Not tolerating passive-aggressive behavior from friends or family.

    + Saying no to last-minute plans that disrupt your schedule.

    + Not over-explaining your decisions.

When you know what matters, setting boundaries becomes easier—because you're not just saying no randomly; you're protecting your well-being.

Step 2: Communicate Your Boundaries Early and Clearly

Boundaries work best when they're set before resentment builds. Too often, people avoid setting them until they've been pushed past their limit, which can lead to abrupt cutoffs, passive-aggressive behavior, or blow-ups.

- Be proactive, not reactive. If you know you don't want to work weekends, let your team know upfront—not when you're already burnt out.

- State them directly. Instead of waiting for someone to cross a boundary and then reacting, communicate it before it becomes an issue.

  Example: Instead of ghosting a friend who constantly asks for favors, you could say:

  - ✦ "I love helping when I can, but I have a lot on my plate right now, so I won't be able to say yes as often."

  - ✦ Don't soften it too much. Avoid saying things like "I'd love to, but ..." if you actually don't want to do it. That leaves room for negotiation. Instead, be clear: "That doesn't work for me."

Step 3: Holding the Boundary Without Over-Explaining

Once you set a boundary, hold it firmly. This is where many people struggle—feeling the need to justify, apologize, or soften their stance. Keep in mind, you don't owe anyone a lengthy explanation for protecting your energy. By holding your boundary without unnecessary explanations, you reinforce self-respect.

- No is a complete sentence. You don't have to follow it with a reason.

PRACTICE SAYING NO

Saying no can feel uncomfortable at first, but with practice, it gets easier. Here are some scripts for common situations to help you navigate them with confidence and grace.

Work Requests

- "I'd love to help, but my plate is full right now."

- "I can't take that on, but I can help brainstorm solutions."

- "I'm not available for extra projects at the moment."

- If a coworker repeatedly oversteps: "I've noticed I've been taking on extra work outside my role. I need to stick to my responsibilities moving forward."

Dating & Romantic Relationships
Saying no to another date:

- "I enjoyed meeting you, but I didn't feel a romantic connection. Wishing you the best!"

Setting a boundary around communication:

- "I appreciate you reaching out, but I need some space right now."

If a partner keeps crossing a boundary:

- "I've mentioned this before, and it's important to me. I need to know my boundaries are being respected."

Friends & Social Invitations

- "Thanks for thinking of me, but I'm going to pass this time."

- "I can't make it, but have fun!"

- "I need some downtime tonight, but let's plan something soon."

If a friend pushes:

- "I really need to prioritize rest, so I won't be going out."

Family Expectations

- "I appreciate your advice, but I need to make this decision on my own."

- "That doesn't work for me, but thanks for understanding."

- "I'm focusing on my well-being right now, and I need to set some boundaries around our conversations."

If guilt-tripped:

- "I love you, but I need to do what's best for me."

REACTIONS FROM OTHERS

One of the hardest parts of setting boundaries is dealing with how others react. But here's the truth: someone else's disappointment, frustration, or confusion is not your responsibility. At first, setting boundaries can feel like drawing a line between yourself and the people you love. You worry—will they be hurt? Will they leave? But the right people don't leave when you honor yourself. They may not always understand immediately, but the ones who are meant to stay will rise to meet you.

- People who respect you will respect your boundaries.

- People who get upset likely benefited from you having no boundaries.

- You can't control their feelings—you can only communicate with kindness and clarity.

If someone gets upset because you said no, that's information for them to process, not something you need to fix. Your job is to stand firm in your truth knowing that setting boundaries is an act of self-care, not selfishness. When you commit to honoring your needs, you stop living in fear of what others think. You stop shape-shifting, over-explaining, and contorting yourself to fit into spaces that were never meant for you. You step into a world where your time, energy, and presence are sacred. A world where love is no longer earned through self-sacrifice but received through self-trust.

When you are clear about what you can give, what you need, and where your limits lie, your relationships stop being tangled in resentment and unspoken expectations. Instead, they become spaces of freedom where you show up fully and love is given freely, not out of obligation, but out of choice.

You are not obligated to be available to everyone all the time.

Read that again and let it sink in. You are allowed to set boundaries. You are allowed to choose yourself. With each small moment of choosing yourself, you will begin to trust that honoring your needs doesn't make you selfish—it makes you strong. So here is your final reminder: *Your needs matter. Your energy is sacred. You are worthy of boundaries that protect your peace.* And today, you choose to honor them.

REFLECTIONS FOR THE ROAD AHEAD:

Like anything new, setting boundaries takes practice. So start small:

- The next time someone asks for your time, and you know you don't have the capacity, try saying, *I can't commit to that right now.*

- The next time you feel pressured to respond immediately, give yourself permission to pause. Not every message requires an instant reply.

- The next time you catch yourself justifying your boundaries, stop. A simple *No, that doesn't work for me* is enough.

CHAPTER 9: AUTHENTIC COMMUNICATION

How Deep Listening and Honest Expression Build Trust

EVERY RELATIONSHIP—whether personal, professional, or romantic—rises or falls on one thing: communication. The way you speak, listen, and express yourself shapes the depth of your connections, the trust you build, and the way people experience you. But real connection isn't just about words. It's about presence. It's about speaking with clarity and confidence while also listening with intention. It's the difference between being *heard* and being *understood*. Authentic communication is about more than just expressing your thoughts. It's about creating conversations that open doors, that make people feel truly seen, that strengthen trust and intimacy. It's the ability to speak your truth without fear of judgment, to embrace the *Let Them* mindset—allowing others to react as they will while you stay rooted in who you are.

In this chapter, we'll explore how to move beyond small talk and into conversations that are deep, real, and transformative. We'll talk about the power of deep listening—why the most magnetic people aren't the ones who talk the most but the ones who make others feel truly heard. And we'll break down how to express your needs, boundaries, and desires with both honesty and grace. Because when you master authentic communication, you don't just become a better speaker; you become someone people trust. You attract the right connections. You build relationships that aren't just fulfilling in the moment but that shape your life in ways you never expected.

Every great relationship—whether it's romantic, professional, or personal—has one thing in common: *depth*. The conversations that shape our lives aren't the ones filled with small talk and polite exchanges; they're the ones where we feel truly seen. Deep, meaningful conversations create lasting relationships. They build trust, forge intimacy, and give us the kind of connections that don't just exist for convenience but actually add to the richness of our lives. Too many of us go through life without that depth. We keep conversations surface-level, we talk about what's easy, we skate around the edges of real connection without ever diving in. And sometimes, we don't even realize how shallow it all is—until we step into something deeper.

I know this feeling firsthand. As I mentioned earlier, when I lived in Phoenix, I thought I had friendships. I was *constantly* surrounded by people—cyclists, runners, athletes who shared my lifestyle. It felt like a community. But when I really looked at it, our conversations rarely went beyond discussing our next race. We connected on activity, not on who we really were. And when life got hard? When I needed something more? Those connections weren't there. When I left Phoenix, I expected at least a few people to check in, to ask how I was adjusting, to make sure I was okay. But the silence was deafening. No one reached out. No one responded to my messages. And I realized something painful but true: proximity doesn't equal depth. Shared interests don't equal true connection.

Fast-forward to now, and the difference is night and day. The relationships I've built since moving—some with people I've only met once or twice—are already deeper than those I had for years. Why? Because we talk about what matters. We share our passions, our struggles, our dreams. I've had casual acquaintances ask me how my book is going, how I'm feeling about a big life change, how I'm *really* doing. And that's when you know it's real.

So, you're asking *"How do I create that?"* How do I move beyond the polite, predictable conversations and into something real? Well, it starts with intention. With the willingness to go deeper—to ask better questions, to listen more fully, to create space for honesty. It's about stepping out of auto-pilot conversations and instead engaging in a way that actually makes people feel something. Because as I've already said, people don't remember *what* you said; they remember *how you made them feel.*

If you want real connection, stop talking just to fill space. Start asking the questions that crack people open:

- What's been lighting you up lately?

- What's been on your heart recently?

- What's something you've been dreaming about but haven't said out loud yet?

Conversations like these build trust. They create relationships that last. And they separate the people who truly see you from the ones who are just passing time. The way you communicate isn't just about words—it's a reflection of your inner confidence. When you trust yourself, you don't feel the need to over-explain, prove yourself, or seek approval in every conversation. You speak with clarity, with ease, with a presence that draws people in.

Think about the people you're naturally drawn to. They aren't the ones who dominate every conversation, who talk just to fill space. They're the ones who listen with presence, who ask the right questions, who make you feel valued just by the way they engage.

That's confidence. Confident communication isn't about being the loudest person in the room. It's about being fully present. It's about knowing that your *words* matter—but so does the way you *listen*, the way you hold space, the way you show up in a conversation.

So, ask yourself:

- Am I just talking, or am I truly connecting?

- Am I engaging in a way that makes people feel seen?

- Am I letting my confidence shape my conversations, or am I still filtering myself for approval?

When you shift the way you communicate, you shift the way people engage with you. You create relationships that are built on real depth, real trust, and real connection. And once you've experienced that? You'll never settle for surface-level again.

I used to think that being liked was the same as being loved.

I convinced myself that if I was agreeable enough, easygoing enough, pleasant enough, then maybe I could outrun rejection. If I could twist myself into whatever shape people needed, I'd always belong. For years, I lived inside that version of myself. I even answered to a name that wasn't mine. People called me Chelsea, and I let them. I let the mispronunciation slide, just like I let everything else slide—my opinions, my boundaries, my truth. Chelsea laughed at jokes that weren't funny. She apologized for taking up air. She made herself small, palatable, and soft around the edges so no one would call her "too much." Approval was her oxygen. She thought if everyone else was comfortable, then maybe she would be, too.

But here's what I've learned: When you seek validation more than truth, you betray yourself. Because if people love you, but you're wearing a mask—who are they really loving? They're loving Chelsea. They're loving the version of you that nods along, that says yes when she wants to say no, that shrinks herself to fit in. And that love? It's not for you. It's for the performance of you. I would rather be loved for who I truly am by a few people than liked by many for a performance. Because when you live for approval, you become a mirror instead of a person, always reflecting back what others want to see, not really yourself. Changing your shape depending on the room. But never fully being *you*.

And sadly, here's the truth no one tells you:

- If you have to perform for love, *it isn't love.*

- If you have to shrink to be accepted, *you aren't truly accepted.*

- If you have to betray yourself to belong, *you don't really belong.*

You may be saying–*Celeste, this sounds really hard.* I really just want to be liked. Here's where we need to learn the mindset shift from seeking validation to standing in our truth. And this is where it gets hard. Because approval feels like safety. Like belonging. Like warmth. And the idea of losing it? *It's terrifying.*

Here's what you have to understand: *Approval isn't safety.* Approval is control. And as long as you chase it, you are handing your self-worth to whoever is willing to give you a little validation that day. And you deserve better than that.

Standing in your truth means realizing that rejection isn't the enemy. It's the filter. The wrong people will leave. The right ones will stay. And the best part? You will finally belong to yourself. It's *really* okay to let people leave. If they judge you, misunderstand you, or dislike you—let them. Let them roll their eyes. Let them talk. Let them twist your words. Because the moment you stop explaining, justifying, proving yourself, *you take your power back.*

Mel Robbins talks about this in her book, *The Let Them Theory.* People will always have opinions. Some will like you; some won't. Some will understand you; some never will. And that's okay. I used to waste so much energy trying to be understood. Trying to convince people I was good, worthy, lovable. *But now?* I don't need them to understand me. I need *me* to understand *me.* Because the only opinion that truly shapes your life is the one you hold about yourself.

So, ask yourself:

- Do I *like* me?

- Do I *know* me?

- Do I *see* me?

When the answer to those questions is yes, nothing else matters.

STOP CHASING APPROVAL

Here's something I wish I had learned earlier in life: *When you stop chasing approval, you stop fearing hard conversations.*

I used to be afraid of something as simple as sending a text message. To begin with, I'd just try to ghost them. But if I had to send a message, I'd draft, reword, soften my words, add exclamation points or emojis just to seem nice. And when I had to say something uncomfortable? I'd send the message—and then block them before they could reply. Because I was *terrified*. Terrified of their disappointment, their anger, their rejection.

But here's what I know now:

- If you're speaking your truth with kindness and clarity, nothing someone else says can shake you.

- If they react poorly, that's their own discomfort—not yours.

- Their expectations of you are theirs to manage—not yours.

You don't have to write a novel to justify your decision. You don't have to over-explain why you feel how you feel. You don't have to convince anyone that your truth is valid. Your truth is valid because it's yours. And if they don't like it? Let them. Because you were never meant to be everything for everyone. You were meant to be fully, unapologetically *you*. And once you step into that? You will never go back.

DEEP LISTENING

Here's an interesting concept: *Most people don't actually listen.* Not really. They hear words, but they don't receive them. They nod. They smile. They say, "That's crazy," or "I totally get it." But behind their eyes, you can see it— they're somewhere else. They're waiting. Waiting for their turn to speak. Waiting to tell their own story. Waiting for a pause they can jump into, like a game of conversational double-dutch. And you can feel it. There's an unspoken, gut-level disappointment when you realize: *This person isn't really here with me.*

You've told a story only to have someone say—"*That reminds me of when I—*" And suddenly, you're not in a conversation. You're in a competition. You've opened up about something vulnerable, only to hear, "*Yeah, I know exactly what you mean, one time I—*" Your moment? It's hijacked. You know that feeling? That moment when you realize, Oh ... we're not actually connecting. This is just a back-and-forth exchange of words. And maybe you do what most people do. You shrink back. You say less. You stop trying. And the conversation? It flattens. It dies. Because deep down, all we really want is to feel seen.

There's a reason why deep listeners are rare—and irresistible. When someone listens to you fully—not just nodding, not just waiting for their turn, but really listening—something shifts inside of you. You relax. Your guard drops. You start talking more and maybe even saying things you didn't expect to share. True listening makes us feel safe. And when people feel safe, they open up. This is why deep listeners are magnetic. It's not about charm. It's not about being the most interesting person in the room. It's not even about having the best things to say. It's about creating a space where people feel so seen, so heard, and so understood that they crave being around you.

Dale Carnegie said, "*You can make more friends in two months by becoming interested in other people than you can in two years by trying to get other people interested in you.*" And that's the irony—the less you try to impress people, the more drawn to you they'll be. Because it's not about you. It's about them.

Studies show that when people feel heard, they:

- Rate the listener as more attractive and charismatic.

- Feel more connected, even after just one conversation.

- Trust the listener more—whether in friendships, business, or romance.

You've had those conversations with someone who is completely hung up on expressing themselves. In those moments, you leave feeling unfulfilled, unseen, and partially annoyed you got stuck having to ask all the questions. But the conversations where someone asks genuine, open ended questions and truly, deeply listens? Those are the conversations that stick with you, and you leave wanting more. *People don't remember what you said. They remember how you made them feel* (Sounds familiar, right?). And the feeling of being deeply heard is unforgettable.

Unfortunately, here's how most people "listen":

- They're in their head, not in the moment.

- They're waiting for their turn to talk.

- They make the conversation about them, not openly curious about you.

It's not malicious—it's just a habit. Most people have never been taught how to really listen. But when you change this? When you start listening differently? People open up to you in ways they never have before. They trust you, respect you, feel connected to you. So let's get into the art of deep listening.

Step 1: Drop the Need to Respond
The biggest mistake people make? They listen to respond, not to understand.

- They're thinking of a clever reply.

- They're waiting for a pause so they can jump in.

- They're more focused on what they will say than what's actually being said.

And you can feel it. But deep listening is different. It means:

- You're fully present.

- You're not mentally drafting your response.

- You're absorbing what's being said—fully, completely, without distraction.

Step 2: Mirror, Don't Hijack

Most people hijack conversations without realizing it. Instead of reflecting their experience, they redirect it.

- "I totally get that, one time I—" (Now we're talking about you.)

- "Yeah, I know exactly what you mean, I—" (Again, back to you.)

Deep listening is about mirroring. Not in a fake, robotic way— but in a way that says: *"I hear you. I see you. I'm with you."* Instead of hijacking, try validating and going deeper:

- "That sounds really tough. How did you handle that?"

- "Wow, that must have been exciting. What was that like?"

- "That makes so much sense. What happened next?"

See the difference? You're not taking the attention away. You're giving them space. And when people feel heard, they keep talking. That's when they start trusting you.

Step 3: Ask Generative Questions
Some responses shut a conversation down in just one sentence.

- "That's cool." (End.)

- "Oh wow, really?" (Dead end.)

- "Huh, interesting." (Now what?)

But generative questions open doors. Instead of stopping the flow, they keep it going. Try asking these questions instead:

- "What was that like for you?"

- "How did that change your perspective?"

- "What ended up happening?"

These types of questions say: *"I care. I'm interested. Tell me more."* And that? That's what makes people feel valued.

Step 4: The Power of Presence
Most people listen while distracted. They check their phone. They glance around the room. They nod absently but aren't really there. And we feel when someone isn't fully present. But when someone gives you their full attention? It's electrifying. It's like the whole world disappears, and for a moment, you're the only thing that matters. That's the power of true presence.

So when you listen:

- Put your phone down.

- Make eye contact.

- Be all in.

Because presence is a rare gift. And when you give it? People feel it deeply.

Step 5: The Unspoken Language of Listening
How you listen without words matters just as much. Your body language, facial expressions, and tone all send a message. Your energy tells people: "I'm here. I care. I'm listening."

Here's what makes people feel truly heard:

- Eye contact that's warm, not intense.

- An open posture—no crossed arms.

- Mirroring their tone and pace naturally.

- Small affirmations ("Mm, yeah, I understand you.")

Here's the bottom line: Most people listen to respond. Few people listen to understand. But the ones who do? The ones who truly, deeply, fully listen? They build unshakable connections.

Because in a world where everyone is desperate to be heard, the rarest, most powerful thing you can do is to be the one who listens.

QUESTIONS THAT OPEN DOORS (INSTEAD OF CLOSING THEM)

Most people ask dead-end questions. "Did you have a good weekend?" "How's work?" "Are you doing okay?" These questions aren't bad. They just don't go anywhere.

Now watch the shift:

- Instead of "Did you have a good weekend?" → "What was the highlight of your weekend?"

- Instead of "How's work?" → "What's something you've been excited about lately?"

- Instead of "You doing okay?" → "What's been on your mind the most this week?"

See the difference? One invites a yes/no answer. The other invites a story. And a story is where connection lives. Great conversations aren't about exchanging facts. They're about opening space for something real to unfold.

So, next time—ask the question that invites more. Because depth starts with the right invitation.

- "What's something that surprised you today?"

- "If you could relive one moment from this week, what would it be?"

- "What's been exciting you lately?"

Knowing When to Hold Space vs. Offer Advice

What's one of the biggest mistakes people make in conversation? They assume every problem needs a solution. Someone opens up about something hard, and immediately you state, "Oh! You should try X." "Have you read this book?" "You know what helped me when I was going through that?" The intention is good. The impact? Not always. Because sometimes, people don't need a fix. They need a witness.

And here's how you make sure you're giving them what they actually need: *Ask.*

"Do you want advice, or do you just want me to listen?"

That one question? Game-changing. Because sometimes, people need space to process out loud without feeling rushed toward a solution. Other times, they genuinely want guidance. When in doubt, let them decide. And if they just need space? Give it.

- Instead of solving, reflect back: "That sounds like a lot to carry." "I can see why that's been on your mind."

- Instead of rushing to reassure, validate: "That makes so much sense." "I'd probably feel the same way in your shoes."

- Instead of fixing, be fully present.

Because sometimes, the most powerful thing you can do in a conversation is simply hold space for someone to be exactly where they are.

THE RIGHT BALANCE OF SUPPORT & INSIGHT

Now—what about when they do want advice? This is where a lot of people swing too far in one direction:

- Some people over-support ("Oh, that's awful! That's so hard! That sucks!"), which can unintentionally keep the person feeling stuck.

- Others over-fix ("You just need to do X, Y, and Z"), which can feel dismissive and make them shut down.

The sweet spot? Balancing support with insight.

- First, acknowledge what they're feeling: "That sounds like a tough spot to be in."

- Then, ask before offering: "Do you want to hear what helped me when I went through something similar?"

- And if they say yes, frame it as an offering, not a directive: "Something that really shifted things for me was _____. It might not be for you, but just throwing it out there."

Support + Insight = A conversation that moves forward without forcing.

REFLECTIONS FOR THE ROAD AHEAD

Mastering authentic communication isn't just about becoming a better speaker or listener. It's about becoming more fully yourself. And when you do that—when you let your voice align with your truth—you don't just connect with others. You connect with your own power. As you move forward and practice the art of authentic communication, ask yourself:

- Am I truly listening?

- Am I speaking my truth with clarity and confidence?

- Am I showing up in conversations with the same energy I hope to receive?

Chapter 10: Professional Relationships
The Art of Magnetism at Work

MAGNETISM ISN'T JUST about attraction in love—it's about energy. It's about how you show up in the world, how you engage with others, and the powerful force you emit when you're fully aligned with your authentic self. This magnetism, when cultivated and harnessed, extends far beyond your personal relationships; it can also influence your professional life in profound ways.

In the workplace, your ability to create authentic, deep connections impacts everything. It shapes your opportunities, your leadership potential, and how effectively you collaborate. Often, we hear the phrase, "It's all about who you know," but the truth is, it's not just who you know—it's how they know you, and how you know them in return. When you form genuine connections with people, you create a bond that goes beyond the surface. It's not just about what you can do for them or what they can do for you but rather the energy exchanged. You become memorable, not because of a flashy resumé or a powerful pitch but because of the lasting impression you leave through your authenticity.

This connection builds mutual understanding. They understand who you are, what you stand for, and what you bring to the table. And you understand them, too. This deeper connection increases the likelihood that when opportunities arise—whether for a promotion, a project, or leadership—you'll be the first person they think of. The relationships you've nurtured work in your favor, allowing you to step into new roles or challenges with a natural ease because your reputation has already preceded you.

When it comes to leadership and collaboration, people often hesitate to step up or voice their worth. But when you've shown up authentically in all your interactions, you don't have to constantly assert your value. The trust and respect you've earned through your magnetic energy speaks for you. People recognize your potential and value because you've already demonstrated it through the way you show up, how you listen, how you lead, and how you support others.

One of the biggest challenges in cultivating this magnetic energy in the professional world is maintaining a balance between professionalism and authenticity. There's often a fear that to succeed you must conform to corporate expectations or lose your true self in the process. But this is a misconception. You don't have to compromise who you are to fit in or to climb the ladder. In fact, staying true to your authentic self is one of the most powerful tools you have. Authenticity attracts, and when you lead with it, you create an energy around you that resonates deeply with others. This is not about being "perfect" or fitting into a mold—it's about being real, being grounded, and showing up with clarity, warmth, and integrity.

When you embrace the duality of professionalism and authenticity, you stop seeing them as conflicting forces. Instead, they work in harmony. You can be professional without losing your unique spark. You can be strategic and ambitious while still leading from a place of genuine connection. This balance doesn't just help you succeed in your career—it helps you build relationships that are enriching and sustainable.

This chapter will explore how to channel that magnetic energy in your professional environment, allowing you to cultivate meaningful connections and create opportunities. It's about mastering the art of being your most authentic self while navigating the complexities of the professional world. So let's dive in and discover how to unlock the power of magnetism at work, where authenticity, energy, and connection become the keys to lasting professional success.

BUILDING TRUST

I didn't come into the professional world with all the answers. In fact, when I was first introduced to NetSuite—a cloud-based business platform companies use to manage their finances, operations, and customer data—I had absolutely no idea what it was. I wasn't trained in it, I didn't study it—I just knew I had to figure it out. So I did what I've always done: I showed up. I took every course I could find. I studied, experimented, Googled late at night, and slowly, I became the person in the room who got things done.

What made this magnetic wasn't that I knew everything—it's that people could trust me to learn anything. That mindset came from years earlier, when my clarinet professor used to say, "If someone asks if you also can play oboe at an audition, you say yes— and then you go home and learn it by Monday." That always stuck with me. Not in a fake-it kind of way, but in a *you can count on me* kind of way. I wasn't pretending. I was practicing confidence, the kind that says, "I might not know it yet, but I will."

Eventually, that energy became my calling card. I had worked closely with a consulting partner on various projects in my old role, and when COVID-19 hit, I reached out and told him I was looking for something new. I didn't pitch myself. I didn't perform. I just said, "I'd really like the opportunity to work for you." And without hesitation, he said yes. He already knew my energy, my effort, my follow-through. That one email led to a new role, a promotion to Director, and later, to becoming a VP.

One of the things he's told me that still means a lot is this:

"If I could clone you, I would. I give you feedback once, and the next time I see you, it's already implemented. That's why I trust you—because you show up consistently as yourself in every situation."

That's what magnetism at work really looks like. It's about being someone people can rely on. Someone who's real. Someone who doesn't need to prove; they just do it.

AUTHENTICITY IN THE WORKPLACE

Professional success doesn't require you to mask your true self or wear a façade. In fact, the more you embrace your authentic self, the more your professional journey will align with your deeper values and purpose. The idea that success means conforming to a set of rigid expectations is a myth. Authenticity doesn't mean being raw, abrasive, or acting in a way that dismisses professionalism. It's about showing up with confidence, warmth, and clarity, and allowing your true essence to shine through in every interaction, without sacrificing the professionalism that's necessary in the workplace.

When you bring your authentic self to work, you naturally build trust. People can sense when someone is being genuine and when they are being guarded or playing a role. This openness fosters a sense of safety and connection in your relationships, whether with your team, clients, or colleagues. Authenticity breeds credibility—it allows others to see you for who you are and what you stand for. And when others trust you, they are more likely to respect your ideas, rely on you for leadership, and champion your success. This is the true power of showing up as your authentic self.

Furthermore, embracing authenticity sets you apart from others in your field. In a world where many people try to blend in or mirror the behaviors and values of those around them, standing firm in your authenticity can create a powerful differentiation. People remember those who are authentic, and it's these genuine connections that open doors to new opportunities—whether it's a job promotion, a leadership role, or an important partnership. You are not just another cog in the machine but someone whose contributions are rooted in a deep sense of purpose, passion, and integrity. This doesn't mean abandoning professionalism or disregarding the expectations of your workplace. It's about integrating who you are into your professional persona in a way that feels aligned, respectful, and effective.

Here are a few practical ways to lean into your authentic self in the workplace:

Lead with Your Values
Know your core values, and let them guide your decisions and actions. When you make choices aligned with your values, you create a consistent, authentic presence that builds trust with those around you.

Be Mindful of Your Energy
Bring warmth and openness into every interaction. Be confident in what you bring to the table, but always remain humble and approachable. This creates a dynamic where your authenticity is evident, and others feel comfortable around you.

Communicate Clearly and Directly
Speak with clarity and purpose, making sure your message is heard without the need for extra drama or flair. People will

respect you for your directness and your ability to communicate effectively.

Honor Professional Expectations

Understand the dynamics of your workplace and adapt your authenticity to fit the situation without losing your core self. This is how you strike the perfect balance between being true to who you are and respecting the environment you're in.

Own Your Strengths

Acknowledge what makes you unique, and lean into those strengths. Whether it's your creative ideas, leadership abilities, or problem-solving skills, allow yourself to shine through your work. Don't diminish your value in an attempt to fit in—your strengths are what will set you apart.

By staying true to your core values, leading with clarity, and fostering genuine connections, you can create an authentic presence that influences every aspect of your professional life. Your authentic self is a powerful tool for success—embrace it, and let it guide you to new opportunities, deeper relationships, and a more fulfilling career.

CREATING CONFIDENCE

Confidence isn't something you "put on" like a super hero's cape. It's something you practice until it becomes second nature. Your brain responds to the signals your body gives it. If you carry yourself with hesitation, your mind registers uncertainty. If you hold yourself with strength, your brain believes you are strong. This is why small physical shifts—how you stand, how you breathe, how you move—can have a massive impact on your self-perception.

Have you ever noticed how wearing an outfit you love changes the way you walk? Or how standing tall makes you feel more powerful? These aren't coincidences. They're proof that confidence is embodied.

Try this:

- Next time you walk into a room, lift your chin slightly and take a deep breath.

- Keep your shoulders back, and imagine your feet firmly planted, like roots growing into the ground.

- Instead of rushing to fill silence, pause. Let your words land.

- Make eye contact—not aggressively, but with intention.

These aren't just postures. They're signals—to your brain and to the world—of self-trust. Magnetism isn't about forcing anything. It's about alignment between your inner confidence and your outward expression.

Here are a few subtle yet powerful shifts to cultivate an effortlessly magnetic presence:

Slow down.
Rushed movements and speech create nervous energy. Give yourself permission to take your time.

Take up space.
Uncross your arms, stand tall, and allow yourself to fully inhabit a room.

Own your stillness.
Nervous fidgeting can make you feel (and appear) unsettled. Stillness radiates confidence.

Lead with your heart.
Physically. Keep your chest open instead of caving inward—this simple shift has a big impact.

Breathe deeply.
Shallow breathing signals stress; deep breathing signals calm authority.

The goal isn't to "perform" confidence. It's to embody it so fully that it becomes who you are. Because the most magnetic person in the room isn't the one fighting to be seen. It's the one who simply is.

Magnetism is rooted in alignment with who you are at your core. It's not about changing yourself to fit the expectations of others, nor is it about trying to please everyone you meet. When you try to be someone you're not just to gain approval or make others like you, you drain your energy and lose your true power. True attraction is magnetic because it's authentic. It comes from living in a way that reflects your values, your desires, and your unique expression. When you're aligned with yourself, you no longer need external validation to feel worthy or seen. This kind of energy is incredibly attractive because people are drawn to authenticity—they feel it on a visceral level.

On the other hand, people-pleasing leads to burnout and disconnection. When you're constantly adjusting yourself to fit others' expectations, you're not living for yourself. And that lack of authenticity repels people, even if they can't consciously pinpoint why. When you stop chasing approval, you free up energy to fully be yourself, and that's when your true magnetism shines.

CHARISMA AND COMPETENCE

Magnetism in the workplace is about cultivating a presence that is both compelling and credible, someone others naturally gravitate toward—not just because they like you, but because they respect you. The most magnetic professionals strike a balance between charisma and competence, warmth and authority, vulnerability and strength. They build deep, authentic relationships while maintaining clear professional boundaries.

Charisma opens doors, but competence keeps them open. You may have a magnetic personality, the ability to engage people easily, and the warmth that makes you likable, but if you lack depth, your influence will only go so far. On the other hand, if you are deeply competent but lack the interpersonal skills to connect with others, you may find yourself overlooked, even if your work is excellent.

True professional magnetism is about blending the two. Charisma helps you connect—it makes people want to engage with you, collaborate with you, and seek your presence. It fosters trust, builds rapport, and makes interactions enjoyable. Competence helps you deliver—it ensures that people take you seriously, that your opinions hold weight, and that you are not just likable but respected. When you merge these qualities, you create a reputation that is both engaging and authoritative—someone people enjoy working with but also someone they trust to get the job done at a high level.

In a workspace, relationships thrive when built on mutual respect and clarity. Yes, you want to be yourself. Yes, you want to foster connection and collaboration. But there is a difference between magnetic connection and overstepping professional boundaries.

- Magnetic connection means being warm, engaged, and open while respecting the context of a professional environment.
- Overstepping boundaries might look like oversharing personal struggles, becoming overly casual with colleagues, or forming relationships that create conflicts of interest.

It's possible to have close professional relationships without losing the distinction between work and personal life. This doesn't mean you can't be friendly—it simply means you're intentional about how much of your personal self you bring into the workspace and how you navigate interactions professionally.

APPROACHABLE AUTHORITY

One of the biggest challenges in leadership and professional dynamics is balancing approachability with authority. If you're too rigid or distant, you risk being seen as unapproachable or intimidating. If you're too informal or casual, you risk losing credibility and respect. The key is to cultivate executive presence, a blend of confidence, warmth, and intentionality in how you communicate and carry yourself:

Stay warm and engaging.
Greet people genuinely. Ask how they're doing. Show interest in their work. Approachability is a strength.

Hold firm to your standards.
Being warm doesn't mean being a pushover. Set clear expectations, hold yourself and others accountable, and make decisions with confidence.

Use intentional body language.
Make eye contact, stand tall, and speak with clarity. Your physical presence communicates just as much as your words.

Communicate with clarity and kindness.
You don't have to be harsh to be firm. You can set a clear standard while still leading with respect.

Magnetic professionals command respect—they don't demand it. They don't have to raise their voices or assert power aggressively. Respect naturally follows because of how they show up, communicate, and lead. The best leaders and professionals are those who can be authentic yet professional, warm yet strong, and vulnerable yet grounded. That balance is where true magnetism lies —when you don't have to perform or prove your worth, but instead, you simply *embody* it.

One of the most striking examples of this in my own life is someone I currently work with—the president of our company. You'd never know it from how he carries himself. He never leads with his title. In fact, he rarely even mentions it unless he's signing an email. Instead, he shows up to every conversation as a human first—present, curious, and intentional. He treats sales not as transactions but as partnerships. His approach is relational, not positional. He talks often about the power of knowing people— really knowing them. What makes them tick, what drives them, what matters most in their world. And he remembers. He circles back. He asks questions that make people feel seen and valued. That's magnetism. Not because he's the president, but because he leads from a place of grounded presence, humility, and trust.

What's just as powerful is the way he gives feedback. It's honest, never sugar-coated, but never diminishing. He admits when he's wrong. He's transparent when he doesn't have all the answers. And that vulnerability doesn't make him weaker—it makes him more trustworthy. It makes people want to work with him, not just for him. He also sets a tone for open communication. While he might not frame it as setting "boundaries," he makes it clear that he wants to be kept in the loop—that he expects people to reach out, to voice challenges early, to let him help navigate solutions before they become full-blown problems. That kind of clarity, availability, and leadership fosters safety and empowerment in a way that is a boundary—one rooted in trust and shared ownership.

GROUNDED VULNERABILITY

But how do you show up with presence, professionalism, and strength and still allow yourself to be real? That's where vulnerability comes in. Not the performative kind, or the overshare-everything-on-Slack kind. But the grounded kind—the kind that says, "I don't have all the answers, but I'll figure it out." Or, "Here's what I need to do my best work." Vulnerability in the workplace isn't weakness. It's a form of quiet power—the ability to be open without unraveling, human without apologizing, honest without losing authority. It creates trust, connection, and space for others to do the same.

Vulnerability in the workplace doesn't mean spilling your deepest fears or sharing personal struggles with your colleagues. But it does mean being real, being open to feedback, and allowing yourself to be seen as human—without compromising strength.

- Vulnerability in leadership looks like admitting when you don't have all the answers, being willing to listen to different perspectives, and owning your mistakes. It makes you relatable and trustworthy.

- Strength in leadership looks like making confident decisions, standing by your values, and guiding your team with clarity and conviction. It ensures that your leadership is respected and effective.

BOUNDARIES IN THE WORKPLACE

Boundaries in the workplace aren't about shutting people out or being inflexible—they're about protecting your energy, maintaining your integrity, and fostering a work environment that is both productive and respectful. Too often, professionals—especially high achievers—fear that setting boundaries will make them seem difficult or uncooperative. But in reality, clear, confident boundaries are the key to sustainable success and strong professional relationships. Strong boundaries actually make you a more valuable colleague, leader, and employee—not a more difficult one.

- **Boundaries create reliability.** When you set limits, you ensure that the commitments you do make are ones you can fully execute. People trust those who follow through.

- **They prevent burnout.** Overextending yourself leads to exhaustion, resentment, and a decline in performance. Sustainable success requires sustainable energy.

- **They reinforce self-respect and invite others to respect you, too.** When you honor your limits, others learn to honor them as well. If you don't take your own time seriously, why should they?

Saying yes to everything doesn't just leave you exhausted—it creates problems for the entire team. When you take on more than you can realistically handle, deadlines slip, quality suffers, and others are forced to step in at the last minute. Overcommitting doesn't just affect you; it affects your team's efficiency, the company's overall success, and even the trust your colleagues have in you.

I once worked with a colleague who had an admirable desire to make clients feel supported and heard. His intentions were solid: he wanted to be the go-to person, the one who always said yes, who made things happen. On the surface, he seemed like a dream team member—always enthusiastic, always promising solutions. But behind the scenes, things started unraveling. He rarely delegated, rarely asked for help, and continually overcommitted himself. He wanted to look like he had it all under control, but the truth was he was juggling more than anyone could reasonably manage. Deadlines slipped. Communication became unclear. Promises made to clients fell through, and team members had to scramble to pick up the pieces. Eventually, this pattern led to frustrated coworkers, lost trust, and even lost clients.

It wasn't because he didn't care—it was because he cared so much that he forgot the difference between being helpful and being overextended. His story is a powerful reminder: saying yes too often doesn't make you a stronger professional; it erodes your ability to actually deliver.

If you're constantly saying yes out of guilt, consider this: a teammate who overpromises and under-delivers isn't being helpful —they're unintentionally becoming a bottleneck. The best way to contribute effectively is to be honest about your capacity and to take on only what you can execute well.

- Overcommitting doesn't just affect you—it affects the trust your team has in you. If you constantly say yes but can't follow through, it hurts your credibility more than if you had set a boundary in the first place.

- Being a team player doesn't mean saying yes to everything. It means being clear about what you can take on, and then following through on it with excellence.

- Workplace respect isn't built on being agreeable; it's built on being reliable. People will value you far more if you are honest about your workload than if you overextend yourself and underdeliver.

PRIORITIZE RESPECT OVER APPROVAL

You don't need to be liked by everyone to be successful, but you do need to be respected. Why? Because in professional environments, respect is the foundation of trust, credibility, and influence. When you prioritize being liked over being respected, you may find yourself avoiding difficult conversations or necessary conflicts. You may hesitate to set boundaries for fear of upsetting others. You might also be over-accommodating and take on tasks that aren't yours to complete. But when you earn respect, you position yourself as a leader, a reliable colleague, and a person whose voice carries weight.

People-pleasing may feel like a survival strategy, but in the long run, it diminishes your impact and erodes your self-respect. Detaching from the need for approval doesn't mean becoming indifferent—it means recognizing that you don't have to be liked by everyone; you just need to be respected. Respect comes from consistency, integrity, and the ability to hold your ground with grace. If people know you as someone who is honest, reliable, and intentional, they will respect you—even if they don't always like your decisions. And in professional dynamics, respect is far more valuable than fleeting approval.

Being respected means that people trust your judgment and take your input seriously. Your boundaries are acknowledged rather than constantly tested. And you most likely have a seat at the table when important decisions are made. The people who matter in your career—mentors, decision-makers, and key collaborators—will not base their view of you on whether you're always agreeable. They will respect you because you show up with clarity, stand firm when needed, and contribute meaningfully. At the end of the day, prioritizing respect over approval doesn't mean being cold or dismissive—it means valuing your integrity, your expertise, and your long-term career growth.

I've seen this play out firsthand. There was a moment recently where a colleague was trying to fix a client issue by suggesting a workaround that made sense on the surface, but from the inside, I knew it wouldn't work. Not because it was a bad idea, but because it wasn't how the system functioned in the first place. That was the moment I stepped in—not to shut the conversation down, but to ground it. I offered a quick clarification about how the process actually worked, and then asked a few questions that helped steer the team back to a productive direction. No one felt embarrassed or corrected—just refocused.

Those small pivots—validating where someone is coming from, bringing clarity without condescension, and asking the right questions—they're what turn messy conversations into moments of alignment. You don't have to be the loudest voice in the room to create clarity. Sometimes, the strongest influence is just knowing when to speak and how to do it in a way that moves the room forward. When you learn to speak with authority while still remaining approachable, people will naturally gravitate toward you. They will trust your leadership, respect your insights, and feel safe enough to collaborate with you.

MASTERING PROFESSIONAL COMMUNICATION

Communication isn't just about transmitting information—it's about building relationships, fostering trust, and creating influence without force.

1. **Professional emails and conversations.** Every email, message, and conversation is a reflection of your professionalism. A well-crafted email isn't just grammatically correct—it's intentional, clear, and structured in a way that makes your message easy to digest. Avoid unnecessary fluff.

Instead of writing, "I just wanted to check in and see if you had any updates," say, "Do you have an update on this?" Respect both your own time and theirs.

2. **Speaking with authority and warmth.** People respond best to confidence that is rooted in certainty, not arrogance. The most magnetic professionals balance strength with approachability—they know what they're talking about, but they also make others feel at ease. Their words are measured, intentional, and free of excessive qualifiers like, "I think," "Maybe," or "Just my opinion, but ..." Drop the verbal hesitations and trust yourself.

3. **Avoiding filler words and over-explaining.** When you minimize your words, you maximize your impact. Confidence doesn't need a cushion. Instead of saying, "I'm not sure if this is right, but ..." say, "Here's what I recommend." Instead of, "I hope this makes sense," say, "Let me know if you have any questions." When you cut the extra words, people naturally listen more closely.

4. **Listen intentionally.** The most charismatic people aren't just great speakers—they're incredible listeners. In a world where most people are waiting for their turn to talk, true presence is magnetic. It makes people feel important, valued, and understood.

5. **Be fully present in every interaction.** Whether it's a high-stakes meeting or a casual hallway chat, your presence signals respect and attentiveness. Put your phone away. Maintain eye contact. Resist the urge to mentally craft your next response while the other person is speaking. Be there, fully. People can feel when you're truly listening—and they can also feel when you're not.

6. **Your body language speaks before you do.** Open posture, a slight forward lean, and engaged facial expressions send a powerful message: *I respect you, and I'm interested in what*

you have to say. Crossed arms, avoiding eye contact, or distracted gestures do the opposite. Your words matter, but your body tells the real story.

7. **Reflect and respond rather than waiting to talk.** Most people listen just enough to figure out what they want to say next. But real connection happens when you pause, absorb, and then respond with intention. Whether it's repeating back key points, asking thoughtful follow-ups, or simply nodding with understanding, these small cues make the other person feel truly heard.

EMOTIONAL INTELLIGENCE

Emotional intelligence is the secret ingredient of every great leader. It's what allows you to read the room, navigate difficult conversations, and inspire trust effortlessly. People with high emotional intelligence don't just understand their own emotions—they understand the emotions of those around them, and they know how to respond rather than react.

Emotional intelligence starts with self-awareness. When you can recognize and regulate your own emotions, you gain control over how you show up. This means staying calm under pressure, responding with clarity instead of defensiveness, and knowing when to pause before speaking. Mastering your emotions doesn't mean suppressing them—it means understanding them well enough to express them wisely.

There was a meeting once where tensions were quietly simmering—nothing explosive, just the kind of low-level frustration that makes people tighten their shoulders and speak a little faster. A project wasn't moving fast enough, and I could feel the pressure rising around me. One of the leads was clearly frustrated, and it would've been easy to either shut down or match their energy just to get through it. Instead, I took a breath and stayed curious. I asked a clarifying question instead of defending the delay. I acknowledged the frustration in the room without making it personal. And then I explained what was happening—clearly, calmly, and without blame. That shifted everything. The tone softened. People leaned in again. We stopped operating from stress and started problem-solving together. That entire moment could've gone sideways, but staying grounded, listening for what wasn't being said, and choosing my response instead of reacting on autopilot completely redirected the energy.

That's emotional intelligence. It's not about being perfectly composed all the time. It's about noticing what's happening in yourself and others and choosing presence over pressure.

Another key factor to emotional intelligence is learning how to balance empathy with decisiveness. Great leaders don't just understand how others feel; they also know how to make strong, confident decisions. Too much empathy without decisiveness can lead to hesitation and uncertainty; too much decisiveness without empathy can create disconnection and resistance. The magic is in the balance—leading with both heart and backbone.

When in doubt, adapt your communication style. Emotional intelligence allows you to read your audience and adjust your approach accordingly. The way you communicate with a high-level executive will differ from how you engage with a direct report. The best leaders have range—they know when to be direct, when to be gentle, and when to simply listen.

- **Mirror, but don't mimic.** When someone speaks, pay attention to their tone, energy, and style of communication. If they're more formal, adjust accordingly. If they're relaxed and casual, allow yourself to be more conversational. This doesn't mean losing yourself—it means creating a bridge between you and the other person.

- **Acknowledge before you respond.** Instead of jumping straight into your own thoughts, take a moment to recognize what the other person has said. A simple, "That makes a lot of sense," or "I see what you mean," makes people feel valued.

- **Use names, reference past conversations, and show that you remember details.** When you say, "How was your daughter's soccer game this weekend?" instead of just, "How was your weekend?" it shows that you actually listen—and that makes people feel seen.

Trust isn't built overnight, and it isn't built with words alone—it's built through consistent actions, follow-through, and emotional intelligence. This means:

- **Be reliable.** If you say you'll do something, do it. If you promise an update, give it. If you don't know the answer, own it. Trust isn't built on perfection—it's built on dependability.

- **Give credit freely.** People trust those who recognize their contributions. A simple, "That was a great idea from Sarah," or "I couldn't have done this without James' insight," strengthens relationships and shows that you're someone who sees and values the team.

- **Stay steady under pressure.** People respect those who can handle challenges with calmness and clarity. Even when things go wrong, if you communicate with transparency and composure, people will trust you more.

Help your team engage in curiosity. Instead of waiting for others to bring up topics you're interested in, show genuine curiosity about them. Ask about their weekend, their projects, their favorite hobbies. When you take an interest in others, they naturally start to reciprocate. If you look for shared experiences or interests, it makes it easier to relate. Even if you don't have obvious commonalities, you can always find something to connect on. If your team loves watching sports, but you don't, you can still engage by saying, "I didn't catch the game, but I saw the highlights—what did you think?" Small efforts like this go a long way. You can also share your passions without expecting others to adopt them. You don't need to hide the things that make you *you*—you just need to present them in a way that invites rather than alienates. Instead of saying, "I don't get how anyone doesn't love running," try, "Running is my favorite way to clear my head—what's yours?"

Celebration and Appreciation

Another important factor in the workplace is celebration and appreciation. People don't just want to be acknowledged—they want to be seen, valued, and appreciated. Try these on for size next time you want to show appreciation:

- **Give specific compliments.** Instead of just saying, "Great job," say, "You handled that meeting so smoothly—I really admired how you kept things on track." Specificity makes praise feel genuine.

- **Express gratitude often**. A simple, "Thanks for taking the time to help me with that," or "I appreciate the effort you put into this," can change someone's entire day.

- **Recognize effort, not just results.** People appreciate when their hard work is noticed, not just when they succeed. Saying, "I saw how much time you put into that—thank you for your dedication," shows that their efforts matter.

- **Be fully present in conversations.** Whether you're catching up in the hallway or in a one-on-one, show that you're engaged. Put your phone down, make eye contact, and give your full attention. Feeling heard is one of the most powerful emotions of all.

Authentic professional relationships aren't built through small talk or surface-level networking—they're built through genuine engagement, trust, and a willingness to truly see and understand the people around you. The more you refine your ability to connect without losing yourself, the more magnetic you become—not just as a professional, but as a person.

POWER STRUGGLES

No matter how magnetic, competent, or confident you are, professional challenges will arise. Power struggles, competition, and self-doubt are inevitable in any career. The key isn't avoiding them— it's knowing how to navigate them with clarity, self-assurance, and a strong sense of identity. The most successful professionals aren't the ones who bulldoze through every challenge or prove themselves at every turn—they're the ones who understand when to engage, when to stand their ground, and when to walk away with their integrity intact.

Power dynamics unfortunately exist in every workplace, but not all power struggles are worth engaging in. Some are natural and necessary—like asserting yourself in a leadership role or negotiating a raise—while others drain your energy and pull you into an unnecessary fight for control.

Power struggles can show up in different ways:

- A peer constantly trying to one-up you in meetings.

- A boss who dismisses your ideas or subtly undermines your contributions.

- A colleague who refuses to collaborate because they see you as competition.

- A gender or authority dynamic that makes you feel unheard or underestimated.

So, how do you navigate these situations without getting sucked into the emotional toll of workplace politics?

Pick your battles wisely.
Not every challenge to your authority or expertise is worth responding to. Ask yourself: *Does engaging in this battle help my long-term goals, or does it just drain my energy?*

Assert yourself without aggression.
Instead of reacting emotionally, state your perspective with clarity and confidence: "I hear what you're saying, but I'd like to add ..." or, "I appreciate your input, but I'd like to clarify my position."

Recognize when disengagement is the most powerful move.
Some people thrive on control and conflict. If someone constantly tries to provoke or belittle you, the most powerful response may be none at all. Silence, a knowing smile, or a strategic redirection can speak louder than words.

A competitive environment can be motivating—but it can also be toxic if it turns into a relentless comparison game. The key is learning how to stay driven without letting competition define your self-worth. Learn to see competition as inspiration, not intimidation. If someone is excelling in an area you aspire to grow in, study what they're doing, learn from it, and use it to level up—without losing sight of your own unique strengths.

We all need to learn that success is not a zero-sum game. Someone else's win doesn't mean your loss. There is room for more than one person to succeed, and the best leaders know that collaboration often creates more opportunities than rivalry ever could. We also need to remember to stay focused on our own lanes. If you're constantly comparing yourself to others, you're wasting energy that could be spent honing your own skills and making your own impact. Instead of asking, "How do I measure up?" ask, "How can I refine my own path?"

The heart of professional success isn't just skill, strategy, or titles —it's presence and energy. The way you carry yourself, the confidence in your voice, the clarity in your decisions, and the warmth in your interactions—these are the things that make you magnetic. Magnetism in the workplace isn't about pushing to be seen or proving that you belong. It's about showing up as your full, authentic self—grounded, confident, and unwavering in your value. It's knowing that you don't have to overpower a room to own it. You don't have to compete for validation when you already recognize your worth. And you don't have to sacrifice your individuality to be respected, admired, and successful.

When you embrace your unique strengths, communicate with clarity and warmth, and establish boundaries that honor both yourself and those around you, you become the kind of professional people trust, respect, and remember because you exude a quiet, undeniable confidence that speaks for itself.

REFLECTIONS FOR THE ROAD AHEAD:
IMPOSTER SYNDROME

Another workplace challenge is impostor syndrome (we'll unpack this more later in the book). Impostor syndrome is that persistent, nagging voice that whispers, *You don't belong here. You're not as good as they think you are. Sooner or later, they'll find out you're a fraud.* It's the paradox of high achievers—the more accomplished you become, the more you doubt your own abilities. But here's the truth: Feeling like an impostor doesn't mean you *are* one. It means you care. It means you're growing. It means you're pushing yourself beyond your comfort zone.

Here's why impostor syndrome happens:

- You're surrounded by talented people and assume they have it all figured out.

- You attribute your success to luck, timing, or being in the right place at the right time.

- You compare your behind-the-scenes struggles to everyone else's highlight reel.

- You believe confidence should come before competence, when in reality, confidence is built through action.

The cure for impostor syndrome isn't waiting to feel worthy—it's owning your value now, even in moments of doubt. Power struggles, competition, and self-doubt will always exist in the workplace. But you get to choose how you respond to them. You get to decide when to engage and when to walk away, how to compete without losing yourself, and how to own your worth even when self-doubt creeps in. True professional magnetism isn't about proving yourself over and over—it's about knowing your value, holding your ground, and leading with confidence, authenticity, and unwavering self-respect.

Here's what you can do to keep imposter syndrome at bay:

- **Acknowledge your expertise.** If you've been hired for a role, trusted with a project, or invited into a room, you belong there. Your knowledge and experience are valid, even if you don't feel like an expert yet.

- **Keep a "wins" folder.** Save emails, messages, or feedback where people have recognized your work. On tough days, revisit it as a reminder that your contributions matter.

- **Shift your focus from proving to contributing.** Instead of obsessing over whether you're good enough, ask: *How can I add value?* When you focus on serving, collaborating, and bringing your best, the self-doubt fades.

CHAPTER 11: FRIENDSHIPS & SISTERHOOD

How Deep, Empowering Friendships Fuel Growth and Success

FRIENDSHIP ISN'T just about having people to pass the time with—it's about who you grow with, who holds space for you, and who challenges you to step into your highest self. True sisterhood is an anchor, a force that fuels confidence, clarity, and success in every area of your life. The right friendships remind you of your strength when you forget it, call you forward when you're playing small, and celebrate you—not just when you win, but through every season.

Yet meaningful and lasting friendships don't happen by accident. They are created with intention, trust, and reciprocity. It's easy to fall into surface-level relationships, ones that exist out of habit rather than deep connection. True sisterhood requires more. It asks for vulnerability, effort, and the willingness to show up—not just when it's convenient, but when it matters the most.

In this chapter, we'll explore what makes deep, empowering friendships so transformative and why they are essential for personal growth. We'll talk about how to create community, whether through personal relationships or structured women's groups, and why surrounding yourself with people who truly see, challenge, and celebrate you is one of the greatest gifts you can give yourself. Finally, we'll dive into practical ways to nurture friendships that feel like home, cultivating the kind of sisterhood that elevates everyone involved. Sisterhood isn't just about connection—it's a catalyst for growth. The friendships you invest in will shape not only your present but your future. Let's explore how to create the kind of bonds that stand the test of time.

SURVIVING OR THRIVING

There comes a moment in every woman's life when she realizes she cannot do it alone. She can be strong. She can be independent. She can carry the weight of the world on her shoulders. But deep down, there's a quiet yearning—one that whispers in the silences between busy days and quiet nights. A yearning to be seen, to be known, to be held in the presence of those who understand without explanation. Because no matter how powerful a woman becomes, she is not meant to rise alone. Sisterhood is not a luxury; it is a lifeline.

It is the difference between merely *surviving* and truly *thriving*. It is the space where masks fall away, where vulnerability is met with understanding, where love is not earned but freely given. A place where your success is never a threat, where your wildest dreams are met with nods of encouragement and a firm, steady, *Yes, you can.* It is in the presence of true sisterhood that a woman remembers everything that she is.

We've all felt it—that moment when you're surrounded by people yet feel completely alone. When conversations skim the surface, never quite touching the depth of what you're truly feeling. When you laugh on cue but leave feeling emptier than when you arrived. This is what happens when friendships exist out of habit rather than intention. Surface-level friendships are built on convenience—proximity, shared interests, a mutual agreement to keep things light. They have their place, but they do not nourish the soul. A soul-aligned sisterhood, though—that is different. That is where real depth begins.

A true sisterhood is not just a group of women who get along. It is a sacred space, a mirror, a forge. It is where you are shaped, refined, and reminded of your strength when the world makes you forget. These friendships are built in moments of raw honesty—the nights spent unraveling fears and stitching dreams together, the sacred trust of knowing someone will hold your secrets with the same care as their own.

True sisterhood is when:

- You can call in the middle of the night, voice shaking, and hear, *I've got you.*

- Your success is celebrated as if it were their own.

- You are held accountable to your highest self, even when it's uncomfortable.

- You can be fully seen without the need to shrink, perform, or prove your worth.

These are the friendships that change you. That call you higher. That remind you of the woman you are capable of becoming. And if you do not yet have this—know that it is possible. Know that you are worthy of it. And know that you do not have to settle for anything less.

THE BIOLOGY OF SISTERHOOD

This feeling we get—the deep exhale of being in the presence of women who get it—is not just emotional. It's biological. Sisterhood is not just a nice-to-have. It is woven into the very fabric of our well-being.

Female friendships reduce stress.
Studies show that when women connect deeply, they release oxytocin, the "bonding hormone," which lowers cortisol and brings a sense of calm and safety.

They increase resilience.
Women with strong friendships recover faster from setbacks, both emotionally and physically.

They boost confidence and ambition.
A Harvard Business Review[1] study found that women with strong female networks are more likely to advance in their careers and pursue their dreams with courage.

They literally extend your life.
Yet another Harvard Study on Adult Development[2] found that the single biggest predictor of long-term happiness and health isn't wealth or status—it's strong, meaningful relationships.

A woman alone can be powerful. But a woman supported by other women? She is unstoppable.

When we stand together, we amplify each other's voices. We turn doubt into belief, fear into action, dreams into reality. We create a world where no woman has to walk alone. So if you find yourself yearning for deeper connections, for friendships that nourish rather than deplete—start here:

- Look for women who make you feel alive, not just entertained.

---

[1] The Secrets of Successful Female Networkers, *Harvard Business Review,* Nov–Dec 2019

[2] Harvard Study of Adult Development, 1938-2000 (also known as the Grant Study)

- Seek out friendships where vulnerability is welcomed, not avoided.

- Be the friend who sees, who listens, who holds space.

Because when you find your true sisterhood, you rise higher. You love deeper. And you finally understand—you were never meant to do this alone.

CHOOSING WITH INTENTION

Before I moved to Washington, most of my friendships were built on convenience. Training buddies who only reached out if there was a race to train for. Coworkers I laughed with during lunch breaks but never heard from once we left the office. I kept trying to make these relationships mean something more—pouring effort in, hoping they'd deepen—but they stayed shallow. I was constantly measuring how much of myself I could safely show. And when I did show more, it often felt like too much. I left conversations more drained than filled, wondering why it never felt quite right.

And then, as if the universe decided it was time, I met my new Best Friend.

It was at a random Meetup event—we were playing corn hole at an outdoor bar. Nothing extraordinary and something I almost didn't go to. But then we locked eyes across the game, and we were wearing the exact same outfit: a white t-shirt and jeans. We burst out laughing. It was so small, but it felt like a signal. Some kind of synchronicity. From that moment, something just clicked. There was no posturing. No holding back. The way we talked felt like skipping small talk and diving straight into the real stuff. Effortless. Open. Safe.

She is the first friend I've had who made me feel whole—not because she completes me, but because I don't have to split myself up to be loved. I can text her at any hour. I can call her crying or celebrating or confused or completely unfiltered. And I never feel like too much. She sees every part of me—the ambition, the softness, the fear, the fire—and holds space for all of it. With her, vulnerability doesn't feel like exposure. It feels like freedom.

A woman's life is shaped by the voices she allows into her world. Who she laughs with, who she cries with, who she turns to in moments of doubt—these choices define her more than she realizes.

Because the company she keeps either fans the flames of her radiance or slowly dims her light.

And here's the truth: you are in control of who sits at your table. The friendships you cultivate are not accidental. They are reflections of your standards, your self-worth, and your willingness to accept or reject what no longer serves you. If you desire depth, you must choose it. If you seek nourishment, you must create it. If you want sisterhood, you must become the kind of woman who attracts it. A radiant woman does not just let people into her life by chance—she chooses with intention.

Some friendships feel like home. They hold you in your joy and your sorrow. They celebrate your wins without jealousy. They push you toward your highest self while reminding you that you are already enough. Other friendships leave you questioning your worth. They exhaust rather than energize. They demand but do not give. They are transactional, heavy with obligation, or laced with subtle competition. And the most dangerous ones? They keep you small. These friendships are built on unspoken agreements to not evolve too much, to stay within the lines, to never outgrow the version of yourself they are most comfortable with.

A radiant woman outgrows friendships that no longer expand her. Not with malice, not with drama, but with the quiet recognition that she is meant for more. And when you realize that certain friendships are costing you your peace, your energy, or your growth, you owe it to yourself to let them go. Not every friendship is meant to last a lifetime. Some are seasonal, some are lessons, and some are weights disguised as companionship. The key is knowing which is which. You get to decide what kind of friendships you allow into your life. Not based on guilt. Not based on history. Not based on how long someone has been around. But based on who they are today and how they contribute to your life.

Ask yourself:

- Do I feel more like myself around this person, or less?

- Do they celebrate my growth, or do they subtly discourage it?

- Do I leave conversations feeling lighter and more alive, or drained and uncertain?

- Do we inspire each other, or do we just fill space?

Choosing depth over convenience and intentionality over obligation means making hard decisions. But it also means creating a life where you are surrounded by women who truly see you, who want you to win, who remind you of your own power when you forget. It means knowing that the right friendships are not about proximity or longevity, but alignment. It means becoming the kind of woman who does not beg for reciprocity—because the friendships she chooses naturally give as much as they receive.

MAKING HARD CHOICES

Sisterhood is not one-sided. It is not about always being the giver, the nurturer, the one who reaches out. It is also not about taking without returning. True friendship is a dance—a natural rhythm of support, of holding and being held, of listening and being heard. If you find yourself always being the one who checks in, always making the plans, always carrying the weight of the friendship—pause. Friendships should not feel like a performance review where you have to prove your worth through effort alone. They should feel like a natural exchange where both people choose to show up, not out of obligation, but because they truly want to.

There was a time in my life when I mistook proximity for connection. I thought I had found a real friendship—someone I could trust, train with, and grow beside. We met at a time when I was aching for closeness, unsure of who I was becoming and deeply craving someone to walk alongside me. So I gave. I invited. I shared. I believed we were building something real. But over time, the dynamic started to drain me. I realized the friendship was built more on convenience than care. We trained together, but it never felt like I was getting stronger. If I accomplished something, there was no genuine celebration—just subtle jabs or silence. If I opened up, I felt exposed rather than supported. The more vulnerable I became, the more I noticed how little space there was for my full self to shine. I began to shrink—not out of humility, but out of self-protection.

And still, I stayed. Because I wasn't strong enough yet to say *this isn't working for me.* I confused overextension with connection. I mistook my own people-pleasing for loyalty.

I thought I was bonding, but I was just bending.

Eventually, I saw it clearly. She didn't want to see me succeed—at least not if it meant I outgrew her. The more I expanded, the more tension grew between us. I realized that the friendship wasn't elevating me. It was holding me down. Letting go didn't happen all at once. But when I finally stepped away, it wasn't with bitterness. It was with a quiet, hard-earned sense of self-respect. Not all friendships are meant to last, especially the ones that can't hold your growth.

A radiant woman renegotiates friendships that are imbalanced. She does not overextend herself for relationships that take more than they give. She does not pour endlessly into people who do not pour back. She does not chase, she does not beg, she does not accept scraps of effort in return for her overflowing love. Instead, she recognizes that energy flows where it is valued. She seeks friendships where giving and receiving happen effortlessly. Where support is not tallied but freely exchanged. Where no one is keeping the score, because love—true love—needs no accounting. And when she finds herself in a friendship that feels one-sided, she does not force it. She steps back, she recalibrates, and she asks herself: *"Does this friendship truly elevate me?"* If the answer is no, she lets go. Not out of anger, not out of resentment, but out of deep self-respect. Because a woman who knows her worth does not settle for anything less than friendships that nourish, uplift, and expand her. And neither should you.

BUILDING COMMUNITY

We are not meant to do this life alone. And yet, as we grow older, real connection can start to feel elusive. Somewhere along the way, making friends stopped being easy. Gone are the days of recess and study groups, of dorm rooms and shared adventures that happened simply because we were in the same place at the same time. Now, friendships require effort. And yet, so many of us find ourselves drifting into loneliness, unsure of how to bridge the gap between wanting deeper connections and actually creating them. Childhood friendships were built on proximity and play—on the simple magic of *I like dinosaurs, you like dinosaurs, let's be best friends*. But now, connection requires something deeper. It is no longer about who happens to sit next to you in class or whose desk is across from yours at work. It is about intention. About choosing to build the relationships that will carry you through this life just as much as you carry them.

But where do we find them? How do we create them? The answer lies in community. Not the kind built on casual socializing, where small talk never scratches past the surface, but the kind forged in spaces where women show up fully. Where conversations go beyond, "How have you been?" to "What's lighting you up right now?" Where masks come off and stories are shared. Where we are seen, not as roles or responsibilities, but as women—whole and real and worthy. This is what sisterhood was always meant to be. *And this is why we must build it.*

Part of the problem? Many people are comfortable living on the surface. They are fine with small talk, with friendships that never ask too much of them. They do not dig deep because they do not want to be seen too clearly. And if you are a woman who longs for more—who craves friendships built on truth, not just convenience—this can be frustrating.

But here is the secret: you are not alone. There are other women out there who want the same depth, the same richness, the same conversations that leave you feeling lit up inside. The challenge is not that these women don't exist—it's that they are *waiting*, just like you. So be the one who reaches out first. Be the one who asks the real questions. Be the one who invites, who initiates, who creates the space for something deeper to unfold. Because the friendships you desire are possible. But they will not happen by accident. You must choose them.

WOMEN'S CIRCLES

There is something sacred about women coming together. It happens around kitchen tables, in cozy living rooms, over coffee cups and candlelight. It happens in structured circles and spontaneous meet-ups, in the quiet space between vulnerability and deep recognition. And in these spaces, we begin to let go. We drop the polished versions of ourselves, the ones that have it *all together*. We stop performing and start speaking from the rawest parts of who we are. And in return, we are met with something rare and life-changing: *understanding*.

This is the power of Women's Circles. These spaces invite depth. They are where we unburden ourselves from the weight of feeling alone, where we hear our own fears and dreams echoed in the stories of others. They are where we say the things we didn't even know we needed to say, and where we are met with nods, with knowing eyes, with the kind of presence that tells us: "*You are not alone. You never were.*"

Isn't that what we are all searching for? The reminder that our struggles are not just ours to carry? The reassurance that our stories, our emotions, our highs and lows—all of it—matter? These spaces are not just social gatherings. They are transformative. And they do not happen by accident. They must be created.

I started my first Women's Circle not because I had all the answers, but because I was longing for something deeper myself. When I left Phoenix, I realized just how much I had been craving real connection—spaces where women could talk about what mattered beyond surface level updates or polite smiles. I wanted to be around people who cared about growing, healing, and remembering who they really are. And I had a feeling I wasn't the only one.

So I created a space—just a simple invitation, really. I didn't know who would show up. I just knew that I had to try. To my surprise, they came. Not just once, but again and again and again. Women who had also been searching. Women who had been walking around with full hearts and no place to put them. They told me, "I needed this." And they kept coming back—not for me, but for what we created together.

We built something sacred: a space rooted in understanding, self-respect, truth, and deep love. It wasn't about performance, or perfection. It was about presence.

Women's Circles are not just about gathering. They are about awakening. They invite us to ask real questions, to hold space for each other, to practice vulnerability in a world that often discourages it. They remind us that we do not need to be perfect to be worthy of love. And most importantly, they teach us that when women come together—not to compete, not to impress, but to truly see one another—something magical happens.

We heal. We grow. We come home to ourselves.

That's why I created *In Search of Us*—to offer you the stories, the language, and the permission to create your own Women's Circle. Because there are women in your city, your community, even your block, who are waiting for someone like you to bring them together.

IN SEARCH OF US

My book *In Search of Us* was written for the women longing for more. For the ones who have spent too many nights wondering why her friendships feel shallow. For the ones who crave soul-deep connection but aren't sure where to find it. For the ones who are tired of waiting for a space to exist and are ready to create it themselves. The deepest friendships are not just built on shared history. They are built on intentionality. They are nurtured through rituals—small but sacred acts that remind us of our bond, over and over again.

Some are simple:

- A weekly coffee date, where phones stay in pockets and attention stays on each other.

- A voice note every Sunday, checking in with honesty and love.

- A handwritten letter, sent just because.

Others become traditions:

- A yearly trip, just the two of you, where you escape the noise of life and truly catch up.

- A birthday ritual—a shared toast, a moment of reflection, a celebration of growth.

- A standing invitation to call, no matter what, no matter when.

These rituals matter. They become the glue that holds friendships together, even through distance, even through time. Because friendships do not last by accident. They last because we choose to show up. Again and again.

So ask yourself: *What rituals will you create?* How will you make sure your friendships are not just something you hope will last but something you actively invest in? Because the friendships that truly nourish us—the ones that elevate, expand, and ground us—are not just found. They are built. And the women who have them? They are the ones who choose them.

You do not need to chase these deep connections. You attract them by being the fullest expression of yourself. When you embody your truth—your values, your passions, your joy—you naturally magnetize others who resonate at the same frequency. This is the power of feminine energy. Feminine magnetism is not about forcing connection. It is about allowing. It is about stepping into the version of yourself that is most alive and letting that energy be the signal that calls in the right people.

How to attract your soul tribe:

Live a Life That You Love
The more joy and passion you infuse into your days, the more others will be drawn to your energy.

Be Open, Be Curious
Say yes to new experiences. Talk to the stranger who intrigues you. Be willing to see people beyond first impressions.

Own Your Worth
When you show up as your full, unapologetic self, the right people will notice. You never have to shrink or dim your light to make space for others. The people who are meant to be in your life will gravitate toward your authenticity and celebrate your unique energy.

Cultivate Inner Confidence
When you know who you are, what you stand for, and what you're passionate about, your energy becomes magnetic. People can feel when you're grounded in your truth, and they want to be around it.

Trust the Timing
The right people will appear at the right time. Sometimes, the soul tribe we're meant to connect with shows up when we've worked through our own growth and are finally ready to receive them. Trust that as you continue on your journey, the people who are meant to walk with you will find their way to you.

LETTING GO WITH GRACE

When you live in alignment with your authentic self, you effortlessly create an energetic space for those who truly belong in your life. And remember, not every friendship is meant to last forever. Some people come into your life for a reason, a season, or a lesson. Knowing when to let go is just as important as knowing how to nurture the ones that truly feed your soul. Letting go of friendships that no longer align with you doesn't mean you have to cut ties abruptly or with animosity. It's about releasing with love, honoring the growth you both experienced together, and moving forward with grace.

How to release friendships with grace:

Recognize the Signs
Pay attention to how a friendship makes you feel. If it consistently drains you, brings up negative emotions, or feels one-sided, it may be time to reevaluate.

Communicate with Honesty
If you sense the friendship is shifting, have an honest conversation. Share how you're feeling, and ask if they feel the same. Sometimes, relationships grow apart naturally, and it's okay to acknowledge that.

Release Without Guilt
Don't hold onto a friendship simply out of obligation. Let go when it no longer serves you, knowing that doing so is creating space for more aligned connections.

Be Grateful
Even when a friendship fades, express gratitude for the lessons it taught you. Every connection, no matter how brief, has a purpose.

Releasing friendships with love and grace creates room for new, more aligned relationships to blossom. Trust that every ending clears the way for new beginnings.

CULTIVATING CONNECTION
True emotional intimacy isn't just built on time spent together; it's cultivated through meaningful conversation, shared vulnerability,

and intentional connection. As you reflect on your friendships, ask yourself: Do they nourish you? Do they challenge and inspire you to be the best version of yourself? Do you feel seen, valued, and supported? And just as importantly—are you offering the same in return?

The friendships that truly elevate you are built on a foundation of mutual trust, respect, and reciprocity. They are not about obligation; they are about alignment. Sisterhood is one of life's greatest gifts, but it's also a conscious choice. Choose friendships that expand you. Choose to be the kind of friend who elevates others. And most of all, choose to build a life surrounded by people who reflect the future you are stepping into—one filled with purpose, love, and limitless possibility.

Here are some prompts and exercises to help you initiate deeper conversations and strengthen your friendships:

The Heartfelt Check-In
Ask your friend, *What's something you've been carrying lately?* This question creates space for vulnerability and invites your friend to open up in a way that brings you closer.

The "Soul Talk" Ritual
Set aside a time to share your biggest dreams, fears, or even moments of doubt. Let your conversations be rooted in real talk about what's alive in your heart. When you share from the depths, you create a bond that is unbreakable.

Gratitude Practice
At the end of each month, take a moment to express gratitude for your friendship. Let your friend know what they mean to you, what you've learned from them, and the ways they've supported your growth. This keeps the connection strong and reminds both of you why you value each other.

The Future Vision
Ask your friend, *Where do you see yourself in five years?* and *What's something you want to accomplish together?* This deepens your connection by aligning on future goals and dreams, creating a sense of partnership.

Emotional Check-Ins
Make it a habit to periodically check in with each other on an emotional level. *How are you really feeling right now?* This keeps the relationship grounded and ensures both of you feel heard and supported.

REFLECTIONS FOR THE ROAD AHEAD

A strong support system isn't built overnight. It's the result of years of deepening connections, sharing vulnerable moments, and consistently showing up for each other. True sisterhood is a bond that weathers the storms of life, providing unwavering support, love, and encouragement. The relationships you cultivate will either expand you or hold you back. True sisterhood isn't about convenience—it's about depth, trust, and the unwavering belief in each other's growth. It's about surrounding yourself with women who uplift you, challenge you, and see you fully, even in the moments you struggle to see yourself.

To cultivate a support system that lasts a lifetime, practice these principles:

Stay Consistent
Strengthening emotional intimacy takes time. Show up, be present, and stay committed to the friendships that matter most.

Encourage Growth
Celebrate each other's wins, support each other's journeys, and hold space for the dreams that haven't yet materialized. A strong support system is one where everyone can thrive.

Communicate Openly
Don't be afraid to have tough conversations. The best relationships are built on honesty, even when it's uncomfortable. Speak your truth, listen deeply, and always seek to understand.

Offer Unconditional Love
True sisterhood is about loving each other through the highs and lows. Offer your love without expectation or condition, knowing that it will be returned tenfold.

SECTION THREE:

EMPOWERED LEADERSHIP

Owning Your Power in Life, Love, and Legacy

THIS SECTION IS at the heart of our journey—where we move beyond simply navigating our lives and start leading them with unwavering confidence, self-love, and purpose. It's not just about surviving the day-to-day; it's about stepping into the power of your choices and aligning your decisions with your highest self.

Leading your own life means having the courage to take ownership of your path even when the road feels uncertain. It means mastering your emotions, developing unshakable inner strength, and cultivating deep self-compassion—fueling not only your actions but also your relationships, conversations, and presence in the world. Here, we'll dive into what it truly means to embody radiance—not as a performance, but as an essence. This isn't about becoming someone new—it's about shedding everything that isn't you and starting to step fully into the brilliance that has always been there.

You'll learn to redefine success on your own terms, move beyond society's narrow expectations, and embrace a version of success that aligns with your passions and purpose. You'll learn to live intentionally, creating a life so deeply fulfilling that it makes you want to leap out of bed every morning with excitement. Through building your own sacred rituals and mindful practices, you'll cultivate routines that both ground and elevate you, helping you harness your energy in powerful ways.

This is also where you will learn to master the art of self-dating —nurturing a relationship with yourself that is just as rich and meaningful as any romantic bond. You'll explore what it means to savor your own company, celebrate your desires, and reconnect with your inner spark.

And finally, you'll tap into the unseen power of presence. You'll learn how to become an energetic force—commanding attention through your own sheer authenticity and unshakable confidence. You'll discover how to walk into any room and own it by being the most effortlessly magnetic person you can be.

As you move through this section, you'll uncover the intersection of radiant self-expression, purposeful living, and the strength to claim your space in the world. This is where you fully step into your power—the radiant woman you were always meant to be.

CHAPTER 12: LEADING YOUR OWN LIFE
Becoming the Architect of Your Reality

MOST PEOPLE spend their lives reacting. They wake up, go through the motions, answer emails, follow schedules, meet expectations—all without stopping to ask: Am I leading my life, or is my life leading me? To lead your own life means stepping out of autopilot and becoming the architect of your reality. It means recognizing that every decision—big or small—either moves you closer to the person you want to become or pulls you further away. It's about making choices with intention rather than letting circumstances dictate your path.

Leadership isn't just about career or authority—it's about how you show up in your relationships, how you navigate your emotions, and how you define your identity outside of external expectations. It's about the habits you cultivate, the routines that set you up for success, and the standards you hold for yourself. Every action you take, from the way you spend your mornings to the way you respond to challenges, is shaping your reality.

So, how do you shift from reacting to creating? How do you align your daily actions with the future self you are becoming? It starts with this knowledge: every decision you make is either a *toward move*—an action that brings you closer to your vision—or an *away move*—a choice that distances you from it.

When faced with a decision, ask yourself: *Would my future self do this?*

- Would my future self choose to stay in bed scrolling or get up and do the morning routine that makes me feel strong and aligned?

- Would my future self avoid the difficult conversation or step into it with confidence and clarity?

- Would my future self numb emotions with distractions or sit with them, process them, and move forward with wisdom?

Leading your own life means making more *toward* moves—even when it's uncomfortable, even when it requires effort. It's about recognizing that every choice compounds over time, shaping who you are becoming.

CREATION MODE

When you live in reaction mode, life feels unpredictable and overwhelming. You feel at the mercy of your circumstances—stressed about work, drained by relationships, frustrated by patterns that never seem to change. But when you step into creation mode, you take radical ownership of your choices. Your reality is not something that *happens* to you—it is something you *create*, moment by moment, through the decisions you make and the energy you bring into the world.

Here's how you step into creation mode:

- Instead of waiting for confidence to magically appear, build it by taking action.

- Instead of hoping for better relationships, cultivate them through intentional communication.

- Instead of feeling stuck in old patterns, rewrite your own narrative by consistently choosing new habits, thoughts, and behaviors.

True leadership begins with radical ownership. This means no longer blaming circumstances, people, or external forces for where you are in your life. It means recognizing that while you can't always control what happens, you can control how you respond, how you grow, and how you move forward. Radical ownership doesn't mean being harsh on yourself—it means being honest. It means acknowledging when you've been making *away moves* and deciding to shift direction. It means understanding that you are not a victim of your life but the *creator* of it.

Self-leadership isn't just about making big, bold moves—it's about the small, quiet moments when you choose yourself. When you stop running on autopilot and start actively shaping the life you want to live. And while the world will try to tell you how to live, what to prioritize, and who to be, the truth is: no one else can lead your life but *you.*

By the end of this chapter, you'll have a clearer understanding of how to step into leadership of your own life—not by forcing control, but by developing deep trust in yourself. You'll learn to make choices that align with your future self, embody confidence in every decision, and take ownership of your path with clarity and purpose. Let's begin.

But how? It starts with three things: intuition, empathy, and authenticity. These aren't just concepts—they are the muscles that shape your reality, the compass that keeps you on course, and the grounding force that allows you to stand tall even when everything around you feels uncertain. I've had to learn each of these the hard way. Let me tell you how.

INTUITION: THE WHISPER THAT KNOWS THE WAY

I'll never forget the moment my stomach dropped. It was my first week of undergrad, and I had just earned a spot in the orchestra as first clarinet. It was a huge deal—music had been a part of my life since I was three. I knew I wanted to get my doctorate in clarinet performance one day, and playing solos on stage was one of the greatest joys of my life.

But there was something else—I had also been swimming since I was six. Against the odds, I had been lucky enough to be selected as a walk-on to the University of Nebraska's Women's Swim Team, coached by Pablo Morales, a legendary coach and swimmer. An incredible opportunity. And then, just like that, I was told I had to choose. Pablo sat me down that Friday and said, "Celeste, you have to pick between music and swimming. Practice times conflict, and we need your full commitment."

I froze. It felt like someone had just ripped me in half. These weren't hobbies; they were two core parts of who I was. How do you choose between two things that have shaped your entire existence? But then, in the midst of my swirling panic, I heard it—a whisper. Not logic, not pros and cons, not what anyone else thought. Just my own knowing.

I already had a rotator cuff injury two years prior. I knew deep down that swimming wasn't going to be my lifelong path. But music? Music would never leave me. Music was something I could grow with, something that would challenge me for decades, something that felt like home.

No one else could have made that choice for me. And in that moment, I realized that leading your own life means knowing when to listen—not to the noise, not to expectations, but to *yourself*.

Empathy: The Shift That Changes Everything

A year ago, I met someone who would become one of the most important people in my life. At the time, I thought I was ready for a relationship. I had just walked away from the altar, left everything behind, and moved across the country. I was trying to rebuild, and in my mind, that meant finding someone to build with. I held onto him tightly, convinced that if I could just make this work, everything else would fall into place. But he kept saying, "I don't want to be in a relationship."

And I didn't understand.

I had put him on a pedestal, painted a picture in my mind of who we could be together, convinced myself that if he just saw what I saw, he would change his mind. And when he didn't, it hurt. But time did something unexpected. It softened me. Over the past year, our relationship has deepened in ways I never could have imagined. Not because I convinced him of anything, but because I stopped trying to control the narrative and started seeing *him*. Instead of fixating on what I wanted him to be, I started to understand who he actually was. His dreams. His fears. His way of moving through the world. And in turn, I started to understand myself better, too.

I used to think empathy was about giving—offering kindness, being patient, forgiving easily. But real empathy? It's about seeing clearly. It's about recognizing that we are all doing the best we can with what we know. It's about allowing people to be who they are rather than who we wish they were. And it's about extending that same grace to ourselves—acknowledging our own struggles, honoring our emotions, and choosing to respond with understanding rather than reaction. I am grateful—so grateful—that he didn't give in just because I wanted him to. Because in not getting what I thought I needed, I found something even greater: a deeper relationship with myself.

AUTHENTICITY: CHOOSING YOURSELF, NO MATTER THE COST

For years, I did everything I could to be liked. I wore the right clothes. I laughed at the right jokes. I agreed with things I didn't actually agree with. At work, I bent over backward to please my bosses. In relationships, I morphed into whatever version of myself I thought would be the most acceptable. I was terrified of rejection. Terrified of being too much or not enough.

And then, one day, I stopped. I stood at the altar, staring down a life that wasn't mine, a version of myself that wasn't real. And for the first time, I chose me. Walking away meant losing a lot. Friends in Phoenix stopped calling. My mom told me to settle. People whispered, questioned, judged. I had spent my entire life making sure I fit in, and now, for the first time, I was completely on my own.

But you know what? I wasn't lost.

Because in the space where other people's expectations had been, I found something else: *myself*. Piece by piece, inch by inch, I started to build a life that felt like mine. I stopped performing, and I started *being*. And the moment I did, everything began to shift. The right people, the right opportunities, the right experiences—they all started finding me. Because when you own who you are, the universe moves to meet you.

210

INTUITION, EMPATHY & AUTHENTICITY: WHAT THEY ARE VS. WHAT THEY AREN'T

1. INTUITION

   What it is: A quiet, deep knowing that guides you toward what feels right even when logic can't explain it. It's the feeling in your gut that nudges you in a direction before your mind catches up.

   What it isn't: Fear, anxiety, or overthinking. Intuition doesn't scream—it whispers. If it feels frantic or panicked, it's likely fear, not intuition.

2. EMPATHY

   What it is: The ability to see and understand people (including yourself) as they truly are without needing to change them. It's recognizing that everyone has their own path, their own timing, and their own struggles.

   What it isn't: Self-abandonment or over-explaining yourself to be understood. Empathy doesn't mean excusing bad behavior or sacrificing your own needs just to keep the peace.

3. AUTHENTICITY

   What it is: Living in alignment with who you truly are regardless of external approval. It's choosing yourself, even when it's hard, and trusting that the right people and opportunities will come when you stand in your truth.

   What it isn't: People-pleasing, performing, or playing small to fit in. Authenticity isn't about being liked—it's about being real.

These three pillars—intuition, empathy, and authenticity—are the foundation of self-leadership. They are the keys to stepping out of autopilot and into the life that is meant for you. So ask yourself:

1. **Intuition**
   Where in my life am I ignoring my inner voice? What happens when I choose to trust it?

2. **Empathy**
   How can I offer myself more compassion in this season? Where do I need to extend it to others?

3. **Authenticity**
   Where am I still playing small? What would it look like to fully own my truth?

Because at the end of the day, no one else is coming to save you. No one else is going to make the hard choices for you. You are the architect of your reality. And the life you want? It starts with you.

REDEFINING YOU

For most of my life, I measured myself by what I achieved. I was an accomplished musician. A doctoral student. A triathlete. I was someone's fiancée, someone's daughter, someone's friend. Every title and achievement stacked neatly together, forming what I thought was my identity. A woman with goals so big they could swallow you whole. Every achievement, every milestone, every title I collected was proof that I was somebody. Proof that I was worth *something*.

But what happens when those labels start to slip?

For me, it happened as I stood at the edge of a life I almost stepped into—walking down the aisle, holding the weight of everyone's expectations, including my own. I had everything that should have made me happy, yet I felt hollow. Because when I stripped away the titles, the achievements, the certificates, I wasn't sure who I really was. And that's the trap. Because when you strip those things away—what's left? We spend our lives being told who we should be. A good partner. A hard worker. A success story. And we chase those things, believing they'll bring us happiness. But what happens when a career shifts? When a relationship ends? When you reach your big goal and *still feel empty*?

If you define yourself by external markers, you will always be at the mercy of things outside of your control. But if you define yourself by what's within you—your values, your mission, your unshakable truth—then nothing can take you away from yourself. So, let's find out who you are beyond what you do. If you want to truly lead your life, you have to know what drives you. Not your job, not your relationships, not what people expect of you—but the essence of who you are and what matters to you.

CORE VALUES

Your core values are the roots of your identity. They are the principles that hold you steady when everything else in life is shifting. They are the unshakable truths that guide your decisions, your relationships, and the way you move through the world. Living in alignment with your values doesn't just mean knowing them—it means making choices that honor them, even when it's difficult.

It means using them as a filter for:

- How you spend your time

- Who you allow into your life

- What paths you pursue

- What boundaries you set

- What you say yes and no to

When you live from your values, you stop outsourcing your sense of self to jobs, titles, or relationships. You stop making decisions out of obligation, guilt, or fear of disappointing others. Instead, you begin leading your own life—one that feels deeply, undeniably right.

Take a moment and ask yourself: What matters to me at my core? What do I stand for, no matter what?

Here are some examples of core values:

- Freedom

- Growth

- Integrity

- Connection

- Adventure

- Authenticity

- Compassion

- Resilience

Now, write down 5–7 words that resonate with you. Don't overthink it. Just write what feels true. If you need a more extensive list, head to *www.myhealingisyourhealing.com* for a guided exercise. Once you have your values, ask yourself:

- Am I living in alignment with these values?

- Where am I compromising them?

- What needs to shift so I can honor them more fully in my daily life?

If you say you value freedom but constantly feel trapped in obligations you resent, there's a disconnect. If you say you value growth but haven't challenged yourself in years, it's time to shift. Living in alignment with your values means making daily choices that honor them. It means using them as a filter for how you spend your time, who you allow into your life, and what paths you pursue. Your core values are your compass. When you use them to guide your choices, you stop chasing a life that *looks* good and start creating a life that *feels* good.

PERSONAL MISSION STATEMENT

Once you know your core values, the next step is creating a personal mission statement—a guiding principle for how you lead your life. Your mission statement is your declaration. It's not about what you do. It's about who you are. And here's the key: You don't write it as something you'll one day become. You write it in the present tense, as if you already are this person. Because the moment you declare it, you start living in alignment with it. This statement becomes your anchor. Your guiding principle. The thing you return to every time life feels uncertain or you need to make a decision.

Examples of Personal Mission Statements:

> I am a woman who lives with fierce integrity. I honor my truth in every decision, speak with clarity and confidence, and never betray myself for approval. My boundaries are firm, my voice is strong, and I trust myself fully.

> I am committed to leading a life of bold self-expression. I do not shrink for the comfort of others. I take up space, share my ideas freely, and embrace my full range of emotions without apology. I create a life that reflects my true essence.

I am a person who chooses joy, adventure, and deep connection. I surround myself with people who inspire and uplift me. I seek experiences that challenge me. I wake up every day with a heart open to possibility, knowing that life is meant to be lived fully.

I am a leader of my own life. I trust my intuition, honor my values, and make decisions with clarity and purpose. I refuse to be led by fear. I choose growth over comfort, authenticity over approval, and self-trust over doubt.

Think about the person you want to be—the most aligned, radiant, powerful version of yourself. Now, declare it. Write a statement that reflects who you are at your core. Let it be a compass that keeps you grounded. And then? Live it. Because when you stop waiting to become yourself and start owning yourself, you lead your life in a way that no one else can.

SELF-TRUST

Self-leadership isn't just about discipline—it's about trust. You can set all the goals, make all the plans, and build all the routines, but if you don't trust yourself to follow through, none of it will stick. Self-trust is the foundation of personal leadership. It's knowing that you are capable of making decisions, handling challenges, and navigating life in a way that aligns with who you truly are. It's not about always getting it right. It's about knowing that you will always have your own back—no matter what.

But self-trust isn't built overnight. It's built through action—through showing up for yourself again and again, choosing aligned action, and proving to yourself that you can be counted on. So how do we strengthen it? Every choice you make is either a *toward* move or an *away* move. Remember:

- Toward moves bring you closer to the life you want to live. They align with your values. They build self-trust.

- Away moves pull you further from yourself. They might feel easier in the moment, but they create self-doubt, frustration, and misalignment.

The more you choose *toward* moves, the stronger your self-trust becomes. Because every time you take an aligned action, you send yourself a powerful message: *I know what I want. I trust myself to show up for it. I can count on myself.*

Here are some examples of toward vs. away moves:

- **Situation: You feel exhausted and overwhelmed.**

  Toward Move (Aligned Action): Resting without guilt, recognizing that your body needs it.

  Away Move (Misaligned Action): Pushing through until burnout, believing that rest is unproductive.

- **Situation: A friend disrespects your boundary.**

  Toward Move: Holding firm, calmly reinforcing your boundary.

  Away Move: Letting it slide to avoid discomfort; later resenting yourself for not speaking up.

- **Situation: You want to be healthier.**

  Toward Move: Making a meal that nourishes you and moving your body in a way that feels good.

  Away Move: Saying, "I'll start next week," and continuing habits that don't align with your goal.

- **Situation:** You have an idea you want to share.

Toward Move: Speaking up confidently, even if your voice shakes.

Away Move: Staying silent because you're afraid of what others might think.

These choices might seem small, but they add up. Every time you choose a toward move, you reinforce self-trust. You teach yourself that you can be relied on to make decisions that support you. Trusting yourself means learning to make decisions with confidence —standing by your choices and pivoting when you decide it's necessary, not because of fear, doubt, or external pressure. Self-trust means knowing that once you make a decision, you don't need to seek endless validation from others. You trust yourself enough to know that you made the best choice with the information and insight you had at the time.

Here's what it looks like:

- When you decide to say no to something, you don't backtrack out of guilt.

- When you choose a new path, you don't let other people's doubts make you question yourself.

- When someone disagrees with you, you don't immediately assume they are right and you are wrong.

HEALTHY PIVOTING
Self-trust doesn't mean you never adjust your course—it means you don't change direction just because someone else questions you. Self-trust isn't about stubbornly sticking to a decision just for the sake of it. It's about knowing when to adjust because it aligns with you, not because you're afraid of judgment.

Examples of healthy pivoting:

- **You quit a job**—not because someone else told you to, but because you know in your gut that it's time for something better.

- **You leave a relationship**—not because someone else disapproves, but because you recognize that you're compromising your core values.

- **You change your mind**—not because you're insecure, but because you've gained new insight that leads to a better choice.

Pivoting from a place of self-trust feels empowering. Pivoting from a place of fear feels disorienting. The difference? When you trust yourself, you know that whatever choice you make, you will handle it.

Self-trust is a muscle. The more you use it, the stronger it gets. And the stronger it gets, the more you become the kind of person who doesn't just follow life—you lead it.

ADAPTABILITY

True leadership isn't about rigidly sticking to a plan at all costs—it's about making empowered decisions while staying open to change. The art of pivoting is about knowing when to stand firm and when to shift without losing confidence in yourself. Many people mistake adaptability for indecision. They think changing direction means they failed, that they "wasted time," or that they should have known better from the start. But the truth is, pivoting is not quitting. It's conscious redirection. It's a skill—one that requires self-trust, self-leadership, and the ability to release attachment to a singular outcome.

We often set goals with a fixed picture of how they should unfold. We decide:

- This is the job I want.

- This is how my relationship should progress.

- This is the only path to success.

When we cling too tightly to one version of the future, we may overlook other opportunities that could be even more fulfilling. Our imaginations are limited; we can't possibly foresee all the extraordinary possibilities that lie ahead. There have been moments in my life where I've stepped into situations and thought, "I could never have dreamed this would be part of my journey."

Releasing attachment doesn't mean giving up on our desires—it means creating space for even greater opportunities to manifest. It involves trusting that if one path closes, another—perhaps more aligned with our true purpose—will open.

Let's be clear: There's a difference between giving up and strategically pivoting.

- Quitting is driven by fear, doubt, or external pressure. It's when you abandon something because it feels hard, uncomfortable, or uncertain.

- Conscious redirection is a decision made from clarity and self-trust. It's when you recognize that a different path aligns better with your values, goals, or well-being.

When you pivot intentionally, you're not running away—you're choosing something better aligned with your goals. Pivoting can feel destabilizing, especially when others don't understand your decision. You might fear judgment, second-guess yourself, or wonder if you're making the "right" move. True leaders don't fear change—they master the art of pivoting. They stand by their choices while remaining adaptable. They trust themselves enough to shift course when necessary, knowing that their growth isn't about sticking to a plan—it's about becoming who they are meant to be.

Here's how to stay confident when plans shift:

Check in with your core values.
If a change is aligned with what truly matters to you, it's not a failure—it's growth.

Reframe the narrative.
Instead of saying, "I failed," try: "I learned something valuable and am making a stronger choice."

Own your decision.
You don't need everyone's approval. You need your conviction.

Trust that every pivot leads somewhere meaningful.
Even if it's unclear now, every redirection is shaping your journey.

EMOTIONAL MASTERY

Emotional mastery isn't a personality trait—it's a practiced skill. And like any skill, it starts with simple tools and moments of awareness. These tools aren't about fixing how you feel; they're about meeting yourself in it. This is where emotional leadership begins—not with control, but with compassion.

I know this difference intimately. There were seasons where I didn't know how to sit with my emotions—so I shopped. I'd find myself wandering through the aisles of Target buying things I didn't need just to distract myself from what I didn't want to feel. Other times, it was a quiet glass of whiskey at night, a ritual of avoidance masquerading as a way to "wind down." But avoidance never made the emotion go away—it just prolonged it. My days felt heavy and directionless because sadness or stress would fester in the background, pulling strings I couldn't see. It wasn't until I learned how to actually sit with discomfort, to name what I was feeling and let it pass through me, that I started reclaiming my power. Emotional mastery gave me my life back—not all at once, but moment by moment.

Emotional Mastery (Healthy Regulation:

- Acknowledging your emotions without judgment.

- Naming and processing your emotions (e.g., "I feel frustrated because ...").

- Allowing yourself to feel emotions fully so they can pass and don't linger.

- Choosing a response that aligns with your values.

- Seeking support when needed.

Emotional Suppression (Avoidance & Numbing):

- Ignoring or denying what you feel.

- Distracting yourself with TV, alcohol, food, relationships, shopping, etc..

- Bottling up emotions until they explode.

- Reacting impulsively or shutting down completely.

- Pretending everything is fine to avoid vulnerability.

Real Strength Looks Like This:

- Sitting with discomfort instead of running from it.

- Acknowledging pain without letting it dictate your actions.

- Regulating emotions in a way that honors both yourself and those around you.

- Giving yourself compassion when you struggle rather than shaming yourself for feeling deeply.

Here's a tool to regulate your emotions without ignoring them. It may feel small, but it creates massive shifts over time. Every time you pause, breathe, and respond with intention, you're rewriting a pattern. You're stepping out of reaction and into alignment.

Pause and Name It
Instead of pushing an emotion away, identify it. ("I'm feeling overwhelmed.")

Breathe and Ground Yourself
Take deep breaths, put your feet on the ground, or do a quick body scan to bring yourself into the present moment.

Ask Yourself, "What Is This Emotion Trying to Tell Me?"
Emotions are messengers. Are you feeling lonely because you need connection? Angry because a boundary was crossed?

Allow Yourself to Feel It Fully
Sit with the emotion without judgment. Let it move through you instead of resisting it.

Choose a Response That Aligns With Your Values
Instead of reacting impulsively, ask, "What action will serve me best right now?"

Express It in a Healthy Way

Journal, talk to a trusted friend, move your body, or create something. Find a way to release it instead of suppressing it.

This is what it means to lead your own life—from the inside out. Mastering your emotions isn't about perfection—it's about presence. When you lead with emotional intelligence, you don't just become a stronger person—you create deeper, more meaningful connections with yourself and the world around you. When we develop emotional clarity, we stop outsourcing our stability to everything and everyone around us. We begin to lead ourselves with calm, confidence, and clarity. And one of the most essential pieces of that is compassion.

COMPASSION IS A LEADERSHIP SKILL

Once we've learned to master our emotions, one of the key skills we need to walk in is compassion, toward ourselves and others.

Toward Ourselves

Self-leadership isn't about being perfect—it's about leading yourself with grace. When you make a mistake, instead of beating yourself up, ask:

- What can I learn from this?

- How can I show myself kindness while still holding myself accountable?

Toward Others

Compassion is the key to strong leadership in relationships. It means:

- Seeing people for who they are, not just how they act in a single moment.

- Leading with understanding rather than judgment.

- Holding space for others without trying to fix or control them.

YOUR FUTURE SELF

Now that you've explored what it means to lead your emotions instead of being led by them, I want to invite you to imagine a future version of you who lives from this space daily. She doesn't run from her emotions—she listens to them. She doesn't suppress her truth—she trusts it.

Your future self isn't someone you meet randomly one day—it's someone you create through your daily actions, choices, and mindset shifts. This process isn't about waiting for a transformation; it's about embodying that version of you *now*, in small and intentional ways, until one day, you realize you have become her.

Future Self Visualization:

Let's try a quick exercise. Close your eyes and take a deep breath. Imagine you are walking through a space—a city street, a coffee shop, a conference, or maybe a quiet, sunlit room. You look up, and then you see her.

You recognize her instantly.

She moves through the world with a quiet confidence, a presence that draws people in. You take in everything about her:

- The way she carries herself—her posture, her movement, the energy she radiates.

- The way she dresses—what is she wearing? How does it reflect who she is?

- The way she interacts with the world—does she smile effortlessly? Does she exude calm, certainty, warmth?

- The way she speaks—what words does she choose? How does her voice sound?

- The way she makes decisions—does she hesitate, or does she trust herself fully?

- The way she nurtures herself—what does she do daily that keeps her grounded and thriving?

- The life she has built—what kind of home does she live in? Who surrounds her? What work lights her up?

Now, as you continue watching her, you realize she notices you, too. She turns toward you and meets your eyes. In this moment, what does she see in you? What does it feel like to be in her presence? Take a moment to absorb everything about her. Let yourself feel it in your body. And now, write it down:

- What does she look like?

- How does she move, speak, and exist?

- What emotions rise up in you as you see her?

- What does being near her make you feel?

- What is she telling you?

This is your future self. She is not a stranger. She *is* you. Now that you have seen her, the next step is closing the gap between where you are and where she stands. Your daily choices shape who you are becoming. Each time you act in alignment with her, you step closer to becoming her. Each time you choose an *away move*, you delay her arrival.

Start with small but powerful shifts:

- Ask yourself in every moment of doubt: What would she do?

- Change your posture to match hers—stand the way she stands.

- Speak the way she speaks—thoughtful, clear, and with conviction.

- Make decisions as she would—without over-explaining or seeking approval.

- Show up in your life as if you are already her. Because you are.

Every aligned action brings you closer until, one day, you look in the mirror and realize: *You have become her.*

If you want a deeper guided experience, you can find the full Future Self Guided Meditation on my website:

www.myhealingisyourhealing.com

THE BECOMING FRAMEWORK

Your evolution is a process. You don't just wake up one day as your highest self—you grow into her. Transformation happens choice by choice, moment by moment. It's not linear, and it's not always easy, but when you understand the phases of your own growth, you can move through them with more intention. I call this *The Becoming Framework* because it's about embracing the journey of becoming the person you are meant to be. It's also a tool you can use.

My framework consists of three versions of myself (when you name yours, you can apply them here):

- Chelsea – The Past Self

- Celeste – The Present Self

- Stella – The Future Self

Each version represents a stage of evolution, and understanding them helps me stay aligned with who I am becoming. I believe in naming these different versions of myself because it makes them tangible. It allows me to recognize old patterns without shame, to honor the work I'm doing now, and to step into my future with confidence. You can do this, too. Maybe your past self is Sarah, or Jessica, or Billie. Maybe your future self is Nova, or Athena, or "The CEO Version" of Me. Whatever resonates with you, name them. Because when you give them names, you can identify them when they show up and choose which version of yourself you want to be.

Chelsea: The Past Self

Chelsea represents who I used to be—the version of me that sought validation instead of self-trust. She was a people-pleaser, always scanning the room to see what was expected of her before deciding how to act. Chelsea avoided difficult conversations. She said "yes" when she meant "no." She was afraid to take up space, to be too much, to disappoint others.

But here's the thing: Chelsea isn't the enemy. She was doing the best she could with what she knew at the time. She developed these patterns because, at some point, they felt safe. And while I'm no longer her, I honor her, because she got me here.

Celeste: The Present Self

Celeste is my current self. She's aware of her patterns. She notices when Chelsea-like tendencies show up, but she doesn't let them drive. She's in the process of stepping fully into her power. She's learning to set boundaries without guilt, to trust her voice, and to prioritize alignment over approval.

But Celeste is still evolving. She sometimes hesitates. She still has moments where she feels the pull of her old habits. And that's okay—because growth isn't about perfection. It's about choosing to move forward, over and over again.

Stella: The Future Self

Stella is who I am becoming. She is the fullest, most radiant version of me. She is unshakable in her values, confident in her decisions, and deeply aligned with her purpose.

I named her Stella because my parents combined the names of my great-grandmothers, Celia and Stella, to create Celeste. But stepping into Stella—the full name—symbolizes my arrival. It is a declaration of who I am meant to be.

I see her so clearly:

- She walks into a room with quiet confidence.

- She speaks on stage without sweaty palms, fully owning her voice.

- She wears tailored blazers effortlessly, embodying power and elegance.

- Her hair is often in a French braid—polished, intentional, and strong.

- She moves through life with certainty, never shrinking, never questioning her worth.

Stella is not a distant dream. She is me. I am becoming her. Every time I face a choice—whether big or small—I ask myself: *What would Stella do?* Would she shrink back or stand firm? Would she seek external validation or trust herself? Would she put off what matters, or would she take action? Every time I make a *toward move* —a choice that aligns with Stella—I bring her closer. The gap between who I am and who I want to be gets smaller. And this is the power of *The Becoming Framework*.

In this chapter, we've taken the first steps toward unlocking your personal leadership, grounding it in your core values and the clarity of your mission statement. You've envisioned your future self—not as a distant dream, but as a real, living, breathing version of you. You've learned how to embrace the present moment, trust your decisions, and navigate the twists and turns of life with confidence.

The truth is, leadership isn't something you just wake up with—it's an evolution. And as you continue on this journey, each choice, each shift, each *toward move* brings you one step closer to the woman you're becoming. It's a process of growth, of continual learning, and of refining who you are. The tools you've learned here —identifying your values, crafting your mission statement, visualizing your future self—are the bedrock on which your radiant life is built. They will serve as the foundation for everything that comes next. But the true magic happens when you commit to embodying them every single day, making choices that reflect the person you are becoming, even before she fully arrives.

So take a moment to reflect: *who are you today, and who are you becoming?* This is the work that will guide you through every chapter to come.

REFLECTIONS FOR THE ROAD AHEAD

You have your own versions of Chelsea, Celeste, and Stella. Maybe you have a Jessie who always plays small, an Alex who is doing the work, and a Phoenix who is your highest self.

So, ask yourself:

- Who was your past self? What patterns and beliefs defined them?

- Who are you now? What work are you actively doing to grow?

- Who is your future self? What do they embody? How do they think, act, and lead?

Then, when you find yourself at a crossroads, ask: *Who am I choosing to be today?* Your future self isn't just an idea. She is real. She is waiting for you to step into her. So, what would she do?

CHAPTER 13: REDEFINING SUCCESS

Creating a Life That Feels as Good as It Looks

SUCCESS IS OFTEN defined by what looks good on paper—titles, achievements, wealth, and social status. It's the version of success that society hands us, the one we're expected to chase without question. And in today's world, social media only amplifies that illusion. We scroll through carefully curated highlight reels, seeing only the best moments of someone's life—the promotions, the picture-perfect vacations, the engagements, the milestone achievements. It creates a false sense of reality, making us believe that somewhere out there, a perfect life exists.

Dating apps play into this illusion as well. We swipe through endless profiles, convinced that if we just keep looking, we'll find someone better, someone more ideal. The grass is always greener, *right*? But what if that perfect version we think exists isn't real at all? What if we've been chasing an illusion, constantly searching for something more, only to feel empty once we get there?

This is the trap of traditional success. We're told that happiness is waiting for us on the other side of achievement—once we get the degree, land the job, buy the house, find the relationship. But what happens when we check all the boxes and something still feels missing?

I know this feeling well because I grew up with a very specific definition of success. My parents were professors, and at our dinner table, success wasn't just an idea—it was measured in degrees, academic achievement, and intellectual status. If I didn't get straight A's, I wasn't worthy. If I didn't go to college, I wouldn't have a future. In my world, success was a title, a paycheck, and a long list of achievements. And for a long time, I believed that was the only path.

But somewhere along the way, I started asking different questions. What if success wasn't about chasing? What if it wasn't about reaching something but about being something? Because the truth is, success that only looks good *but doesn't feel good* is just another empty illusion. The real challenge—the real transformation —comes when we stop performing success and start embodying it.

What if instead, we focused on being the person we *want to be* right now? Living in alignment with who we are, doing the things that bring us joy and fulfillment—not for validation, not to impress anyone, but simply because it *feels good*? How do we redefine success so that it aligns with personal fulfillment rather than external validation? That's what this chapter is about—stripping away old definitions, unlearning what we thought success had to be, and creating a version of success that isn't about proving anything to the world. It's about living in a way that feels deeply, genuinely good—from the inside out.

REDEFINING SUCCESS

Success has long been defined for us before we ever have a say in it. From the moment we're old enough to understand achievement, we're handed a checklist—one that's been reinforced by our families, schools, workplaces, and the world around us. Job titles, salaries, degrees, marriage, children, homeownership, luxury vacations—these are the markers of a "successful" life, at least according to the traditional script. The more of these boxes you check, the more validation you receive. But what happens when you follow the script and still feel *empty*? Or when you don't follow it and feel the weight of judgment pressing down on you?

If we strip away the external validation, what actually makes a life feel meaningful? What feels like success to you? Not what looks good on paper. Not what earns applause. But what makes you feel fulfilled when no one else is watching?

People rarely showcase their struggles, doubts, or failures. *Why is that?* Why are we so hesitant to reveal the moments when we feel lost, unworthy, or uncertain? Do we believe that admitting our struggles makes us less valuable? That people will judge us if we're not always thriving? Social media and societal norms push us to present a curated version of our lives, one that highlights our wins while keeping our hardships hidden. But the truth is, no one's life is a constant highlight reel. Behind every seemingly perfect existence, there are unseen hardships—people who feel unlovable, who doubt themselves, who lose jobs, experience heartbreak, or silently carry grief. In a world where everyone seems to be thriving, who wants to be the one to say, *I'm struggling*?

We're conditioned to celebrate success and conceal struggle, but by doing so, we create a false standard—one that makes others feel like they're failing simply because they're experiencing what's actually *normal*. When we only see success, we begin to expect it as the default. And yet, the reality of life is both joy and sorrow, gain and loss, expansion and contraction. The key to redefining success isn't to eliminate the lows; it's to embrace them as an essential part of a meaningful life.

If every day was a ten, how would we ever recognize a moment as extraordinary? If life was nothing but success, achievement, and fulfillment, those peak moments we chase would start to feel ordinary. The excitement of hitting a milestone would fade because it would no longer feel like a milestone—it would just be normal. When success becomes our baseline, we lose the very thing that makes it feel meaningful in the first place.

And so, we begin chasing more—the next goal, the next achievement, the next validation—believing that this time, it will bring the rush we're looking for. But without contrast, even the greatest wins lose their magic. The key isn't just to stack more highs on top of each other. It's to embrace the full spectrum of life, knowing that the lows are what make the highs feel like highs. True fulfillment isn't about avoiding struggle; it's about learning to sit with it, knowing that it's what gives depth to our joy.

The trick is learning how to live through the lows—to trust that the ten's and eleven's will come again. To understand that life moves in cycles, that our relationships, successes, and failures all ebb and flow. That the struggles do not define us, but our ability to move through them does. Success isn't about maintaining a perfect upward trajectory. It's about living fully—through both the exhilarating moments and the ones that bring us to our knees. The moments of doubt, the failures, the unexpected turns—these don't diminish our success; *they define it*. Because in the end, success isn't just about what we achieve—it's about how deeply we experience the life we're living.

The pressure to conform is immense. We're conditioned to believe that the safest, most acceptable path is the one society has already laid out for us. There's an unspoken rule that deviation is risky—that if we don't follow the standard timeline, we'll be left behind. But who actually decided these rules? Who says you have to do things in a certain order, by a certain age, in a certain way?

I've felt this pressure firsthand. As a 36-year-old woman who is not married and does not have children, people ask me *why*. They assume something must be missing, that I must be searching for what they believe I lack. *"Don't you want love?"* they ask. Yes. Of course, I do. But I refuse to sacrifice the fullness of my life just to fit into a version of love that isn't aligned with me. I know what I want my life to feel like, and I refuse to settle for anything that doesn't meet that standard.

That's the key: knowing yourself deeply enough to trust that your version of success is valid, even when others don't understand it. Choosing your own path means embracing the discomfort of being different. It means standing firm in your choices, even when others question them. It means having the self-worth and self-love to recognize that other people's discomfort with your choices is theirs to carry—not yours. You don't need permission to build a life that makes sense to you. The timeline you've been given is not a rulebook; it's a suggestion. And if it doesn't fit, you have every right to rewrite it. Because real success isn't about meeting external expectations. It's about living in a way that feels deeply right for you.

THE COMPASS WITHIN

We've talked about stepping outside of societal expectations and defining success on our own terms. But once we remove external validation, what's left? What does success actually feel like when it's not measured by job titles, paychecks, or applause? This is where we shift from achievement-based worth to embodied worth. Instead of defining ourselves by what we accomplish, we start defining ourselves by who we are and how we feel. True success isn't just about what we do—it's about how we experience our own lives.

Success without fulfillment is empty. You can climb every ladder, earn every accolade, and still feel like something is missing. That's because fulfillment isn't something we achieve—it's something we cultivate. It comes from aligning our lives with what genuinely matters to us.

So how do we even begin to figure out what success means to us? Try answering these questions:

What makes you feel alive?
Think about the moments in your life when time disappears, when you feel fully present, when joy comes effortlessly. What were you doing? Who were you with?

What fills you with purpose?
Purpose isn't always about career or grand missions. It can be found in the way you nurture relationships, the way you create, the way you make space for yourself and others.

What satisfies you beyond external validation?
If no one was watching, if no one could measure or judge your success, what would still feel deeply right?

When we start answering these questions, we begin to see that success isn't about reaching a destination—it's about how we live every day.

When we tie our worth to achievements, we're always at risk of losing ourselves.

The moment we fail, the moment we fall short, our self-worth crumbles. But when we build a foundation rooted in self-trust and self-identity, we become unshakable. What true success looks like is not a life that looks impressive from the outside, but a life that feels deeply fulfilling from the *inside*.

THE ACHIEVEMENT CHECKLIST

I grew up believing that success was a finish line. A series of checkboxes. A thing you earned by being the best. My parents made it clear that excellence wasn't just encouraged, it was required. My mom would say, "I'm a college professor. I know these things." And that was that. Straight A's weren't an achievement, they were the bare minimum. A B+? That was a mistake, something to be corrected.

And it wasn't just academics. Every part of my life was measured by achievement. First-chair clarinet wasn't just about my love for music—it was about proving I was the best. Swimming wasn't about feeling powerful in the water—it was about hitting AAA times, standing on the podium, being the fastest girl in the event. And every milestone came with a reward. Ice cream after a recital. A t-shirt or a keychain from the swim meet when I hit a PR. Every success was followed by something tangible, reinforcing the idea that winning meant earning love, attention, and approval.

So I kept going. Because what else was there? I followed the conveyor belt laid out in front of me without questioning where it was leading.

- Get into college? Check.

- Audition for your master's degree? Check.

- Audition for your doctoral degree? Check.

- Get a job? Check.

- Get married? Have kids? Keep going. Keep achieving.

But here's the thing about conveyor belts: They don't let you stop and ask if you actually want to go where they're taking you. I reached the end of the track and tripped off.

I had a Doctorate in Clarinet Performance. I had done *everything right*. I had followed the plan. But for the first time, I looked around and realized—I didn't want this life. I didn't want to fight for an underpaid teaching job in some small town I had never heard of. I didn't want to compete against dozens of other doctoral students for the same scraps of opportunity. I didn't want to spend the rest of my life in a reality that didn't feel like mine.

For the first time, there was no next step. No next checkbox. No applause for achieving the thing I was supposed to achieve. Just silence. Just *me*. And that was terrifying. Because if I wasn't the girl with straight A's, the first-chair clarinetist, the fastest swimmer, the doctoral student, then who was I? I had spent my whole life defining myself by my accomplishments. Without them, I felt like I had nothing. *Like I was nothing.*

So, I started over. From the bottom. I taught myself new skills. I rebuilt my identity piece by piece. I found my way into business, into leadership, into a whole world I had never imagined for myself. And for the first time, I wasn't chasing something just to prove I could. And still—that old voice crept in. Shouldn't you be achieving more? Shouldn't you be doing something *impressive*? Because success was still whispering to me in the language I had been raised with. But now, I had a choice. I could let it control me, or I could redefine what success even meant.

I started asking myself—what if success wasn't about what it looked like from the outside? What if success was a feeling? And when I asked myself that, success started showing up in ways that had nothing to do with titles or paychecks or applause.

Success became:

- The night I hosted a women's group and saw the look on every single woman's face as they exhaled—realizing they weren't alone.

- The moment someone messaged me after an event and said, *"This changed my life. I didn't know I needed this."*

- The day I opened my milestone jar and found a tiny note celebrating the email I got from the Olympia Symphony Orchestra asking me to sub for third chair clarinet—not first, not second, just third—and feeling so proud because I was playing music again for the joy of it.

That's success. Not proving myself to the world. But creating a life that feels full.

New Definitions

So, what does success really mean? How do we strip away the old definitions and build something new? We start by asking the real questions:

- **What are my core values?** *Mine are creativity, compassion, community, and determination. When my life aligns with these, I feel successful.*

- **What actually makes me happy?** If no one was watching, if there were no awards, no promotions—what would still bring me joy?

- **What impact do I want to make?** Not in the way the world expects, but in the way that feels meaningful to me.

And the biggest one:

- **Who am I when I'm not achieving?**

Because success isn't just about the big moments. It's about *this* moment. Right now. Living a life that feels good from the inside out.

I don't measure success by external validation anymore. I measure it by the strength of the women who show up at my women's group, the friendships I've built, the nights I laugh until my stomach hurts, the runs where I feel my body getting stronger, the wonderful conversations that leave me thinking about them for days. Success isn't a ladder. It's not a race. It's not a destination. It's a life you feel deeply. One that makes you want to wake up every morning and do it all over again. And that's exactly what I've built.

So, how do we stay connected to this new version of success? Here's what's helped me:

Reflection
Checking in—am I still in alignment with what actually matters to me?

Gratitude
Recognizing the small wins, the moments that make life rich.

Intentional Living
Making choices that align with my values, not what looks good on paper.

Letting Go of Comparison

Staying in my own lane. Trusting that my version of success doesn't need to look like anyone else's.

Success is not the titles, the paychecks, or the highlight reels. It's the moments of pure fulfillment, the things that set your soul on fire, and the life that feels undeniably yours. It's not a finish line to cross or a checklist to complete. It's a journey—one where joy, growth, and alignment reign over validation from the outside.

This is your invitation to redefine success on your own terms. Step out of the boxes others have put you in. Break free from the paths you're told to follow. It's time to take charge of your own happiness. Take charge of your own success. You're not waiting for the world to tell you that you've made it. You are already here. You are already succeeding. Now, step into it. Own it. *Your* life. *Your* success. *Your* rules.

CHAPTER 14: THE ART OF SELF-DATING
Becoming the Love You Seek

WHAT IF I told you the most important relationship you'll ever have is the one you have with yourself? The one that begins the moment you're born and continues until your very last breath. It's easy to spend so much of our lives seeking validation, affection, and love from others—but what if, instead, we poured that same love and attention back into ourselves?

The idea of dating yourself might sound a little unconventional, but hear me out. Think about it: If you're going to be with yourself for your entire life, shouldn't you make that relationship as rich, fulfilling, and exciting as any romantic relationship you could have? Why settle for anything less?

In this chapter, we'll explore how to fall in love with your own life—how to cultivate a meaningful, dynamic relationship with yourself that doesn't rely on external validation but instead is rooted in deep self-love, self-discovery, and self-acceptance. When you know yourself, love yourself, and trust yourself, all of your other relationships—romantic, family, friendship, work—become mere complements to the amazing life you've already built.

You don't need anyone else to define your happiness or your success. When you fall in love with your own life, you begin to realize you already have everything you need to be happy, whole, and fulfilled. It's time to take yourself on adventures, explore new passions, discover what nourishes your soul, and create a life that feels as vibrant as your dreams. Because at the end of the day, the only relationship you can guarantee is the one you have with yourself. Let's dive into how you can make it the most meaningful one you'll ever experience.

Let's start with a story. A tale as old as time.

Since I can remember, the world had filled my head with whirlwind love stories ever since the first time I watched Sleeping Beauty. Prince Charming finds his princess, falls in love with her beauty, they ring their wedding bells, and off into the sunset they ride. Happily ever after.

Story after story told us that if we could just be beautiful enough, desirable enough, agreeable enough—someone would choose us. Love would save us. And if we could find it, and keep it, we'd finally be happy. Finally be enough. I believed this. Ate it up. I turned over rock after rock searching for love. Kissed every toad, hoping he'd turn into someone who would complete me. I begged for a ring. Walked him into the store. Pointed at it. I dropped hints like breadcrumbs for months, hoping he'd propose and we'd start our real life. Because that's how I thought it was supposed to happen. Because that's what I thought I needed.

That ring, that wedding, that life—those were the milestones that would prove I was worthy. That I was wanted. That I had arrived.

Until the moment I found myself walking down the aisle, white dress, hair curled just right, father by my side, guests wiping tears and smiling because I looked so happy … and I felt nothing but dread. All I could think was: *Why am I here? What am I doing? Whose life is this?* And it hit me. This was never mine.

This dream I'd been chasing, this conveyor belt of life—date, marry, have children, smile on cue—it wasn't built for me. It was built for someone else's idea of a successful woman. And I had spent years trying to contort myself to fit inside it.

That day, I didn't say "*I do.*" I said *I don't.* I said *I don't* to pretending. *I don't* to disappearing into someone else's story. *I don't* to handing my worth over to someone else to define.

And instead, I said *I do* to myself. To the woman I had lost. To the life I hadn't yet written. To the truth that was begging to be lived.

And that's when I started dating myself. Not in the cutesy "treat yourself" way, but in the deeper, truer way. I started showing up for myself with curiosity. With presence. With reverence. I started listening. Feeding myself not just food, but joy. Space. Peace. Celebration. I gave myself slow mornings and solo walks and real affection. I stopped waiting for someone else to say, *You matter,* and began showing myself that I did.

Self-dating isn't about pretending you're your own boyfriend. It's not about putting on red lipstick and taking cute selfies and calling it empowerment—unless that actually nourishes you. It's about tending to your relationship with yourself the way you would with a partner you adore. With honesty. With intentionality. With commitment.

Because when the world stops texting you back ... When no one posts the comment you hoped for ... When the wedding bells are long gone, or never came ... *You* are still there. And that relationship with yourself? It's the only one you can guarantee for a lifetime.

We weren't taught how to *love ourselves*. We were taught how to be *chosen*. But the art of self-dating is choosing yourself, day after day, with joy, with truth, with power. It's not a backup plan. It's not a consolation prize. It's the foundation for everything else. Because when you stop begging for scraps of love and start feeding yourself a full, nourishing feast of self-worth, you stop chasing what was never meant for you. And in that space, life finally begins to rise up and meet you. Not because you followed the script. But because you wrote your own.

When you date yourself, you take the time to get to know who you really are without the distractions of what others think or expect of you. Think about dating someone new—how you're curious about their life, their likes, dislikes, hopes, and dreams. You're eager to learn what makes them tick, what excites them, and what brings them joy. You make an effort to understand their needs and desires. *Why wouldn't you do the same for yourself?*

Self-dating is about embracing the concept that you are your most important companion. Here's the secret: your happiness and satisfaction in life should come from within, first and foremost. When you learn to love yourself, everything around you becomes the complement to that love—not the foundation of it. You are whole. You are complete. When you get to know yourself and take care of your own needs, you're not seeking someone else to "complete" you—you're bringing your best, most fulfilled self to every relationship that comes your way.

Dating yourself isn't about being alone forever or avoiding connections with others; it's about understanding that you don't need someone else to make you feel whole. When you're comfortable with yourself, others can come alongside you, and together you can learn, grow, and share life's adventures. But, *and this is important*, you should never depend on someone else to feel whole. If that relationship, that job, or that phase of life ends, you need to be able to stand on your own without losing who you are.

Now, think about how much energy and time you put into nurturing your relationships with your friends and loved ones. You listen to them, you show up for them, you give them your time, you care about their needs, and you invest in their growth. But how often do you show up for yourself in the same way? How often do you pause to ask yourself what you truly need, what excites you, what nourishes your soul? Self-dating is about making time for yourself in a way that aligns with your personal desires. You begin to ask yourself: What do I love? What brings me joy? What do I need to feel fulfilled? What are the little things that make my life feel richer, brighter, and more alive? This is where curiosity comes in —getting to know yourself on a deeper level, not just in terms of your likes and dislikes but in terms of how you want to experience life.

And the beauty of this? When you're already content in who you are, the relationships you have with others become an extension of that contentment, not a means to fill a void. Self-dating is about creating a fulfilling life from the inside out—one where you are the best partner you'll ever have. You're the one you're with all the time, so why not make the relationship with yourself the most exciting, meaningful, and fulfilling one? Because, in the end, when you truly understand and love yourself, everything else in life falls into place.

So ask yourself: How can I date myself today? What can I do to show up for me the way I would for a loved one? You deserve to know yourself, care for yourself, and be as excited about your own journey as you would for anyone else. Let the adventure begin with you—because when you do, the rest of life will follow.

REDISCOVERING YOU

In the journey of self-dating, a crucial part of building a relationship with yourself is rediscovering who you are at your core. This isn't just about the big moments of self-realization; it's also in the tiny, everyday details. Do you know what makes your heart race with excitement? Have you ever thought about what really lights you up in the most unexpected ways? Maybe it's peanut butter over Nutella (I know, it's a big decision). Or maybe it's salsa dancing over improv comedy. These might sound trivial, but they matter. They show us how much joy and wonder we can discover in the simple things when we stop long enough to check in with ourselves. When was the last time you allowed yourself to just be in the experience without worrying about the result? That's the key to reconnecting with your passions—it's about being present in the moment and tuning in to your desires without judgment.

Now, ask yourself: What haven't you tried yet? What would happen if you gave yourself permission to explore new things? Whether it's picking up a hobby you've always been curious about, like playing a musical instrument, or something completely outside your comfort zone, like signing up for a pottery class or even trying improv, the possibilities are endless. You won't know what excites you until you step outside of your routines and give yourself permission to explore the unknown.

Self-connection and discovery require curiosity—getting to know yourself in the same way you would a new person you're interested in. If you were dating yourself, what questions would you ask? What would you want to know about your own likes, dislikes, and dreams? Exploring these questions leads you to the heart of what makes you tick. What makes you feel alive? What are you avoiding because you're afraid you might not be good at it? Do you shy away from things like singing or painting because you're worried about the judgment of others, or is it because you haven't yet connected with the joy those activities might bring?

It's easy to get caught up in the expectations of others—family, friends, society, even social media—and forget what it feels like to truly explore ourselves. When we stop and listen, we often discover parts of us that we didn't even know existed, or parts we've long forgotten because we've been too busy chasing someone else's version of success.

There was a moment—it was a random Saturday, nothing special about it—when I realized I had been waiting for someone to knock on my door. Like, *literally*. I was sitting in my house, sipping lukewarm coffee, scrolling on my phone, and it hit me—no one knows I'm here. No one is coming to save me. Not because I'm not worthy, but because I've made myself invisible by waiting to be chosen instead of choosing myself. That night, I sat down and made a list of things I was curious about. Pottery. Salsa dancing. Improv. Singing out loud in the car without skipping the high notes. I wasn't looking for mastery. I was just … *curious*.

A few days later, I went to an improv class. I didn't know anyone there. I was nervous—my whole body felt like static electricity. What if I wasn't funny? What if I froze? What if everyone could see how much I didn't belong there? But I stayed. I stepped into that room, and when it was my turn, I said yes to the scene, even though my voice trembled. I said yes to being ridiculous, to making stuff up on the spot, to laughing at myself. And on the drive home, I realized something powerful: I wasn't scared because I was bad—I was scared because it was *new*. And that's not something to be ashamed of. That's something to celebrate.

I didn't wait for anyone to invite me. I didn't ask for permission. I decided to get to know myself, and in doing so, I heard a voice I hadn't listened to in years: *my own*. I learned that the only person who can hear me screaming from the inside is me. And the only one who can pull me into the life I'm meant to live ... is me.

Let yourself be new to yourself. Don't rush the process. Curiosity leads to deeper connection—it gives you the space to explore your preferences, passions, and quirks without pressure. In doing so, you cultivate a well of creativity and excitement that becomes the foundation for the most fulfilling relationship you'll ever have: *the one with yourself.*

GETTING TO KNOW YOU

So, let's start small. Think of a few simple questions you'd ask a date—things like:

- What's something you've always wanted to try but never had the courage to do?

- What makes you feel most alive, even if it's just for a moment?

- What's a small, everyday pleasure that lights you up?

From there, create a list. It might be a combination of activities, feelings, or even foods (hello, peanut butter). What gets you curious, joyful, and excited? The point is that rediscovering your inner desires and passions isn't about following a to-do list or achieving a certain level of success—it's about being with yourself in the moment, exploring your preferences, and allowing yourself to evolve along the way.

When was the last time you spent an entire day with yourself, doing what you wanted on your own terms without worrying about the expectations of anyone else? Being comfortable with your own company is one of the most powerful foundations of self-love. When you're truly at ease with yourself, you begin to build a life that is satisfying, fulfilling, and completely your own. You no longer rely on others to fill gaps in your life because you've learned how to fill them yourself. And that's when true empowerment happens—when you know you can stand alone and still feel whole.

Self-dating is about taking yourself on adventures, exploring new experiences that replenish your soul, and allowing yourself to grow through those experiences without the pressure of needing someone else to be there. This doesn't just mean romantic relationships; it means creating a life where you enjoy the world around you—alone, in full ownership of your happiness and your well-being. You're free to choose what excites you, to venture into new hobbies, to take that class you've always wanted to try, or sign up for that spontaneous weekend getaway. The power of saying "yes" to yourself is liberating, because you're the one steering the ship.

You might be asking, *"What happens when you spend your time doing things that genuinely fill your heart with joy?"*

The answer is pretty neat. You start meeting other people who are also creating fulfilling lives for themselves, people who are excited about their own journeys. When you're busy enjoying life, you don't need anyone else to validate you. You don't need them to say yes to you, because you've already said yes to yourself. You go out, try new things, and discover what feels right. You don't need to worry about anyone else's opinion or approval because you've already established your own worth through your actions.

One of the most freeing aspects of self-dating is setting boundaries with others. By giving yourself permission to explore new experiences without needing the approval of others, you get to choose where your energy goes. If you try something and you don't like it, that's okay. No one has to validate that decision but you. You're in control. Maybe you went to that sushi bar and realized it's not your thing? No problem. You just move on to the next adventure. You get to decide what stays in your life and what doesn't.

And here's the kicker: When you take up space in your own life, you stop settling for relationships that don't serve you. If someone doesn't align with your energy, it's okay to walk away. You're not dependent on them for your sense of fulfillment. You can simply move on, knowing that there's someone else out there who will align with who you are. You can move forward with a light heart because you're no longer carrying the weight of needing someone to "complete" you.

Creating this rich, independent life means you're always in the driver's seat. The choice to fill your days with things that fuel your soul and keep you centered is yours, and when other people come into the picture, they do so because they see you living a life that's full of purpose and joy. They want to be part of that energy. And if they don't fit? It's fine. You don't need to make excuses, and you don't need to explain why you're moving in another direction. You're living for you, and the right people will come alongside you as you journey forward.

Raising the Bar

There was a season in my life where I kept asking, *Why do people keep treating me like I'm optional?* Like I was the backup plan, the afterthought, the one they reached for only when it was convenient. I kept attracting people—friends, partners, even coworkers—who would take and take and never give. Who would disappear when I needed them most. Who would say "I care" but act like I didn't matter.

And then, one day, it hit me. They were just following my lead. I was the one abandoning myself first. I was the one saying yes when I wanted to say no, keeping quiet when something hurt, brushing off my own needs to keep the peace. I thought being easygoing made me lovable. I thought being low-maintenance made me worthy. But all it really did was teach people how to treat me—and I was setting the bar *way too low*.

So I started making small shifts. I stopped answering texts out of obligation. I said no to plans when I needed rest. I paused before people-pleasing and asked, *What do I actually want right now?* And then I gave *myself that.* I stopped waiting for someone else to show me I mattered—and started doing that for myself. And slowly, something magical happened: the energy around me shifted. The friendships that were one-sided faded away. The men who only offered crumbs disappeared. But in their place? People who listened. Who cared. Who reciprocated. Who saw me. Because now, I was seeing myself, too.

I wasn't begging for love anymore. I *was* love—and that became the new standard. It's one thing to say, *love yourself.* However, it's another thing entirely to look in the mirror—physically, emotionally, mentally—and face the parts of yourself that feel unlovable.

MEETING YOURSELF FULLY

Self-intimacy isn't just about celebrating the parts of yourself that are easy to love. It's about meeting yourself in the moments when you feel insecure, messy, or lost. It's about learning how to show up for yourself when shame creeps in, when you feel like you're failing, when old wounds resurface and you just want to turn away. Because the truth is, there are parts of you that you've ignored, hidden, or numbed out for a reason. *They're painful.* They remind you of mistakes, disappointments, or the times you weren't chosen, weren't seen, weren't enough for someone else. But here's the thing—you can't build a loving relationship with yourself by only loving the easy parts.

So, *how do you begin to love the harder parts?* How do you stay present with yourself when you'd rather look away?

1. **Get Curious About Your Inner World**
   If you're struggling to love a part of yourself, ask yourself:

   - Where did this belief come from?

   - Is it actually true, or is it just something I was taught to believe?

   - If my best friend had this insecurity, what would I say to them?

   For example, if you struggle with feeling like you're "*too much*"—too loud, too ambitious, too opinionated—where did that come from? Did someone tell you that growing up? Did you shrink yourself to make others comfortable? If so, why are you still carrying that belief as if it's fact?

   Curiosity is what unlocks self-intimacy. Instead of judging yourself for your thoughts, feelings, or past actions, ask questions. Why do I react this way? What am I afraid of?

What would it look like to meet myself with understanding instead of frustration?

2. **Make Space for Your Stuck Parts**
   There are parts of you that feel like they haven't moved in years. Patterns you keep repeating. Fears you keep bumping up against. The instinct is often to bulldoze through them—to force yourself into growth or change before you're ready. But self-intimacy means sitting with those stuck places. It means acknowledging them instead of rushing past them.

   Instead of saying, I should be over this by now, try saying, *I see that this still hurts.* What do I need to feel safe enough to move through it?

   Healing isn't linear. Some lessons take time. Some wounds need more than just a new mindset; they need patience, compassion, and a willingness to sit in and feel through the discomfort instead of shutting it down or numbing it out.

3. **Learn to Hold Contradictions**
   Self-love doesn't mean fixing every flaw. It means making peace with the fact that you are a whole person—beautiful, imperfect, evolving. It means accepting that you can be confident and still have insecurities. You can be independent and still crave deep connection. You can be strong and still have tender places inside you.

   Too often, we believe that we have to be one thing or another —that if we struggle with self-doubt, we must not be confident. That if we have wounds, we must not be healed. But self-intimacy means holding space for all of it. It means saying:

   - I am a work in progress, and I am already enough.

   - I am healing, and I am whole even as I grow.

- I can love myself even in the moments I don't feel lovable.

4. **Rewriting the Way You Speak to Yourself**

   Your inner voice is always speaking—so what is it saying? Is it encouraging? Compassionate? Or does it echo the voices of past criticism, rejection, or shame?

   If your self-talk leans negative, it's not because you're broken. It's because somewhere along the way, you learned that voice. Maybe it was a parent who was hard on you. A teacher who told you you'd never be good enough. A past relationship that made you question your worth. That voice isn't you—it's just something you absorbed. And the best part? You can change it.

   Start small. The next time you catch yourself saying, "I'm so stupid for making that mistake," pause. Reframe. *I'm human. I'm learning. I get to try again.* If you look in the mirror and think, "I hate my body," shift it to: *This body has carried me through everything. I want to learn to appreciate it.* It's not about fake positivity—it's about giving yourself the grace you'd give anyone else.

5. **Treat Yourself Like Someone You Love**

   Think about someone you love deeply. How do you show up for them? How do you reassure them when they doubt themselves? How do you celebrate them when they accomplish something? Now ask yourself—do you do that for yourself?

   Self-intimacy isn't just in the way you think; it's in the way you act toward yourself:

   - Do you take care of your needs, or do you neglect yourself?

   - Do you listen to your body, or do you push it past exhaustion?

- Do you make space for joy, or do you feel guilty for resting?

Loving yourself in action means prioritizing yourself—not as an afterthought, but as a standard. It means treating yourself with the same love, patience, and care that you so freely offer *others*.

Self-intimacy is about embracing all of you. The easy parts, the messy parts, the evolving parts. It's about learning to be fully present with yourself—not just when you're winning, but when you're struggling, when you're healing, when you're in the thick of it.

And the most beautiful part? The more you deepen your relationship with yourself, the more you realize that you are never truly alone. Because at the end of the day, no matter what happens —no matter who comes and goes—you always have you. And that relationship is worth everything.

SELF-LOVE IN ACTION

Self-love isn't just a concept—it's something you do. It's in the way you show up for yourself, prioritize your needs, and create a life that feels aligned with who you truly are. But so often, we treat self-love as something abstract, when in reality, it's built through small, intentional actions every single day. It's all about turning self-love into a practice. How do you actively cultivate a deeper connection with yourself? How do you move from knowing you should love yourself to experiencing that love in real time?

1. **Getting Curious: Journaling Prompts for Self-Discovery**
   Journaling is one of the most powerful tools for self-connection because it slows down your thoughts and brings awareness to what's happening inside of you. If you want to

strengthen your relationship with yourself, start with curiosity.

Use these prompts to explore your inner world:

- What are activities, hobbies, or experiences I've always wanted to try but haven't? What's stopping me?

- What makes me feel the most alive, and when was the last time I experienced that feeling?

- What are five things I genuinely love about myself— physically, emotionally, mentally?

- Where in my life do I feel disconnected from myself? What might help me rebuild that connection?

- What does self-love look like to me in action?

This isn't about writing the "right" answers—it's about giving yourself the space to be honest. Let your answers surprise you.

2. **Breaking Through Fear: What's Holding You Back?**
   For every dream, experience, or act of self-care you've put off, there's usually a reason. Maybe it's fear. Maybe it's self-doubt. Maybe it's the belief that you don't have time or that it's not for you.

Take a moment to reflect:

- What's something I've been wanting to try but haven't?

- What's the story I tell myself about why I can't do it?

- Is that story true, or is it just fear trying to protect me?

Then, challenge yourself to take one small step forward. Remember: fear shrinks when you take action. If you've always wanted to learn an instrument, sign up for a beginner class. If you've wanted to travel solo, start with a weekend getaway. When you prove to yourself that you can do the things that once scared you, your world expands.

3. **Creating a Self-Care Routine That Nourishes You**
Self-care isn't just bubble baths and spa days—it's the daily practice of taking care of your body, mind, and soul. The way you treat yourself physically, mentally, and emotionally is a reflection of your self-relationship.

Think about these categories:

Body
How do you care for your physical well-being? This includes movement, rest, nutrition, and the way you treat your body.

Mind
What do you consume? Are you filling your mind with things that uplift and inspire you, or things that drain you?

Soul
What makes you feel deeply connected to yourself? Maybe it's meditation, creative expression, or time in nature.

Here's an exercise to try: Create a self-care menu—a list of activities that nourish each part of you. This way, when life gets busy, you have a go-to list of ways to reconnect with yourself.

INVEST IN YOURSELF

When you invest in yourself—when you love, nurture, and prioritize your own well-being—you create a foundation that impacts every other relationship in your life.

You Show Up More Fully in Relationships
When you are deeply connected to yourself, you don't enter relationships (romantic, familial, or friendships) from a place of need—you enter from a place of wholeness. Instead of looking

for someone to complete you, you're simply looking for people who add to your already rich life.

This changes everything:

- You stop tolerating relationships that drain you.

- You attract people who respect, uplift, and support you.

- You communicate your needs without fear of rejection.

You become the kind of person who doesn't need to be chosen—you choose yourself. And ironically, this makes you even more magnetic to others.

Your Confidence Becomes Unshakable

When your happiness isn't dependent on external validation, you move through the world differently. You trust yourself. You take up space. You make decisions based on what feels right for you, not what will please others.

- You stop over-explaining or justifying your choices.

- You feel comfortable spending time alone.

- You embrace both your strengths and imperfections without shame.

Confidence isn't about being perfect—it's about deeply knowing and accepting yourself.

You Become More Resilient

When you have a strong relationship with yourself, setbacks don't break you. Disappointments don't shake your sense of worth. You know that no matter what happens, you always have you.

You learn to navigate:

- Rejection without internalizing it as personal failure.

- Change without feeling lost or untethered.

- Loneliness without believing it means something is wrong with you.

When you trust yourself to handle whatever comes your way, life feels less like something that happens to you and more like something you are actively creating.

You Become Magnetic to Opportunities & Love
When you are deeply engaged in your own life—trying new things, prioritizing joy, taking care of yourself—you naturally attract people and opportunities that align with you.

People are drawn to those who are genuinely living. When you love your own company, take yourself on adventures, and create a life that excites you, you naturally meet others who are doing the same. Instead of waiting for love, friendships, or success to find you, you're out there living fully—and the right people and opportunities gravitate toward you as a result.

FALLING IN LOVE WITH YOUR LIFE

Imagine this: You wake up in the morning, and instead of groaning about another Monday or counting down the days until the weekend, you feel excited—not because something extraordinary is happening, but because your life itself is extraordinary. Because you've built something so full, so rich, so *you*, that every day feels like a gift.

This is what happens when you fall in love with your own life.

Real fulfillment isn't waiting for you in some future moment. It's right here. It's now. And it begins with how you love yourself and the life you're creating. There is something profoundly freeing about realizing that you are enough—that your own presence is enough to fill your life with meaning, joy, and adventure. When you treat

261

yourself like someone worth knowing, worth cherishing, worth celebrating:

- You stop waiting for someone else to say yes to your dreams —you say yes to yourself.

- You stop seeking approval from others because your own approval is enough.

- You stop putting your happiness on hold and start living— right here, right now.

You become the main character of your own story, not waiting for love or success or the "perfect moment" to find you, but creating those moments for yourself.

Think about the feeling of being in love—not just with a person, but with life itself. That electric, full-hearted aliveness. The way colors seem brighter, experiences richer, and everything feels touched by a kind of magic. That feeling isn't reserved for romance. It's something you can cultivate within yourself every single day. It's in the way you savor your morning coffee, the way you laugh at your own jokes, the way you take yourself on adventures just because you deserve to experience joy.

Falling in love with your own life is about showing up for yourself in a way that makes you excited to be alive. It's about creating a world where you don't need permission to feel happy, to feel free, to feel deeply, undeniably yourself. When you live this way —when you wake up each day thrilled to be you:

- Your energy shifts, and people notice. You attract experiences, opportunities, and relationships that align with the vibrant life you've created.

- You stop fearing rejection or loneliness, because you know you will always have yourself.

- You become magnetic—not because you're trying to impress anyone, but because you radiate the kind of joy and confidence that only comes from someone who is truly living.

At the end of the day, this is what it's all about: creating a life so fulfilling that you go to bed grateful for another day well-lived, and wake up excited to do it all over again. Not because every day is perfect, but because every day is yours.

Because you are fully alive. Because you have chosen yourself. Because you are living a love story with you.

And that is the most beautiful love story of all.

SECTION FOUR:
EMOTIONAL WISDOM & RADIANT LIVING

Mastering your emotions to live with depth, authenticity, and unshakable confidence

EVERYTHING WE'VE EXPLORED so far—self-awareness, self-trust, self-expression, purpose, and presence—culminates in this: your emotional wisdom. This is the final part of the journey where we integrate everything we've learned, not just intellectually but emotionally, so that it fully becomes who you are.

True radiance isn't just about what you do; it's about how you feel as you move through life. It's about living with emotional depth, presence, and an unwavering connection to yourself, no matter what challenges arise. In these next chapters, we step into the final layer of self-mastery—the art of navigating your emotions with wisdom, grace, and power.

Your emotions have never been obstacles to overcome. We will learn to see them as teachers, guiding you toward deeper self-awareness and alignment. Your emotions are a source of immense power, and when you learn to understand, honor, and heal them, you unlock an unshakable confidence that radiates through every part of your life.

This section is not about controlling your emotions or numbing them. It's about allowing yourself to feel fully without being consumed or controlled by those feelings. It's about responding to life from a place of grounded self-trust rather than reacting from fear or insecurity. It's about learning to navigate difficult emotions without abandoning yourself in the process.

In this section, we will explore how to transform self-doubt into self-trust, fear into confidence, and pain into wisdom. You will learn how to stand unwavering in your truth, let go of what no longer serves you, and live in a way that honors your deepest self. This is where you stop seeking radiance and start being it.

By the time you finish this section, you won't just understand what it means to live as the radiant woman—you'll embody it. You'll walk through life with a presence that is magnetic, unshakable, and entirely your own. And from this place, anything is possible.

This is your invitation to step into the most powerful, emotionally wise, and fully alive version of yourself.

CHAPTER 15: RADICAL SELF-ACCEPTANCE

Embracing Your Whole Self—Flaws, Strengths, and Everything in Between

RADICAL self-acceptance isn't just about confidence—it's the foundation for a deeply fulfilling life. It's the difference between constantly trying to prove your worth to the world around you and just simply knowing that you are enough exactly as you are. We live in a world that teaches women to seek validation from everywhere except within themselves. Approval from men. Praise from friends. Likes on social media. Recognition at work. It's like we're constantly asking, *Am I okay? Do I belong? Is this enough?* without realizing we are allowed to give ourselves our own permission. Here's the real question for you: Why do we need permission to exist exactly as we are? Why do we measure our worth in how well we fit into a mold someone else created?

Self-improvement is not the same as self-acceptance. You are not a fixer-upper. You don't have to earn your place in the world by being more productive, more beautiful, more likable. Growth is wonderful, but not because you need to be "fixed." You are already whole. Radical self-acceptance means embracing every part of you—the strengths, the flaws, the messy, complicated, brilliant layers that make you *you*. It's about letting go of the exhausting need to be chosen and instead choosing yourself, fully and unapologetically. Because the moment you stop waiting for the world's permission to be yourself? That's the moment you become unstoppable.

Let's be honest. Everyone has something about themselves they wish they could change. Maybe it's a physical feature, a personality trait, or something in their past they can't seem to let go of. But here's the truth—what you see as a flaw, someone else might admire, envy, or even find beautiful.

Think about it. You might obsess over the cellulite on your legs while someone who has struggled with their weight for years sees your body and thinks, *She's stunning*. You might hate how your voice sounds, but someone else hears warmth and wisdom in every word you say. You might feel self-conscious about being too quiet, but to someone overwhelmed by the noise of the world, your presence feels like peace. We spend so much time believing we are "less than," without realizing that our so-called imperfections are what make us unique, relatable, and real. The things you criticize about yourself are often the very things that make you *you*.

For years, I believed my body was something I had to shrink, fix, or apologize for. As a lifelong swimmer and Ironman athlete, I developed a strong, muscular frame. I remember standing in front of the mirror, seeing broad shoulders, a barrel chest, defined legs, powerful arms—and yet all I could think about was how I didn't look "feminine enough." How my body felt too heavy, too solid, too much. I weighed close to 180 pounds. And even though I knew it was mostly muscle, I carried a quiet shame around that number. I'd think, If I weighed less, my joints wouldn't ache so much during marathons. If I were lighter, I'd be faster, more graceful, more worthy of admiration.

But over time, I started to look at my body not as something to punish but as something to honor. These legs have carried me across dozens of finish lines. These arms have powered me through miles of open water swims. This body—this strong, steady, incredible body —has never given up on me, even when I've doubted it. And that number on the scale? It doesn't tell the story of my strength, my grit, or my endurance. It doesn't speak to the discipline it takes to train day after day or the joy I feel when I'm moving through the world in full expression of who I am. So now, when I catch myself critiquing my reflection or comparing myself to someone smaller or more feminine, I ask: *What if I saw my body as a masterpiece in motion, not a project in need of fixing?*

Because the truth is: I don't have to change to be worthy. I already am.

Your body—exactly as it is—carries you through life every single day. It walks you into new opportunities, hugs the people you love, heals itself after exhaustion or injury. It deserves kindness, not criticism. And the same goes for the parts of yourself beyond just the physical. Instead of picking yourself apart, start appreciating what you bring to the world. Your laugh, your kindness, your ability to make people feel seen—these are the things that matter.

Let's review some exercises we can use to reframe your own Negative Self-Perceptions:

The Mirror Exercise
Every morning, look at yourself in the mirror and find one thing to appreciate. It doesn't have to be physical—maybe it's your resilience, your humor, or the way your eyes light up when you talk about something you love. Speak it out loud: *I love my* _____ *because* _____.

Rewriting the Story
Take a perceived flaw and reframe it. If you've always thought, *I'm too emotional*, shift it to: *I am deeply feeling and intuitive, which allows me to connect with others on a meaningful level.*

The Love Letter
Write a letter to yourself as if you were writing to your best friend. What would you say about her? How would you lift her up? Then, read it out loud.

When you stop treating yourself like a problem to be solved and start treating yourself like someone worthy of love—flaws and all—you unlock a confidence that no amount of external validation could ever give you. That being said, we all have our own internal safety police, the strong voice in our head that tells us we're not good enough, smart enough, attractive enough. It didn't just appear out of nowhere. It was planted. Maybe it was a comment from a parent, a teacher, a friend, or even something unspoken by a younger you but deeply felt. Maybe it came from watching the way women were treated around you, the expectations placed on you, or the times you were made to feel like you had to earn your worth.

Over time, these external voices become internalized, repeating like a broken record. And after a while, you don't even question them. You just assumed they were true. But here's the thing—your inner critic isn't you. It's a collection of past experiences, outdated beliefs, and other people's projections. And once you recognize that, you can start to take your power back.

Imagine talking to a close friend the way you talk to yourself. You wouldn't say, *You're so lazy. You'll never get this right. You're such a mess.* No—you'd encourage her, remind her of her strengths, and help her see the bigger picture. So why not offer yourself that same kindness?

Rewiring your own negative self-talk starts with awareness. Pay attention to the words you use when you think about yourself. When you catch a critical thought, pause and ask:

- Would I say this to someone I love?

- Is this thought actually true, or is it just familiar?

- Where did this thought originally come from?

- What's a more supportive way to frame this?

For example, if you think, *I always mess things up,* shift it to: *I'm learning and growing, and mistakes are part of that process.* If you catch yourself thinking, *I'm not enough,* challenge it: *According to who? I define my own worth.*

Let's be honest. Most of us are conditioned to seek external approval. We wait for someone else to say we're doing a good job, that we're lovable, that we're enough. But what if you didn't need that? What if you gave yourself the validation first? A lot of the time, when we're looking for permission—from a partner, a boss, a friend—it's because we haven't given ourselves permission yet. And once you do? The need for outside approval starts to fade.

Here's how you can start finding ways to validate yourself instead:

Acknowledge Your Own Effort
Instead of waiting for praise, recognize what you're proud of. Say it out loud: *I handled that really well. I showed up fully. I'm proud of myself for trying.* (Better yet, do this in a mirror and look yourself in the eyes when you say it!)

Set Your Own Standards
Instead of asking, *Is this okay?* ask, *Do I feel good about this?* Instead of wondering if you measure up to someone else's expectations, ask, *What do I want? What feels true to me? Does this align with my core values?*

Trust Your Own Approval First

The moment you stop outsourcing your worth, you step into a whole new kind of freedom. You realize that you don't need anyone else to tell you that you're good enough. You just are.

Self-validation is a skill—one that takes continual practice. But every time you choose to be your own source of approval, you weaken the grip of your inner critic and strengthen the voice of self-trust. And that is the foundation of true confidence.

Let's get one thing straight: self-acceptance doesn't mean you stop growing. It doesn't mean you never change or that you throw your hands up and say, *"Well, this is just who I am forever."* That's not what we're doing here. Self-acceptance means you stop beating yourself up for not being "there" yet. It means you allow yourself to be here—fully present in who you are today while still holding space for the person you're becoming.

You can love yourself and still want more for yourself. You can accept your flaws and still want to improve. You can be proud of how far you've come and yet also excited about where you're going. You're not a fixer-upper. You're not broken. You're a whole, evolving, beautiful work of art in progress. And when you accept yourself as you are today, you free up the energy that used to go into shame and self-doubt and redirect it toward growth, curiosity, and becoming. That's not settling. That's liberation!

Taking up space is an act of self-respect. It's the deep knowing that you matter—your voice, your presence, your ideas, your energy. So speak a little louder. Take your time when you answer. Don't apologize for existing or for feeling or for needing. Let your full presence be felt, even in silence. Because when you stop shrinking, you invite others to expand, too. Becoming unapologetically you isn't a one-time decision. It's a daily devotion. A conscious choice to live in alignment with your truth—over and over again.

Here are a few small-but-mighty practices to anchor into your full self:

Start your day with self-acknowledgement.
Before the world gets a say, remind yourself who you are. Say it out loud: *I am allowed to take up space. I trust myself. I like who I'm becoming.*

Say what you mean.
Practice speaking to yourself with clarity and honesty, even when your voice shakes. Especially when it's easier to stay quiet.

Dress in a way that reflects how you feel inside.
Show up in your body like you mean it.

Choose alignment over approval.
When you're tempted to say yes just to be liked, pause. Ask: *What do I really want? What feels most true to me?*

Living in alignment doesn't mean that you never falter. It means you continue to come back to yourself again and again, even when things get tough. You begin to learn to trust your own rhythm, your own inner compass. You live like you have nothing to prove—because you don't. That's what being unapologetically you is all about: living as if you already belong—because you do.

Let's just pause here for a breath because this part matters. You are already enough. Not once you hit your next goal. Not once you "fix" the things you've been taught to hate. Not once you feel more healed, more accomplished, more like someone else. But right now. As you are. Messy. Brilliant. Still figuring it out. You are worthy of your own love and kindness—no exceptions, no disclaimers. You don't need to earn your own acceptance. You don't need to wait for someone else to say, *"Yes, now you're finally lovable."* That moment is not coming from the outside. It's coming from you!

Stop waiting for permission to fully love yourself. You don't need it. You never did. Go ahead and stand in front of the mirror and look at the woman you are—the woman who's carried you through every moment. The one who's tried so hard, even when she felt unseen. The one who's still here, still rising. Tell her: *You are already enough. And I've got you now.*

Let this be the moment you finally, truly give yourself permission to be you.

CHAPTER 16: HEALING WITH GRACE
Letting Go of the Past and Finding Inner Peace

LET'S be really honest—healing is definitely not this magical moment where one day you wake up, your heart no longer aches, your past no longer lingers, and everything makes perfect sense. That's the myth we've been sold, right? But the truth? Healing is quieter than that. Slower. More painful. And a whole lot more human.

You don't just move on from the things that broke you wide open. You integrate them. You learn how to carry them differently. Lighter. Softer. With more grace. Healing doesn't mean pretending the past didn't happen. It means learning how to honor it without letting it define you. It means saying, *yes, that hurt me ... and I'm still here, still loving, still becoming.*

To heal with grace is to stop punishing yourself for being affected by your old pain. It's to hold compassion for the version of you who didn't know what you know *now*. It's trusting that the slow unfolding of growth is still movement—even on the days it feels like you've slipped backward. Unfortunately, the past doesn't disappear. But its grip loosens when you meet it with patience instead of shame, when you see it as a teacher instead of a sentence.

This chapter is about finding your peace—not by erasing your history, but by learning how to live with it gently. You are not broken. You are becoming whole. And that process is sacred.

There was a time I had built an entire future in my mind with someone I loved deeply. We had plans, inside jokes, shared routines. I had wrapped my identity around the shape of us, and somewhere along the way, I stopped imagining a life without them in it. So when I decided to walk away, I didn't just lose a person—I lost my *storyline*. A version of my life I had gripped so tightly that letting it go felt like death. And for a while, it was. Not a dramatic kind of death, but a quiet one. The kind where you're sitting on the floor of your own life, surrounded by memories and unfinished dreams, wondering how to begin again when all the maps you made were now useless.

It wasn't just heartbreak—it was the loneliness that came after. The echo of what could have been. The anxiety of not knowing who I was without them. I was scared to be alone with myself, because in the silence, all the *what-ifs* and *if-onlys* grew louder. So I filled the space with distractions, with busyness, with running and striving and doing. I smiled when I didn't feel like it. I pretended I had it all figured out. But deep down, I knew that version of my life—the one I had clung to—was gone. And it took me a long time to even want to get close to that truth. To sit still. To stop performing my own healing and actually feel it. To stop making my grief a backdrop for resilience and instead let it just be what it was: *Heavy. Tender. Real.*

But eventually, I was tired of carrying the weight of a story that no longer served me. I didn't want to use it as a shield or an excuse anymore. There was too much life left to live. I was too curious about who I might become. And so, I began the slow, sacred work of making peace with the quiet. Of listening inward to the voice I silenced. Of embracing this new version of me—not as a backup plan, but as the *main character* all along.

That's what healing with grace looks like. Not pretending the pain didn't happen, but choosing to grow around it. Not erasing your history, but refusing to be defined by the ache of it.

LETTING GO OF THE PAIN

So, let's talk about why we hold on to pain even when we say we want to let it go. The truth is, sometimes pain becomes familiar. We start to wrap our identity around it. We replay the moments that broke our hearts, not because we like suffering, but because some part of us still wants it to turn out differently. We hang on to the imagined versions of the past or a fantasy of how the future could have looked, and we get stuck there—gripping tightly to a reality that doesn't exist. Will never exist. That's where suffering lives: in resistance to what actually *is*.

Sometimes we even cling to our pain because it makes us feel safe. Because it gives us something to point to—*this is why I am the way I am*. We use it as an excuse *not* to change. And yet, holding onto it doesn't protect us. It just weighs us down.

Letting go doesn't mean pretending it didn't hurt. Because it did. And probably still does. It doesn't mean rushing to provide forgiveness or plastering a smile over your wounds. It means feeling it fully—letting the sadness, the anger, the grief move through you like a storm. Because if you never let yourself feel it, if you dissociate from it or distract yourself from embracing it, you'll always be carrying a piece of it quietly, subtly, everywhere you go.

This is how you begin to release emotional baggage without bypassing your truth. You acknowledge what happened. You give yourself permission to feel all of it—not just the parts that are convenient or easy to explain. But *all of it*. And then, gently, when you're ready, you start to loosen your grip. Not because the pain wasn't real, but because you deserve to be free.

Letting go is not forgetting. It's saying: *this shaped me, but it does not own me.* You can honor your past without being defined by it. You can carry your story with grace instead of grief.

And that, right there—that's when the healing truly begins.

FORGIVENESS IS FREEDOM

Forgiveness isn't saying what they did was okay. It's not letting someone off the hook or pretending it didn't hurt. Forgiveness is about *your* freedom. Because when you carry resentment, it lives in your body. When you replay what happened over and over again, you're the one feeling that same sting every time. And while anger might feel powerful at first—it burns hot and fierce—resentment is heavy. It lingers. It drains you. It quietly whispers that you are still stuck in that moment, still defined by what they did.

But you're not.

Forgiveness is how you set yourself free. It's how you say, *I choose peace over punishment. Not for them, but for me.* It's a quiet reclaiming of your energy. It's the moment you say: *You don't get to live in my mind, in my heart, in my nervous system anymore.* And then—maybe even harder still—you begin the work of forgiving yourself.

Because sometimes we're carrying guilt or shame that isn't even ours to hold. Sometimes we blame ourselves for not knowing better, for staying too long, for not speaking up, for letting someone treat us a certain way. But you're allowed to look back at past versions of yourself and offer her compassion instead of judgment. She was doing the best she could with what she knew. And the fact that you see it differently now? That means you've grown. Letting go of self-judgment doesn't mean you don't take responsibility—it means you stop punishing yourself for being human.

So here it is: Forgiveness is not forgetting. It's remembering and choosing to release the weight of it anyway. It's saying: *I've carried this long enough. I choose peace now.* For them, maybe. But mostly—for you.

INNER PEACE

Here's the hard truth—inner peace doesn't just happen. It's something you cultivate—bit by bit, breath by breath. And sometimes, in the middle of the chaos or the grief or the overstimulation of life, it's easy to forget that you can create calm. You have the tools. You just have to remember to reach for them.

When in doubt, try one of these tools:

- **Mindfulness.** It is our anchor. It brings you back from spiraling into the past or spinning out into the future. It says: *Come home. Right here. Right now. Breathe.* It's not about clearing your mind—it's about noticing what's there without judgment. It's the pause between the trigger and the reaction. The space where choice lives.

- **Journaling.** A sacred place to pour out the thoughts that are too heavy to carry. You don't have to censor yourself. You don't even have to make sense. You just let it out. Write what you're really feeling, even if it's messy or angry or scared. Because the page can hold what your body doesn't need to carry anymore.

- **Visualization.** Picture what peace looks like for you. Maybe it's a place. Maybe it's the version of yourself who's moved through the pain and is smiling again, grounded again, clear again. Let her guide you. Let that image pull you forward when the present feels too thick with emotion.

- **Somatic Practices.** Things like deep breathing, stretching, shaking, humming, dancing—these are how you let your body finish what your mind keeps trying to process. Emotions aren't just thoughts. They live in your cells, your posture, your nervous system. And movement is how they leave.

- **Create your own rituals for peace.** This may be the most important tool. Not routines. *Rituals.* Tiny sacred practices that remind your body and spirit: *You are safe. You are loved. You are okay.* Maybe it's lighting a candle and pulling a moon card. Maybe it's a bath, or a walk with no phone, or five deep breaths with your hand over your heart.

These aren't fixes. They're invitations. To soften. To reconnect. To make space for stillness in a world that rarely offers it. And the more you reach for these tools, the lighter you'll begin to feel—not because everything is perfect, but because you're not carrying it all alone anymore.

So as we conclude, remember that healing doesn't mean you just forget. It doesn't erase what happened or that you pretend it didn't shape you. It just means you stop letting it harden you. You stop carrying it like armor and start walking forward more lightly—with open hands instead of clenched fists. Choosing healing over resentment is a quiet rebellion. It's saying, *I deserve peace.* Even if I never get the apology. Even if they never understand. Even if the wound was deep and the scar still aches sometimes. I still choose peace—because it's mine to claim.

You don't have to be completely healed to move forward. You just have to be willing. Willing to feel. Willing to let go, layer by layer. Willing to trust that your softness is strength and your grace is a power that doesn't need to shout.

So as you keep walking—maybe slower, maybe steadier—hold these truths close:

- I release what no longer serves me.

- I forgive, not because they deserve it, but because *I do.*

- I honor my journey, every messy, beautiful step.

- I am whole, even as I heal.

- Peace is not a destination—it's the way I choose to move through the world now.

You're doing it. You're already becoming the woman who walks through life with quiet confidence, with radiant ease, with a heart that stays open—even after it's been broken. And that is nothing short of powerful.

EMOTIONAL RESILIENCE

We tend to think of resilience as being rock-solid—unmoving, unshakable, or unbothered. But true emotional resilience isn't about being unbreakable. It's not about building walls or pretending nothing touches you. It's about learning how to bend without snapping. It's about holding space for your pain while also holding onto your power.

Emotional resilience is the quiet strength that says, I can feel this and still move forward.

It's the moment you sit with your heartbreak instead of numbing it. It's when you pause and breathe through the anger instead of lashing out. It's when you choose to stay with yourself in the dark knowing the light is coming—not because someone told you it would, but because you trust that you can find your way there.

This is the kind of strength we're talking about in this chapter—not the performative kind, not the type that pushes emotions away and pretends that everything's fine. This is emotional intelligence paired with emotional courage. It's the decision to show up with compassion for yourself, especially when everything feels like it's falling apart. Because real resilience is built when we learn to sit with what hurts without losing ourselves in it or hiding from it. It's adaptability, strength, and self-trust braided together into something unshakable—not because it doesn't feel, but because it does. Because it dares to.

We've all been there—those moments when a wave of emotion crashes into you so hard, it feels like you might drown in it. Maybe it's shame after an argument, heartbreak that sits in your chest like a stone, or the quiet numbness of burnout that creeps in slowly and silently. Our instinct is to run. To numb. To distract. To fix.

But the real work? It begins when we stop running. When we sit still, and listen.

From a young age, most of us were taught that certain emotions are "bad" or "too much." Crying means you're weak. Anger means you're difficult. Sensitivity means you're unstable. So we start learning how to suppress it. We smile when we want to scream. We shrink when we want to speak. We say "I'm fine," when we're absolutely not. *But* emotions aren't problems to solve. They're messages. They're clues. And when we learn to sit with them—really sit—we gain access to what they're here to teach us. Emotional resilience isn't about *not* feeling things. It's about allowing yourself to feel everything fully and then still choosing to stay rooted in yourself.

That means giving yourself permission to feel the sadness without rushing to fix it or drown it out with distractions. It means recognizing that anxiety is sometimes your body trying to signal something is out of alignment. It means sitting in discomfort without immediately turning on Netflix or reaching for the glass of wine or doom-scrolling for the next two hours. It's hard. But it's worth it. Because when you stop turning away from your emotions, you begin to understand them. And when you understand them, you reclaim your power.

There was a time in my life where silence felt dangerous. Not just uncomfortable—*dangerous*. Like if I stopped moving, or thinking, or consuming, I'd be swallowed whole.

So I didn't stop.

I texted people constantly—waiting, hoping for someone to respond. And if they didn't? I spiraled. Not hearing back made me feel like I didn't matter. Like I'd done something wrong. Like I was forgettable.

I bought things I didn't need. Sometimes it was little things—another book, more earrings. Other times it was big things—clothes I wouldn't wear, courses I wouldn't finish. Amazon boxes at the door made me feel like something was happening in my life. Like progress. Like forward motion. But it was just another distraction.

And when all else failed—wine. Not a glass. Usually two. Sometimes three. Not for the taste. Just to blur the edges.

And it all worked—for a while. It kept me busy enough to not notice the emptiness. To not feel the shame. To not admit how lonely I was, even when I was surrounded by people. But deep down, I knew what I was doing. I knew I wasn't okay. Because the second I was left alone, without a screen, or a reply, or a new thing arriving in the mail—I unraveled. I'd call it boredom, But it wasn't boredom.

It was *withdrawal*.

I was addicted to external noise—validation, attention, the buzz of "maybe this will make me feel better." And without it, I felt like I didn't exist.

What changed wasn't sudden. There was no big crash. Just this one moment when I realized: *I'm exhausted by my own life.* I wanted to stop needing everything outside of me to feel okay *inside* of me. And the only way out was to stop running. So I started sitting. First, for five minutes. Then ten. Then longer. It was awful at first. My thoughts were loud. My body was restless. My hands itched to reach for *something*. But slowly, beneath the noise, I found a quiet voice. One I hadn't heard in years.

She wasn't asking for more. She was asking to be *felt*.

That was the beginning of everything. Not the healing, not the wholeness—just the beginning. The moment I stopped filling the space and started listening to what the space was trying to show me. And at first, the listening was rough. My inner voice didn't speak in wisdom or love right away. She spoke in grief. In irritation. In hunger. She sounded a lot like shame at first—because I had confused her with every voice I had absorbed over the years: *You're too much. You're falling behind. You should be doing more. Why can't you just be happy?*

But over time, as I kept showing up—sober, quiet, present—the voice softened. She got clearer. More nuanced. Less like a drill sergeant, more like a trusted guide. She started saying things like: *"You're allowed to rest." "That didn't feel good—and you don't have to override it." "This isn't your pace. You're allowed to slow down." "It's okay that you want more. You're not too needy. You're waking up."*

And that was the moment I realized I hadn't just been avoiding my emotions. I'd been avoiding myself. The part of me that knows. The part of me that had been trying to get my attention for years— not with punishments, but with invitations. Invitations to come home. To take off the mask. To stop performing wholeness and to start practicing honesty. Authenticity. The more I listened, the more I trusted myself. And the more I trusted myself, the more I stopped needing the world to constantly affirm that I was okay. Because *I* could affirm it.

I could hear the signal before the spiral. I could feel when I was abandoning myself again. I could feel when I was about to numb something that really just needed to be held. And most of all, I could feel when something was a "yes" because it brought me peace, not just relief. And when something was a "no" because it made me small, even if it looked shiny. That's what emotional safety looks like. Not a perfect, regulated life. But a relationship with yourself where you listen first—before the world gets a vote.

Try this practice on for size:

Next time a big emotion hits—don't run. Instead, ask yourself three questions:

1. What am I actually feeling right now? (Not just "bad"—but is it anger? Fear? Grief?)

2. Where do I feel it in my body? (Is your chest tight? Is your jaw clenched?)

3. What might this emotion be asking me to pay attention to?

Give it five minutes. Set a timer. Breathe through the discomfort. Let it be there. Then decide: *What do I need? What feeling am I trying to change right now? What would feel like support in this moment?*

You may be surprised to find that just naming your emotions is enough to soften their grip. Pain will visit you in this life—there's no getting around that. But allowing yourself to suffer under that pain? That's optional. That's where your power lies.

LESSONS IN THE HARD PLACES

There's a kind of magic in learning to transmute your pain—not by ignoring it, not by pretending it didn't happen, but by turning it into something useful. Something that deepens you. Something that makes you wiser, stronger, and more open-hearted than you were before. This is the art of emotional alchemy. And it starts with one question: *"What is this here to teach me?"* Not why did this happen to me, but *what can I learn from it?* Because when you stop seeing your pain as punishment and start seeing it as a portal, you begin to move from victim to creator.

I remember as a child, my mom wanted so badly to protect me from mistakes. She just wanted me to be happy. But in trying to create a perfect life, she unintentionally tried to shield me from the very things that would've made me stronger. Mistakes. Hard moments. Failing and getting back up again. And I needed those moments. We all do. The scraped knees, the rejections, the failures, the heartbreaks. Because every single one of them can become fuel for growth—if you let them. My dad used to say, "If you can't climb up, you can't climb back down." He wouldn't lift me to the top of the jungle gym, no matter how much I begged. He wanted me to figure it out. To build that muscle. To earn my way up so I could find my way down. That lesson stayed with me. Because emotional strength isn't handed to you. It's built.

When you start looking at life that way, you begin to realize that the hardest seasons are often the most transformative ones. You can either stay stuck in the narrative of what hurt you—or you can write a new story where that same pain becomes the very thing that shapes your wisdom.

Let's try out a practice on a past memory:

Reflect on a moment in your life that hurt. Something that cracked you open, maybe even broke you a little. Ask yourself:

- What did I learn about myself because of that experience?

- What strength did I discover that I didn't know I had?

- What new values, boundaries, or clarity emerged?

Write it down. Reclaim it. Turn it into your own fuel.

Emotional resilience isn't just about bouncing back once—it's about becoming the kind of person who knows they can rise again and again. Not because life gets easier, but because you get stronger. This isn't about gritting your teeth and powering through. It's about learning how to tend to yourself. To develop the inner scaffolding that holds you steady even when the world tilts.

CHAPTER 17: OVERCOMING IMPOSTER SYNDROME
Stepping into Your Power and Owning Your Success

OKAY, LET'S JUST say it—imposter syndrome sucks. It's that little whisper in the back of your mind saying, *"Are you really good enough?"* even when you're sitting in the room you worked your entire life to be in. It shows up when you're about to raise your hand in the meeting, launch the project, pitch the idea, post the thing, go after the dream—and it says, *"Wait ... who do you think you are?"*

Sound familiar? Yeah. Me, too.

For a long time, I lived inside that voice. I thought I had to be perfect and achieve to be worthy. That unless everything I produced was pristine, impressive, gold-star-ready, I didn't deserve to take up space. I was a full-on, all-apologies, straight-A, overachieving, perfection-obsessed woman. And for a while, it worked. I got the degrees. I got the accolades. I climbed the ladder. But inside, I was exhausted. I wasn't thriving—I was performing. Performing excellence. Performing worthiness. Performing confidence. Performing *me.*

And the thing is, I never felt like I had actually arrived. I always thought there was some invisible finish line, and maybe everyone else had the instruction manual, and I just missed the day they passed it out. I was terrified that someone would see through me and say, *"She doesn't really know what she's doing."* And that would be it—my cover would be blown, the impostor-police would come and take me away, and I would have to start over covered in a blanket made of my own shame.

But here's the truth that changed everything for me: *everyone feels like that*. No one actually has it all figured out. Everyone is living in some version of their own self-doubt. And no, they are not thinking about you as much as you think they are. They're thinking about themselves. Just like you are.

The other truth I learned—and this one hit me hard—is that feeling like a fraud doesn't mean you don't belong. It means you're growing. It means you're stretching beyond what's comfortable. It means you're doing hard things. And of course your brain wants to throw up warning signs when you're doing something new. It's wired for safety, not success.

So in this chapter, I want to pull back the curtain on imposter syndrome—not just from a theoretical lens, but from my own lived experience. I want to talk about the thoughts that loop in our heads, the stories we tell ourselves, and how we can rewrite them. I'll share what helped me go from shrinking in rooms I had already earned the right to be in to walking in like I belonged there all along.

Because I do. And so do you.

This chapter is about you reclaiming your success. Not as a fluke. Not as luck. But as a reflection of who you've always been becoming. It's time to stop auditioning and start owning your place in the world. Let's do this, together.

BREAKING THE CYCLE

Let's start with the loop. You know the one. The *"I'm not good enough." "I shouldn't even be here." "Someone else could do this better." "Why did I say yes to this?" "What if they find out I have no idea what I'm doing?"* loop.

These thoughts are like horrible hold music that never shuts off. They play on a loop in the background of your mind, and after a while, you stop noticing them—but they're still shaping every decision you make. And they're sabotaging you. Silently. Strategically.

Because what happens when those thoughts are running the show? You *hesitate*. You overthink. You second-guess. You edit your brilliance down to what feels "acceptable." You decide not to post that video, not to speak up in that meeting, not to launch that idea, not to talk to that cute guy, not to follow the nudge. You tell yourself you'll do it tomorrow. When you feel more ready. When you feel more confident. When it's "*better.*"

But the truth? Tomorrow doesn't come! Because confidence doesn't come before you take the leap—it comes after. It's a muscle that grows through action.

I know this because I lived in that loop. I lived with that soundtrack blasting through my brain. I'd stare at something I created and think, *This isn't good enough.* And then I'd make it better. And better. And better. And eventually, I wouldn't put it out at all. Because perfectionism told me it still wasn't ready. And underneath that perfectionism? Fear. The fear that I wasn't enough. The fear that someone would judge me, that I'd fall flat, that I'd fail publicly. I wasn't avoiding failure—I was avoiding shame.

I remember sitting on the floor of my office, staring at the draft of my last book, completely paralyzed. I had poured months of work into it—hours of organizing my thoughts, refining ideas, trying to say something that mattered. But as I stared at all the pages, all I could think was: *Who am I to write this?*

That inner critic wasn't quiet. It said: *You've only just started this journey. You're not an expert. What if people laugh at this? What if they roll their eyes? What if no one even reads it?*

I started editing again. And again. And again. Not because the book needed it—but because I was terrified. Terrified someone would see through me. That they'd realize I wasn't this wise, radiant, put-together woman—just someone trying her best, figuring it out as she went along. And underneath all that editing was a secret I didn't want to admit: I wasn't afraid the book would fail. I was afraid *I* would fail. That I would be the one judged, misunderstood, dismissed.

That fear nearly stopped me. But then I remembered something I had told other women in my group, over and over: *"You don't have to be the most qualified. You just have to be willing."* So I let the book be imperfect. I let it be honest. I let it be enough.

And finally, I put it out into the world. Because I knew that sharing it—even imperfectly—was more than enough. That moment taught me something powerful: *fear doesn't always mean stop.* Sometimes, it just means you're doing something that matters, and even if it's scary, you should keep moving forward.

RETRAINING YOUR BRAIN

And here's where the science comes in: your brain is wired to protect you, not to promote you. It's designed to scan for threats, to anticipate worst-case scenarios, to keep you safe and alive. Back when we were living in tribes and foraging for food, that threat-scanning was essential. But now? It's not the tiger outside the cave —it's your boss. Your inbox. The stage. The comment section. Strangers. Family. Friends. Your own potential.

Your brain doesn't know the difference between "this is *unfamiliar*" and "this is *unsafe*." So when you try something new or big or bold, your brain sends up the red flags. And if you're not aware, you take those warning signs as truth. And so you stay small. You stay safe. You stay stuck. But here's what you need to remember: just because a thought *feels* true doesn't mean it *is* true.

That's where our work begins—learning to recognize the thought, then to pause and reframe. So here's a simple framework I use when impostor thoughts start circling like hungry vultures:

Notice the Thought.
Start by naming it. *"I'm having the thought that I'm not good enough."* Just that one little phrase—"I'm having *the thought* that ..."—creates space. It helps you step out of the story and see it for what it is: a pattern, not a prophecy.

Ask: Is This True?
Not "does this *feel* true," but *is it true*? What are the actual facts? What's the evidence that supports this, and what evidence contradicts it?

Ask: What Else Could Be True?
If I'm thinking, "I'm not qualified," what else could be true? Maybe: "I've worked hard for this," or "I bring a unique perspective," or "I'm learning as I go, and that's okay."

Reconnect to Your Why.
Why are you doing this? Who are you here to serve? What part of you knows this matters? Your why will ground you when your mind wants to run wild.

Move Anyway.
You don't have to feel 100% ready. You don't need to silence every doubt. You just need to take the *next step*. One small act of courage builds the trust you're craving.

Here's what I want you to know: self-doubt doesn't mean you're broken. It means you're human. But you don't have to let it drive. When you learn to recognize the lies your mind tells you and rewrite the thoughts in your own voice, that's where your power comes back. That's when you stop waiting for permission and start moving from self-trust. You're not behind. You're just beginning to hear yourself clearly.

Owning Your Accomplishments

Now, let's talk about something women don't talk about nearly enough: *being proud of ourselves.* Not quietly proud. Not low-key, humble-brag proud. I mean fully, unapologetically, heart-bursting, dancing-in-your-kitchen, tears-in-your-eyes proud. And yet, how many of us downplay our wins? How many of us say, "*Oh, it was nothing,*" when it was everything? How many of us shrink in rooms where we should rise?

Why? Because we're taught that owning our success is dangerous. That it's arrogant. That it might make other people uncomfortable. That being a radiant woman somehow dims someone else's light. And let's be real: there's an extra layer of complexity when it comes to feminine energy and power. We're navigating this weird tightrope where we're told to be confident, but not too confident. Assertive, but not aggressive. Soft, but not weak. Successful, but not intimidating.

It's exhausting.

And the truth is: sometimes it feels embarrassing to shine. To say, "*I'm amazing at this.*" To post the win. To tell someone, "*I worked so hard for this, and I'm so proud.*" Even writing that sentence makes me slightly want to cringe. But you know what? *It shouldn't.*

Because dimming yourself to make others comfortable doesn't serve anyone. Not you, not them, not the world. You're not helping anyone by pretending to be less than you are. You are allowed to own your success without apology. You are allowed to be joyful about your life. And in doing this, it allows other women to bask in the glory of their own successes, too!

I started practicing this in small, private ways—like talking to myself in the mirror. I'd look at my reflection and say, *"I'm proud of you."* Sometimes I'd cry. Sometimes I'd laugh. Sometimes I'd roll my eyes because it felt so cheesy—but I did it anyway. Because I knew the most important person who needed to witness my growth ... *was me.*

Then I created something I call the milestone jar.

Every time I had a win—big or small—I'd write it down and stick it in the jar. It didn't have to be flashy. Sometimes it was: *I had the hard conversation with grace.* Sometimes it was: *I submitted the proposal even though I wanted to quit.* And sometimes it was: *I ran 26.2 miles and cried through the last one, but I didn't stop.* Or: *I brought my book into a bookstore and asked if they'd carry it—even though my voice was shaking.* Or: *I walked into a room full of women I didn't know, and led a circle, and they stayed.* Or: *I posted something I was scared to share, and people told me it made them feel seen.*

These moments? They added up. And you know what? I could look back and see my growth. I had proof. I had evidence of my becoming. There's something about seeing your wins collected in one place that changes you. You stop second-guessing your worth and start remembering it. You stop waiting for permission to be proud and start giving it to yourself. You start holding space for your own brilliance instead of hiding from it.

And slowly, being proud doesn't feel embarrassing anymore. It starts to feel like the truth.

That's what celebrating yourself does. It creates a record of your own expansion. But here's the most powerful shift: *learning to celebrate yourself without guilt.* No disclaimers. No self-deprecating jokes. *Just truth.* You're not celebrating to prove anything. You're celebrating to remember who you are.

THE COURAGE TO BE YOU

Confidence isn't about who you think you *should* be—it's about showing up as who you *actually* are. For the longest time, I thought I had to show up as Stella—my radiant woman "future self" alter ego. She's bold, clear, powerful, and magnetic. I'd ask myself, *"What would Stella do?"* And while that can be a helpful compass, I started to realize something. I was trying to become someone who didn't even exist yet. I was performing confidence instead of embodying it.

So, here's what I've learned: *there is no finish line.* There is no perfect version of you waiting at the end of the road. You're not trying to become someone else—you're returning to yourself. Stella isn't the end goal. She's just a compass. She's a reminder to me of what alignment feels like. But I don't need to *be* her. I just need to be me, right now, in truth.

Confidence is showing up in honesty. It's owning where you are, today, in this moment. It's being okay with not knowing what's going to happen, but trusting yourself anyway.

So I challenge you: stop waiting to feel *"ready."* Stop holding your breath until you become a future version of yourself. Start celebrating who you are *now*. Speak your wins out loud. Honor your efforts. Smile at yourself in the mirror. Be proud without hesitation. Because you don't have to become someone else to be worthy. You already are.

Let's get one thing straight: confidence isn't something you wait around for. It's something you build—moment by moment, breath by breath, choice by choice. Confidence isn't loud or flashy. Sometimes, it's a whisper: *I can try again.* Sometimes, it's a hand on your own heart. A deep breath before the next step. A quiet refusal to abandon yourself in the middle of the storm. You don't have to wait until the fear is gone to move forward. You just need to move forward with it.

FIGHTING THE VOICES IN YOUR HEAD

Imposter syndrome creeps in when you're stepping into a new level, speaking up, showing up more fully, or doing something you've never done before. So instead of trying to "get rid of it," I want to give you real tools to meet it when it shows up.

Let's keep this toolbox handy for the next time your impostor flying monkeys take flight:

> **Name the narrative.**
> When you hear the voice in your head saying, *"Who do you think you are?"* or *"You're not good enough,"* pause. Call it out. Literally name it out loud: *"Ah, that's Chelsea, my imposter voice again."* By naming it, you separate yourself from it. You remember: this is not you. This is an old pattern trying to keep you small.

Ask.
What's the fear under this? Imposter syndrome is often fear wearing a mask. Fear of failure. Fear of rejection. Fear of being "too much." Identify what your imposter thoughts are trying to protect you from. Once you name the fear, you can speak directly to it with compassion.

Practice courageous truth-telling.
Say it out loud. Write it down. Share it with a trusted friend. *"This is hard for me." "I'm scared, but I'm still doing it."* Confidence grows when you let your truth breathe instead of keeping it locked inside.

GIVE YOURSELF ROOM TO GROW

Let's be honest—some moments hit harder than others. You freeze. You want to disappear. You wonder if you're really cut out for this. In those moments, I want you to remember something really simple.

It's okay. It's okay to have doubt. It's okay to feel scared. It's okay to not know what to do. But what matters most is what you do next. If you freeze this time, that's okay. Next time, you'll remember this moment, and maybe you'll shift just a little. That's all confidence really is—tiny shifts made over time. A quiet stacking of self-trust. One choice. Then another. Then another.

Every time you choose courage, even in the smallest way, you're building a new foundation inside yourself. And sometimes the most courageous thing is being kind to yourself. Saying, "I'm not there yet, but I'm getting there." "I'm proud of how far I've come." "I trust myself to keep going." You don't have to get it perfect. You don't have to fake it. You just have to keep choosing yourself. Confidence isn't a destination—it's a relationship. One you get to deepen every day.

Let me say this as clearly and directly as I can: *You are not an imposter.* You're a human being who is growing. You're someone who has worked hard to get where you are. You're someone who dares to care deeply about the quality of what you do, and sometimes that care gets tangled up in fear. But that doesn't make you a fraud. That makes you real.

The fact that you question yourself doesn't mean you're not worthy. It means you give a damn. It means you're stepping outside of your comfort zone. It means you're expanding into new territory. And every time you show up anyway, despite the voice in your head that says you're not ready, you are proving to yourself that you are. So, let's stop waiting for permission. Let's stop minimizing our wins. Let's stop shrinking just to make other people feel more comfortable. Own your voice. Own your work. Own your joy. Because you're still here. Still showing up. Still growing. Still choosing yourself. That is what makes you radiant.

If no one has told you this lately, let me be the one to say it: *I'm proud of you.*

For reading this chapter. For wrestling with your doubt instead of letting it win. For daring to become the woman you were always meant to be. You don't have to be loud to be powerful. You don't have to be perfect to be worthy. You don't have to be fearless to move forward.

You just have to keep choosing yourself. Again. And again. And again.

Chapter 18: Judgment Detox
Releasing the Weight of Other People's Opinions

THERE IS A SPECIAL kind of freedom that tastes like fresh air. It's the moment you realize: the outside world is going to think what they think anyways, no matter what you do. So you might as well show up fully and let go of what you can't control. It's not that the fear of judgment disappears overnight—it's that you get tired of editing yourself for people who are still unable to see the whole picture.

Let's be real here: if we let ourselves spiral over every thought someone might have about us, we'd never leave the house. We'd never speak up. We'd never try anything new. We'd be too busy second-guessing how we look, how we sound, what we said, whether it was too much, not enough, or just plain weird.

And all of that fear? It keeps us small. It chips away at our boldness, our joy, our creative spark. It makes us contort ourselves into versions of us that are less true and more *"acceptable."* But here's what changed the game for me: I finally understood that people's opinions of me were never really about *me*. They were projections—reflections of their own insecurities, their own limitations, their own rules about what's acceptable. When you start to realize that you are a mirror for everyone else (and vice versa), you begin to understand that the things they don't like about you are reflections of things they are working on, and the things they cherish about you are things they hope to someday become.

The truth? We're all walking around with our own shit. Someone might be short with you because they had a bad day. Someone might make a passive-aggressive comment because they don't know how to own their envy. Someone might misunderstand you, judge you, dismiss you—and it still has nothing to do with you. Once you become aware that we are all just eight-year-olds in adult bodies, unsure of how to handle all of our big emotions, you start to understand this concept a little more. It's not about you. It never was.

Have you ever had moments where you shrank because you were afraid someone was watching? Held back from posting something you were proud of because you were worried it would come off as too much? Muted yourself in rooms where you should've stood tall? I certainly have. *But I'm done.* Because I know now: trying to manage everyone else's perception of you is a full-time job—and it's not one I'm interested in keeping anymore.

This chapter is about learning how to *let go*. Let go of needing to be liked. Let go of needing to be perfect. Let go of the exhausting loop of second-guessing and self-censoring. It's time for your Judgment Detox. Not because judgment doesn't exist—but because it doesn't deserve that much power over you anymore. Let's unhook. Let's get free. Let's finally stop asking for permission to be who we already are.

LET THEM

Learning to let people think whatever they want—and then going ahead and doing what I was going to do anyway changed my life There was a time I needed people to understand me. To see me the right way. To validate that I was a good person, that I was smart, that I wasn't too much, or too loud, or too ambitious, or too emotional, or too anything.

I used to twist myself into knots, especially when I was stepping into a new version of myself. When I started doing Ironmans, when I got the VP job, when I started posting about self-love and healing—I felt this wave of *"what will they think?"* crash over me. Every. Single. Time. The fear was so loud it nearly drowned out my own truth.

But here's that truth unpacked: you can't control what someone else sees. You can't control what they project, how they receive you, or what judgments they've already made based on their own lens. That's where Mel Robbins' *Let Them Theory* hit me right in the gut. And I'm not going to lie, it landed right when I needed it the most. When I heard her say things like: *Let them misunderstand you. Let them think you're too much. Let them roll their eyes when you talk about healing, or mindset, or inner radiance. Let them.* I realized—It's not my job to chase after everyone's approval. It's my job to stay aligned with my own truth.

Here's the thing—validation from others might feel good for a moment, but it's like sugar. A quick hit, a temporary high, then you crash. But self-trust? That's protein. That sustains you. And I've learned this the hard way, especially when people didn't get what I was doing. When I shifted my content, when I became softer but stronger, when I started talking about becoming the radiant woman —it confused people. Some people backed away. Some said nothing. Some projected their own discomfort with change.

But guess what? I kept going. Because I wasn't doing it for applause. I was doing it because it was true.

So here's how we begin detaching from external validation: You get really honest about whose opinion is actually driving your choices. And then you ask yourself: *Do I trust myself more than I trust their perception of me?* Because trusting yourself doesn't mean you never feel doubt. It means you feel the doubt and still walk forward. It means you remind yourself: They don't need to understand it. They don't have to believe in it.

They're not walking your path—you are.

And when you start focusing on your own path, not someone else's, you realize that the opinions that once had power over you begin to fade into background noise. You don't need to convince anyone that you're worthy. You already are. You don't need to wait for their permission. You already have your own.

So let them think what they think. Let them be confused. Let them stay where they are while you grow where you're going. Because the people who are meant to be in your life—the ones who truly see you—don't need an explanation. They just recognize the light in you and say, *I see it, too.*

THE TRAP OF PERFECTIONISM

Let's just call this one out: Perfectionism isn't about high standards —it's also about fear. It's fear of criticism. Fear of rejection. Fear that if it's not flawless, then you're not worthy. But here's what perfectionism really does—it tricks you into holding everything hostage.

Because if you never finish the thing—never send the email. Never launch the business. Never share the post. Never say what you really want in that relationship—then no one can criticize it. No one can reject it. And you never have to face the pain of, "What if I'm not good enough?"

So you keep perfecting. Tinkering. Over-editing. Rewriting. Waiting for the right moment.

But let me ask you—how long have you been waiting? Perfectionism keeps your power locked in a cage. And self-judgment is the warden.

The truth is, people can't love what you don't share. You can't grow from work you never complete. And you can't expand into the person you're becoming if you're still stuck trying to please an imaginary critic who's never satisfied. You know how many times I've made a mistake in front of people? Tripped over a sidewalk in the middle of the day? Legs flying, full-on stumble. Did anyone laugh? Maybe. Did I? Definitely.

Because what are you gonna do? Hide from the sidewalk forever?

I used to make mistakes and then spiral—go into this deep well of overthinking and embarrassment and judgment. Now I trip, and I keep walking. Or I laugh. Or I shrug. Because mistakes aren't proof that you're a failure. They're proof that you're in motion. Failure isn't the opposite of success—it's just part of it. And when you start rewiring how you see failure, it becomes data, not identity. It becomes an experience, not a sentence.

So here's what I want you to start practicing—self-acceptance even in the midst of judgment.

Because the truth is, sometimes people *will* judge you. Sometimes you'll fall short of your own expectations. Sometimes you'll try, and it won't land. But here's what matters: Can you hold compassion for yourself in those moments? Can you say, *"I still love me?"* Can you keep going, even when it's messy?

Start there. Start by talking to yourself like you would a best friend. Start with these daily practices I've used to break the grip of self-judgment:

The mirror check-in:
Look at yourself in the mirror every morning and say one kind, real thing. Not fluffy. Not fake. Something true. *"You're doing your best today." "You showed up even though you were scared." "I'm proud of you for trying."*

The three grace points:
At the end of the day, write down three moments where you could have judged yourself but instead, you chose grace. Maybe it's when you got distracted mid-task and forgot what you were saying, or didn't speak up even though you had something to share, or you needed rest, so you let the dishes sit in the sink. Write it. Release it. Let it be okay.

Celebrate the imperfect win:
Every time you do something before it's perfect—that's a win. Post the thing. Send the message. Speak up before you feel fully ready. Let that be your rebellion.

You need to be in the arena, not perfecting your armor in the locker room forever. You can trip over your own shoelaces and still be powerful. You can mess up and still move forward. You can feel judged—and still love yourself through it. Because the goal was never perfection. The goal is freedom.

Dealing with Criticism

Something in this process that is hard to overcome: there's a particular kind of sting that comes from receiving criticism when you've poured your heart into something. Especially when it's from someone close to you. Someone whose voice has shaped you. Someone you wanted to be proud of you.

I remember when I first shared my women's group vision with my dad. I was so excited. I had this fire inside me, a clear sense of purpose and direction. And I wanted to share it with him—not just because he's my father, but because he had created something similar in this same space many years ago. A men's group that had lasted decades.

So I shared my plans, my heart, and the book I was working on. And then ... he started correcting me. Offering his opinions. Giving suggestions on how I should do it differently.

And I spiraled. Not because what he said was wrong or even harsh—but because I wasn't grounded in my own truth yet. I hadn't built up that layer of self-trust strong enough to hold my vision steady in the face of someone else's input.

And that's what criticism can do if we're not anchored. It can shake you. Make you question yourself. Make you shrink. But here's what I've learned since then: Other people's opinions are just information. That's it. Not commandments. Not prophecy. Not truth.

Information.

And it's up to you to decide what you do with it.

Maybe you take a piece of it and integrate it. Maybe you say, "*Thank you for sharing,*" and keep it moving. Maybe you set a boundary, change the subject, or just let it slide off your skin. Because when you are deeply aligned with your truth—when you know your values, your mission, your heart—criticism doesn't have the same power. It might sting for a moment, but it doesn't stick.

And that's the foundation of unshakable self-trust. It's not about ignoring feedback or pretending you don't care. It's about knowing who you are so fully that other people's doubts can't take root in your soil.

Let's explore some daily practices for staying grounded in your authenticity:

The Alignment Check

Every morning, ask yourself:

- What do I believe in?

- What matters most to me today?

- What am I creating or contributing that feels true to who I am?

This is about staying rooted in your why so when the winds of criticism come through, it doesn't uproot you.

Criticism as a Mirror

When you receive feedback—especially the kind that triggers something—pause and reflect:

- Is there truth in this for me?

- Or is this reflecting the other person's fears, limitations, or preferences?

Sometimes criticism says more about their worldview than your worth. Discernment is key.

Talk to Your Inner Voice First
Before seeking validation, go inward:

- What do I think?

- What feels right to me?

- Would I still choose this path even if no one else approved?

When you build the habit of consulting your own voice before others', you create an unbreakable inner compass.

Anchor Phrases
Create a few personal mantras that bring you back to yourself. Not fluffy affirmations but grounding truths.

- "I know who I am."

- "I trust the pace and direction of my path."

- "I can receive feedback without losing myself."

Repeat them when the world gets loud.

Release with Intention

When you feel yourself spiraling, say it out loud or write it down: *"This is not mine to carry."*

And then let it go.

Because sometimes you need a physical or verbal signal to remind yourself you don't have to hold onto the weight of everyone else's thoughts. Standing strong in your truth is a daily practice. It's not about being unshakable all the time. It's about being able to return to yourself again and again—after the sting, after the spiral, after the moment of doubt. You're not required to prove your worth. You're just asked to live it. Loudly. Softly. Joyfully. Honestly. But—*Your* way.

YOUR LIFE IS YOURS

Really—you are free. That's the truth they never teach you in school. The truth that gets buried under years of trying to be liked, trying to be good, trying to fit into whatever version of life you were told was acceptable. But here's the reminder, in case no one has ever said it clearly to you: *Your life is yours.* That's not up for debate. No one else gets to live it. No one else has your vision, your voice, your knowledge. No one else has your laugh, your weird quirks, your brilliant perspective. And no one else has the right to decide what's *too much* or *not enough* for you.

You get to decide.

You get to shape this life in the way that feels honest to your soul —even if it doesn't make sense to anyone else. Even if people have opinions. Even if they don't understand. Because that's not your job. That was never your job. Your job is to live. Fully. Bravely. Unapologetically. To show up in your skin and know that your presence is not a problem. To be proud of yourself without permission. To make bold decisions without explanation. You don't owe anyone a watered-down version of your truth.

So, take the long walk in the direction of what lights you up. Let them think what they want. Let the judgment come and pass like clouds. Let go of the pressure to prove or explain. You're not here to be understood by everyone. You're here to be you. And if that ruffles feathers, or stretches expectations, or inspires someone else to break free, too—then good. Let it. Because a free woman gives other women permission to liberate themselves.

So, breathe deep. Stand tall. Trust your heart. And walk forward, not with armor, but with radiance.

You're free. You always were. Now go live like it.

CHAPTER 19: PURPOSEFUL LIVING

Falling in Love With Your Own Life

WE'VE EXPLORED THE ART of self-dating—how to build a relationship with yourself that makes your life feel rich and full. But the real magic happens in the day-to-day. A fulfilling life isn't just made up of big, exciting experiences—it's built in the ordinary, in the way you move through your routines, in the rhythm of your life. What if, instead of rolling over and groaning at your alarm, you felt a quiet thrill in your chest because you get to live another day in a life that feels like it was made for you? This is what purposeful living creates.

Most of us wake up and go through the motions, not realizing that our daily habits are quietly shaping our entire existence. It's easy to believe that a meaningful life is something we'll arrive at once we hit a milestone—the dream job, the perfect relationship, the right number on the scale. But what if fulfillment isn't waiting for you some day in the future? What if it's being built, moment by moment, in the way you move through *today*? Purposeful living isn't about filling your calendar with productivity. It's about creating a rhythm that brings you joy. It's about knowing when to push forward and when to rest, when to challenge yourself and when to surrender. It's about crafting a life that feels like an extension of who you truly are—one that honors both your ambitions *and* your well-being.

Too often, we chase external markers of success, thinking they'll bring us fulfillment. But remember: the real magic isn't in how your life looks—it's in how it feels. It's in the small, intentional choices that shape your days, the rhythms that ground you, the moments of joy you allow yourself to savor. The way the morning light filters through your window. The first deep breath before the day begins. The simple rituals that make you feel like you.

THE POWER OF INTENTIONAL LIVING

Intentional living is about designing a life that feels like home. One that meets you where you are, supports you through every season, and makes you fall in love with the simple act of waking up in the morning. Because when you wake up every day excited to live, that's when you know you've built something truly extraordinary. At the heart of this is sacred structure—the understanding that discipline and freedom aren't opposites but *partners*. Structure isn't meant to confine you; it's meant to hold you, to create the foundation for a life that feels expansive rather than restrictive. When you create intentional rituals and routines, you free yourself from the weight of decision fatigue. You move through your days with ease, not because your routines are rigid but because they are yours.

So, what if you started looking at your routines as sacred? What if every small act—your morning coffee, the way you move your body, the way you speak to yourself—became a deliberate choice to create the life you *want* to be living? What if, instead of just structuring your day, you infused it with meaning? That's the difference between a routine and a ritual. Routines keep life moving. They help us stay organized, efficient, and productive. But rituals? Rituals bring us home to ourselves. They take the ordinary and transform it into something intentional, something alive with purpose. The distinction is subtle but powerful:

- Routine is what you do. Ritual is how you do it.

- Routine is brushing your teeth. Ritual is taking a deep breath, feeling gratitude for the body that carries you, and then beginning your day.

- Routine is drinking your coffee. Ritual is savoring the warmth, allowing it to be a moment of stillness before the world rushes in.

So, which one do you need? The truth is, *it's both*. The structure of routine gives your day rhythm, but the intention of a ritual gives it meaning. When you blend the two, you create a life that feels both grounded and alive.

The way you begin your morning influences everything. How you show up for the first moments of your day sets the tone for how you carry yourself, how you make decisions, and how you interact with the world. This isn't about forcing yourself into rigid discipline —it's about finding what feeds you. What makes you feel centered, awake, and connected to yourself and your life? What small, simple acts make you excited to step into the day?

For me, it's journaling first thing. A deep breath. A few quiet moments of meditation and stretching. Then I practice my French, a small commitment to learning, before making my coffee—but not before drinking a full glass of water. Every part of my morning is intentional, designed to nourish me before I pour my energy into anything (or anyone) else.

Your sacred ritual doesn't have to look like mine. It doesn't have to be long or complicated. It just has to matter to you. A well-designed daily practice isn't just about getting things *done*—it's about creating touch-points of presence throughout your day. These small moments remind you that you are here, you are alive, and your time is sacred.

Try creating yours:

Morning grounding
How do you want to feel today? What's one small thing that would support that feeling?

Midday reset
A walk, a stretch, a deep breath—something that interrupts autopilot mode and brings you back to the present.

Evening closure
How do you want to end your day? A gratitude practice? A moment of reflection? Something that signals to your body and mind that you are complete for the day.

It's easy to wait for the big moments—vacations, celebrations, milestones—to feel alive. But true radiance comes when you find meaning in the smallest things. What if washing the dishes became a moment of mindfulness, a pause in your day rather than a chore? What if your daily walk became a moving meditation, a way to reconnect with yourself and the world around you? What if every sip of water, every deep breath, every small act was a reminder that you are here, in this body, in this moment? Purposeful living isn't about grand transformations. It's about noticing. About choosing. About making even the smallest parts of your day *yours*.

SEASONS OF ENERGY

We all know that energy isn't constant. We often expect ourselves to perform at the same level every single day, but life isn't linear—it moves in rhythms, cycles, and seasons. Just like nature, we have times of expansion and times of retreat, moments of high energy and moments where we need deep rest. Purposeful living isn't about forcing yourself to be consistent; it's about learning to work with your natural ebb and flow instead of against it.

Just as the world around us shifts with the seasons, so do we. Have you ever noticed how different your energy feels in the height of summer compared to the quiet of winter? In the summer, when the days are long, I wake up naturally with the sunlight. The early morning birdsong makes me feel refreshed, and I crave time outside —whether it's a run at sunrise, paddle-boarding in the evening, or simply taking my yoga practice outdoors. My days feel more open, more expansive.

In the winter, when the darkness lingers, I'm drawn to slower, more introspective rituals. Cozying up with a book, lighting candles, making sure I'm intentional about nurturing my mental health. It's a season of restoration, of gathering my energy rather than constantly expending it.

When we acknowledge these shifts, we stop fighting ourselves. We stop expecting summer-level energy in the middle of winter. Instead, we learn to adapt, designing our routines to support us rather than constrain us. Rather than rigid routines that demand the same output every day, what if your structure was flexible? What if you designed your life to evolve with you instead of feeling like you're constantly failing to keep up?

This means:

- Giving yourself permission to do less when you need rest without guilt.

- Leaning into moments of high energy and letting yourself expand without burnout.

- Crafting routines that can shift depending on the season—both the literal seasons of the year and the seasons of your life.

Some seasons are for growth and momentum. Others are for slowing down and integrating. The key is recognizing where you are and giving yourself the grace to move accordingly.

CREATING A FRAMEWORK

Let's create a toolbox so you're able to build a framework of purposeful living for yourself:

1. **Create rituals that support your nervous system.**
   Your nervous system is the foundation of emotional resilience. When it's fried, your emotions feel louder and more overwhelming. When it's regulated, you're more grounded and clear-headed.

   Daily rituals like:

   - Breathwork (even just three deep breaths in a moment of tension)

   - Taking a walk without your phone

   - Drinking water before reacting

   - Journaling your thoughts instead of spiraling

   - Creating space to pause before responding

   These small acts teach your body: *I am safe. I can handle this.*

2. **Talk to yourself like someone you love.**
   This sounds simple. It's not. Most of us talk to ourselves in ways we would never speak to someone we care about.

   You're going to mess up. You are going to have moments where you snap, freeze, cry, avoid, or say the wrong thing.

That doesn't mean you've failed. That means you're human. Building emotional resilience means creating an internal environment where you are safe to be imperfect—and still worthy.

Start small: When something goes wrong, say, *"I'm doing the best I can right now."* And let that be enough.

3. **Stay connected to what centers you.**
   The most resilient people I know aren't always the strongest —they're the most rooted in something deeper than the moment. Maybe that's your values. Your purpose. Your faith. Your body. Your breath. Your people.

   When life shakes you, go back to what steadies you. Write it down. Keep it close. These are the anchors that keep you from drifting too far from yourself. You're not meant to be unshaken. You're meant to know how to come back to yourself.

You've been through more than you give yourself credit for. There were moments you didn't think you'd make it through and yet here you are. Still breathing. Still becoming. Emotional resilience isn't about avoiding pain or pretending you're okay when you're not. Real resilience is quieter than that. Softer. It's in the moment you choose to feel instead of flee. The moment you offer yourself grace instead of judgment. The moment you get up—not with force, but with faith.

This isn't about becoming a version of you that doesn't get hurt. It's about remembering that when you do, you know how to heal. That you have the tools. That you have the wisdom. That you have the strength—even when you forget you do.

So to end, let's reflect:

- When was a time you didn't think you'd make it through but you did?

- What did that teach you about yourself?

- What have you survived that has shaped your strength?

- And how can you honor that version of you—the one who rose?

Write it down. Speak it out loud. Remember it. You're not just surviving anymore. You're rising with intention. And every time you do, you're rewriting the story of your strength. You are the evidence of your own resilience.

FINDING YOUR OWN RHYTHM

Your ideal rhythm is unique to you. Maybe your energy flows differently with the moon cycles, or maybe you find that your creativity peaks at night while your physical energy is highest in the morning. Pay attention. Track how you feel. Notice the patterns in your motivation, your focus, your desire for rest. When you stop trying to force yourself into an artificial sense of consistency and instead honor the natural rhythm of your life, everything begins to feel more effortless. Life doesn't have to be a constant push—it can be a dance, moving in harmony with the seasons, the cycles, and you.

Most people think of discipline as something restrictive—rules, obligations, and rigid schedules that take the joy out of life. But true discipline, when done with intention, is the opposite. It creates freedom. When you build habits that support you, life feels lighter. You don't waste energy debating whether or not to do something— you simply do it. You're not weighed down by unfinished tasks, nagging thoughts, or the mental clutter of procrastination. Instead, you move through your days with ease, knowing that your systems are holding you up rather than holding you back.

Have you ever noticed how much mental space undone tasks take up? The dishes in the sink. The laundry waiting to be folded. The email you meant to send yesterday. Every time you see them, you think, *I need to do that,* and it drains your energy—even if you're not actively doing anything about it.

But what if, instead of letting things pile up, you handled them now?

- Wash the dish immediately after eating. No lingering mess. No extra stress. Just a clean, open space.

- Put away your clothes as soon as they're dry. No piles waiting to be dealt with later. No running out of socks and having to rummage for a pair.

- Respond to that message or email right when you think of it. No mental load of remembering to get back to it.

This is what discipline really does—it removes unnecessary friction. Instead of carrying around the weight of unfinished tasks, you create instant clarity and space for what truly matters.

Every time you follow through on what you said you would do, you prove to yourself that you can be relied on. That you're someone who keeps promises—to others, yes, but most importantly, to yourself. And that's where confidence comes from. If you tell yourself, "I'm going to the gym today," and then you don't, you subtly teach yourself that your word doesn't matter. That what you say isn't final. But when you show up—even if it's just for five minutes—you reinforce the belief that you're someone who follows through.

If starting is the hardest part, make it easy:

- Set a two-minute timer. Commit to just beginning. Whether it's stretching, writing, reading, or practicing an instrument, once you start, momentum will usually carry you forward.

- Remove the friction. Want to journal in the morning? Keep your notebook by your bed. Want to work out? Lay out your clothes the night before. Make the choice obvious and effortless.

This isn't about forcing yourself. It's about showing up—even in the smallest ways—so that over time, discipline becomes second nature. Discipline doesn't mean micromanaging every moment of your day. The goal isn't to squeeze every ounce of productivity out of life—it's to create enough structure so that there's room for spontaneity.

When your essential habits and systems are in place, you don't have to worry about falling behind or losing momentum. Instead, you create space for unexpected joy. Spontaneous bike ride? You can say yes, because you've already handled what needed to be done. Last-minute adventure? No stress, because your life isn't in chaos. A slow, unstructured afternoon? Enjoy it fully, without guilt, because you know your foundation is solid.

Discipline isn't about restriction—it's about freedom. Freedom from mental clutter. Freedom from unfinished tasks. Freedom to fully live—because you're not carrying the weight of everything undone.

The Practice of Joy

Joy isn't something we stumble upon—it's something we cultivate. It's woven into the small moments of our day, hidden in the ordinary, waiting for us to notice. But because of the way our brains are wired, we're often too busy scanning for problems to truly see it. Our survival instincts are strong. The human mind naturally fixates on threats, uncertainties, and potential dangers. This negativity bias once kept us alive, but now it often keeps us distracted from joy.

And beyond that, many of us don't allow ourselves to feel joy at all. We treat it like a reward we haven't yet earned, a luxury to indulge in once everything else is done. But joy isn't something we can postpone and expect to revisit later—it lives in the now. That fleeting burst of beauty, that laugh, that warm sunlight moment on your skin—it will pass whether or not you let it in. You don't get to come back and re-feel it. You either embrace it now, or it's gone. So, if we want more joy in our lives, we have to train ourselves to linger in it.

This is the power of lingering in joy:

When you see something beautiful, pause.
Take it in for just a few extra seconds. Let the colors, the textures, and the feeling settle into your body.

When you smile, hold it for a moment longer.
Notice how it feels. Let the warmth spread.

When something makes you laugh, laugh fully.
Let yourself feel the joy instead of moving on too quickly.

When you experience delight, stay in it.
Savor the sip of coffee. Absorb the feeling of fresh air on your skin. Listen fully to your favorite song.

At first, this might feel unnatural—almost like you're forcing yourself to hold onto happiness. But over time, these small moments add up. The more you embrace joy, the more it shows up for you. The key to daily joy is making those moments a priority. What makes you feel most alive? What are the moments that light you up?

- If dancing fills you with energy, start your morning with a dance party in your kitchen.

- If being outside refreshes you, schedule time to walk, hike, or simply sit in nature.

- If creativity fuels you, carve out time for writing, painting, or music.

- If deep conversations make you feel connected, intentionally reach out to people who inspire you.

The more you integrate these joy-filled activities into your routine, the less life feels like something you're just getting through and the more it feels like something you're actively creating.

FINDING INSPIRATION

There will be days when life feels uninspired. When the routine feels dull. When joy feels distant. That's why it helps to have a go-to list of ways to reset.

I keep a running list of things I can do when I feel bored, restless, or uninspired—some at home, some out in the world. I categorize them so I don't have to think too hard when I need a shift in energy. Here are some of my examples:

Movement
Go for a run, take a dance class, stretch, try a new workout.

Rest & Reflection
Meditate, journal, take a bath, listen to calming music.

Creativity & Growth

Read a new book, try a new recipe, learn something new, start a DIY project.

Adventure & Play
Visit a new coffee shop, go on a spontaneous day trip, explore a part of town I've never been to.

By having this list ready to go, I don't get stuck in indecision when I need a change. I just pick something—and that small action is usually enough to shift my entire mood.

Try out this Exercise: **Try creating your own list. What categories does yours contain? How many of these items have you never done before? How many of them excite you just thinking about doing them?**

At the heart of it all, this is about more than just routines, discipline, or daily joy. It's about crafting a life that feels good to live in—not just from the outside, but from the inside out. A life where you wake up each morning with a quiet excitement, knowing that the way you move through your days is fully aligned with who you are and who you're becoming. The truth is, joy lives in the margins of ordinary life, waiting for us to notice it in the small decisions we repeat each day. When we train ourselves to notice joy, linger in it, and create more of it, life starts to feel richer, lighter, and more alive. And isn't that what we're all really searching for?

You don't have to overhaul your entire life overnight. You just have to start.

- Start by listening to what feels right for you.

- Start by creating space for what lights you up.

- Start by showing up for yourself in small ways, over and over again.

And one day, you'll look around and realize you've built a life that doesn't just look good on paper—but one that feels like home.

So, here's your invitation:

- What if every morning felt like an opportunity instead of an obligation?

- What if, instead of going through the motions, you designed your days with purpose?

- What if you approached life with the quiet confidence that you are not just existing, but truly living?

It starts with intention. With presence. With choosing, moment by moment, to create a life you want to wake up to. A life that feels like yours.

CHAPTER 20: THE RADIANT WOMAN FRAMEWORK
Unlocking Your Fullest Expression

RADIANCE ISN'T a piece of clothing you put on. It's not a script you memorize, a posture you practice, or a persona you step into when the world is watching. It's something you become. And more than that, it's something you already are.

For too long, we've been taught that confidence is something we perform, that power is something we prove, and that self-worth is something we earn. But here's the truth: Radiance isn't something outside of you—it's already within you, waiting to be uncovered.

This chapter isn't about giving you another self-improvement checklist. You don't need more rules, more things to "fix" about yourself, or more ways to curate the "perfect" version of you. This is about unlocking the most powerful, unapologetic, fully-expressed version of who you already are.

The Radiant Woman Framework used in this chapter is not about adding more. It's about stripping away the conditioning, the expectations, the quiet compromises you've made just to fit in. It's about stepping out of performance and into presence. Because a truly radiant woman doesn't need to perform confidence—she *is* confidence. She doesn't need to seek validation—she is the validation. She doesn't need permission to be herself—she simply is.

In this chapter, we break it all down—the roadmap to stepping into your fullest expression, how to integrate these principles into your leadership, relationships, and daily life, and most importantly, how to move beyond passive self-improvement into full embodiment. This is about owning your power, not just conceptually but in every room you walk into, in every word you speak, and in every decision you make. The journey to radiance isn't about becoming someone new. It's about coming home to yourself. Let's begin.

WHAT IS RADIANCE?

I remember the first time I saw her—a woman who embodied radiance. Not on a screen. Not behind a filter. Not perfectly posed or chasing attention. She was just … in the world. Waiting for her coffee. Talking to someone in the checkout line. And still, she turned heads. Not because of what she wore, but because of how she *wore herself*. There was something in the way she stood—rooted, relaxed, unbothered. Something in how she spoke—clear, kind, not rushed. Something in the way she saw you—not as someone to impress but as someone to connect with. You could feel her presence before she said a word. And when she did speak, you leaned in—not because she was loud, but because she was undeniable. She felt … full. Like she had nothing to prove. Like her power didn't come from performance; it came from being deeply, truly herself. And you didn't just want to be her; you wanted to know her. To sit next to her. To be in her orbit. To understand how she could be so at ease, so clear, so vibrant. She didn't shrink. She didn't puff up, either. She just was. And when she looked at you, you didn't feel judged or overlooked. You felt seen. Like you mattered.

A radiant woman isn't performing—she is embodying. She walks through life as her fullest self, unapologetically and powerfully, because she is no longer tethered to self-doubt, old narratives, or societal expectations that ask her to shrink. Instead, she owns her space, moves with confidence, and invites others to do the same.

That's the kind of radiance we're talking about here. Not just external glow but the inner fire of a woman who's come home to herself. A woman who leads, loves, speaks, and moves from deep alignment. She may be rare—but not mythical. She's rare *because* she's real, and most people haven't yet dared to live that fully. But you can. You already carry the same spark. The question is: *are you ready to fan it into flame?* This radiance is something you cultivate, step by step, as you align with your most authentic, empowered self.

That's where *The Radiant Woman Framework* comes in. This framework is a roadmap—a guide to help you reflect, align, integrate, and evolve. It is built on these core pillars of radiance:

Self-Expression
Living and speaking your truth without fear or hesitation.

Self-Acceptance
Embracing every part of yourself, including the parts you once hid.

Self-Empowerment
Stepping fully into your personal power and claiming your life as your own.

Self-Respect
Honoring your boundaries, needs, and desires.

Community & Connection
Cultivating meaningful relationships rooted in authenticity and vulnerability.

When these elements come together, radiance is inevitable. It is not just about feeling confident—it's about becoming unshakable. This framework is designed to guide you through the transformation from simply existing to fully embodying your radiance. Each step builds upon the next, leading you toward a life of authenticity, confidence, and deep fulfillment.

The R.A.D.I.A.N.C.E. Framework

R – Reflect: The Foundation of Self-Awareness

Before you can *become*, you must first *see*.

I used to mistake approval for identity. If people liked me, if they validated me, if I was useful or impressive or chosen, then I must be doing something right. But I started to notice something strange. I was in rooms full of people who admired me, and I still felt invisible. Not because they weren't looking at me, but because *I* wasn't looking at me. I had built an entire version of myself around what I thought would be lovable. And I'd never paused to ask, *But do I even love this version?*

Reflection started in tiny ways. In the way I felt exhausted after certain conversations. In the quiet moments, walking alone when I first moved to Olympia, wondering why I still didn't feel like myself. In the realization that I was still trying on different faces, hoping one of them would finally feel like home.

But what shifted everything was this: *I started catching glimpses of the real me.* In my unfiltered laughter. In the things I didn't say out loud but felt deeply true. In the relief I felt when I stopped performing—even just for a minute. I didn't discover who I was all at once. I recognized her in contrast—in the spaces where I finally felt aligned and in the ones where I didn't. That was when I realized: I hadn't lost myself. I'd just stopped looking. And now, I was ready to see.

Reflection is about uncovering the stories you've been telling yourself, the beliefs you've inherited, and the ways you've shaped yourself to fit into spaces that were never meant for you. Self-awareness is the foundation of transformation. When you reflect deeply, you reclaim the truth of who you are.

To begin your path in Reflection, let's explore these thoughts:

- What narratives have you absorbed about your worth?

- What identities have you worn to be accepted?

- Where have you been holding yourself back?

A – *Align*: Living in Full Integrity with Yourself

Radiance requires alignment—your values, desires, and actions all must match.

For a long time, I didn't know who I was outside of proximity. I didn't just adapt to the people around me. I *absorbed* them. Their passions became mine. Their routines, my structure. Their preferences quietly replaced my own.

Most of the time, it was a man. And being close to him felt like an identity. If he loved it, I loved it. If he was happy, I was okay. I wore their lives like costumes. And the scariest part? *I didn't even know I was doing it.* I thought I was just being easy to love. But underneath it all, I was disappearing. I stopped asking what I wanted. I stopped listening to the small voice inside that whispered, *This doesn't feel like you.* I kept saying yes when my body said no. I kept shape-shifting, hoping someone would finally choose me. But even when they did, I still felt hollow. Because what they were choosing wasn't me. It was the version I'd sculpted to be acceptable to them.

And when the relationship ended? I wasn't just heartbroken. I was lost. Like I'd handed over the map to myself and forgot to make a copy. That's when I realized how deep the misalignment had gone. And that radiance—real radiance—couldn't grow in that soil.

So I started asking real questions. *What are my values? What do I stand for, even when no one's watching? What do I love, even when no one else cares?* The answers didn't come fast. I had to experiment. To try things on. Some things felt awkward, forced. But others landed like truth in my bones. And I learned to listen. I let go of what wasn't mine. I stopped editing myself to fit someone else's life. I stopped shrinking to be chosen. And as I aligned with myself, the exhaustion faded. The confusion quieted. And for the first time in a long time, I felt solid. Rooted. At home.

A woman out of alignment feels disconnected, lost, and exhausted because she is constantly performing rather than *being*. To step into radiance, you must bridge the gap between who you are and how you show up in the world. True confidence comes from this inner congruence—when your outer life is a reflection of your deepest truths.

To live a life of Alignment, this means:

- Choosing what truly fulfills you over what simply looks good on paper.

- Living in integrity with your values no matter how inconvenient it may be.

- Releasing anything that no longer serves your highest self.

D – Discover: Claiming Your Unique Light

Every woman has a unique radiance—a light only she can bring into the world.

But for most of my life, I didn't know what mine looked like. I had spent so long trying to blend in, shrink down, and belong that I forgot what it meant to *burn bright*. When I finally stopped performing for acceptance and let myself exist in the quiet of my own company, I realized I had no idea what I even liked. Not just what I was good at *but what made me come alive.*

So I made a list. A ridiculous, wonderful, sprawling list of every possible version of me I'd ever wondered about. Pottery. Improv. Salsa. Swing. Aikido. Piano. Poetry. I hunted down events on Meetup and Eventbrite, wandered into art classes and movement spaces, walked into rooms where I knew *no one*. Not to impress anyone. Not to build a resumé. But to discover who I could become when no one was scripting the scene but *me*.

And in those moments, in those awkward first steps and beginner's bruises and belly laughs, I felt joy. Not just happiness but *aliveness*. And I started to notice the patterns: which spaces felt like a full-body yes. Which ones woke up the parts of me I hadn't met before. I stopped asking, *What should I be doing?* and started asking, *What makes me feel like myself?* And slowly, the answers came. Not all at once. But enough to follow.

This was the beginning of discovering my light. Not as a role to play or a box to check but as a living, breathing expression of who I really am. A woman who plays. A woman who explores. A woman who is willing to be surprised by the brilliance that has always been waiting inside her. The more you lean into your authentic brilliance, the more magnetic you become.

Discovery is about reclaiming your essence—as yourself:

- What are you passionate about?

- What makes you feel most alive?

- What gifts do you bring to the world effortlessly?

I – *Integrate*: Embodying Self-Acceptance

Healing isn't just about uncovering wounds—it's about integrating the lessons you've learned.

For so long, I lived in a quiet war with myself—a constant undercurrent of shame, guilt, and self-judgment that shaped everything I did. I was chasing approval, hoping that if I just fixed this or became better at that, I would finally be enough. But no matter how hard I tried, there was always a part of me I was running from.

That part of me carried the wounds I was too scared to face: the mistakes I replayed in my mind, the voices that whispered I wasn't worthy, the shadowy places where I tucked away my truth so no one else would see it. It wasn't just about feeling imperfect. It was about feeling broken and unlovable. And that hurt ran deep, deeper than any accomplishment or external validation could reach.

Then this year, I started doing something that felt almost impossible: standing in front of the mirror every morning and saying, *I love you*. At first, the words felt like a lie. The woman staring back was a stranger, someone I didn't recognize or trust. I was groggy, unpolished, and vulnerable in ways I hadn't allowed before. But I kept showing up. Day after day, whispering those words, asking, *What do you need today?*

And slowly, painfully, I began to see her—the parts of me I'd hidden, denied, and judged. The guilt, the shame, the fear—they didn't disappear, but they stopped ruling me. I learned to say, *I see you. I hear you. You're still worthy of love.*

Integration wasn't about erasing the past or pretending it didn't hurt. It was about holding every fragment of myself—the light that shines bright and the shadows that linger quietly beneath. Learning to meet those parts with quiet compassion, to recognize the weight they carry, and yet, to offer them space to simply be.

There's a certain grace in allowing yourself to exist fully—without judgment, without the need to fix or hide. It's a tender kind of courage, this gentle acceptance, showing up for yourself in the raw, in the places you once wished to escape. And in that presence, the fractured edges begin to soften, and a deeper kind of wholeness takes root, not perfect, not polished, but utterly real. It's in this unfolding—the weaving together of all you are—that radiance quietly awakens. No longer a performance, no longer a mask, but a quiet, steady light, burning with the truth of your own story. And in that light, you find your breath again—unhurried, unguarded, finally free.

Radiance comes from wholeness, not perfection. A truly radiant woman has walked through the fire, faced her shadows, and come out on the other side with deeper wisdom, compassion, and strength. This is where you stop seeking outside approval and start living your life for yourself.

Integrating your life means:

- No longer running from your past but embracing the wisdom it gave you.

- Letting go of guilt, shame, and self-judgment.

- Fully accepting every part of who you are—light and dark, strength and softness.

A – *Awaken*: Activating Self-Empowerment

To awaken radiance is to step fully into your power.

I remember standing backstage with my clarinet in hand, heart pounding so loud I could hear it in my ears. I was about to walk out and perform a solo with the orchestra—completely from memory. No safety net. Just me, the lights, the stage, and every eye on me. The fear was real. What if I squeaked? What if I forgot a note? What if the silence after I finished wasn't admiration but disappointment? I didn't feel ready. But I walked out onto the stage anyway.

To awaken radiance is to step fully into your power—and for me, that awakening didn't arrive wrapped in certainty or confidence. It came through action. I learned to walk into rooms before I felt like I belonged there. To breathe through doubt. To play anyway. I had to act first. To stand in my power. To trust the moment and the music. To trust the universe would meet me exactly where I was—and most importantly, that I would meet myself there, too.

That night on stage, I didn't play perfectly, but I played from something deeper. And when it was over, I realized that power isn't built by waiting to feel fearless. It's built by walking forward anyway. This was a lesson my heart taught me slowly—not through applause or perfect performances, but by learning to trust who I am beneath the noise. Even when I don't have all the answers, I know now that I am enough. I'll find my way, note by note.

This kind of awakening doesn't happen all at once. It's found in small, everyday acts—saying yes to yourself, following the quiet pull of your own growth, taking the next brave step even when the outcome is unclear. Every time I pushed past hesitation, I wasn't just building confidence; I was reclaiming my power. Owning my space. Sharing my gifts without apology.

The shift from hiding to shining didn't happen in one bold moment. It happens in a thousand tiny ones. Choosing to trust. Choosing to act. Choosing to keep showing up. And now, when I walk into a room—even if my heart races—I know I belong. Not because I'm flawless. But because I'm fully myself. And that is the source of true radiance.

Awakening your power is the shift from:

- Seeking external validation → Trusting yourself completely
- Playing small → Owning your space unapologetically
- Hiding your gifts → Sharing them freely with the world

N – *Nurture*: Protecting Your Light Through Self-Respect

A radiant woman does not burn herself out to keep others warm. She honors her boundaries, protects her energy, and prioritizes her well-being.

I didn't always know how to do this. I remember the first time I consciously chose to end a friendship. It wasn't explosive; it was quiet, stretched out over time, but inside, I knew the connection no longer served me. Still, I wrestled with it. I ran through endless scripts in my head—what to say, how to say it, whether it was okay to say it at all. It felt terrifying. I was afraid of being mean, of hurting someone, of being "too much" or "too sensitive." But what I came to understand is that respecting someone else doesn't mean betraying myself. So I took a breath, and I said the words I needed to say. With kindness. With clarity. And when I did, something shifted—not just in that relationship, but in me. I didn't have to carry the weight of it anymore. I had listened to myself and honored what I heard.

That moment became a turning point. I started paying attention to what my gut was telling me—those subtle, inner cues that whispered: this feels off, or I need more of this, or I simply need rest. I learned that saying yes to everything wasn't noble; it was a slow erosion of my peace. Now, I give myself permission to cancel plans without guilt. To say, "I need today for me." To rest when I'm tired. To leave the phone unanswered and the inbox unchecked. I've learned that restoring myself isn't optional—it's vital.

And that self-respect extends outward, too. Like choosing to send the text instead of ghosting after a date. Being honest with someone rather than stringing them along. Saying, "Hey, you're not in alignment with what I'm looking for, but I wish you well," and meaning it. Because the people who are meant for me, they'll show up, and they'll stay. And I'll be ready for them because I'm not exhausted from chasing what isn't aligned.

Protecting my light means I get to offer the best, most full version of myself not just to others, but to me. My energy is sacred.

My peace is earned. And my boundaries are love in action—for myself first and for everyone who truly belongs in my life. When you nurture yourself, your light expands, rather than dims.

Embodying self-respect looks like:

- Saying no without guilt.

- Giving yourself rest without needing to earn it.

- Surrounding yourself with people who uplift and support your growth.

C – *Connect*: The Ripple Effect of Radiance

Radiance is not solitary—it is shared. A woman who stands fully in her power elevates those around her. She creates spaces for deep, meaningful connections because she herself is rooted in authenticity.

When I lived in Phoenix, I felt profoundly disconnected. I didn't have a close circle of women, or anyone, really, who helped me see myself more clearly. I was surviving, not growing—floating through the days without many mirrors, without deep conversation, without anyone to challenge me or hold space for me. And because of that, I stopped asking questions, not just to others but to myself.

When you're standing on your own, it's hard to imagine what's even possible. Your world becomes as small as your circle, and when your circle is just you, everything starts to shrink. Your vision, your creativity, your belief in what life can hold. There were so many things I didn't even know I could become simply because no one around me was becoming them, either.

And in that space, I realized something: if I wanted deeper connection, I had to be the one to create it. It started small. I stopped staring at my phone in line at the coffee shop and looked up instead. I smiled. I complimented someone on their jacket. I asked how their day was and meant it. And you know what happened? I watched their entire posture shift. I watched their eyes light up. It was just 30 seconds, maybe less, but something happened in both of us—an energetic exchange, a brief but powerful moment of being seen. And that moment didn't end with them. They carried that feeling into the next conversation, and the next.

That's how the ripple starts.

When I began showing up more authentically, when I led with curiosity instead of assumption, compassion instead of retreat, I didn't just begin connecting with others. I began feeling more connected to my own life. I felt more vibrant, more alive, more awake. And I finally started attracting people who were doing the same thing. Women who weren't afraid to go deep, to be vulnerable, to cheer each other on, to ask bigger questions and sit with real answers.

Those connections reminded me who I was. They invited me back into my power. They helped me remember that community doesn't just support radiance; it amplifies it. We all just want to be seen. And in a world that makes that harder every day, being the one who looks up—who really sees people—is a radical act. When you choose to connect, when you choose to truly witness another human being, you're not just offering them something. You're reminding them—and yourself—that we're never actually alone. This is how a radiant woman changes the world. With presence.

With curiosity. With connection. True radiance does not compete—it inspires.

Connection is about:

- Attracting relationships that reflect your highest self.
- Creating community from a place of wholeness.
- Lifting others as you rise.

E – *Evolve*: The Endless Becoming

Radiance is not a final destination—it is a continuous unfolding. A radiant woman is never static. She is always learning, growing, expanding into new versions of herself. She does not fear change—she welcomes it.

I used to think evolution was something that happened in big, dramatic moments. That transformation was some lightning-strike, life-altering event. That one day, I'd arrive at "the version" of me I was meant to be, and everything would settle there. But now, standing at the threshold of 40, I've never felt more alive—not because I've arrived, but because I finally understand I never will. And that is the most thrilling part.

For the first time in my life, I feel at peace with who I am and wildly curious about who I am still becoming. I love my life—truly love it. Not because it's perfect, but because it's mine. Because I've learned how to be in a relationship with myself. Because I trust myself now. I ask questions. I listen for new truths. I follow what lights me up, not out of desperation, but out of joy.

And the most beautiful part? I know there are decades ahead of me to keep unfolding.

There's a strange, powerful freedom that comes with that realization—that these next 40 years can be filled with even more love, more learning, more softness, and more strength. I don't crave a different life anymore. I crave a deeper life. Deeper understanding. Deeper connection. Deeper embodiment of the woman I already am and the woman I'm still yet to meet within myself.

This, to me, is radiance: not something you chase, but something you grow into. Over and over. Like shedding old skin and blooming again and again, without apology. I used to think transformation was a single event. Now I see it as a rhythm. A dance. A lifelong dialogue with my own spirit. And I can't wait to keep evolving, not because I need to become someone else but because I love the woman I am becoming more and more every day.

Evolution is the ultimate embodiment of radiance. It's trusting yourself to navigate the unknown. You embrace transformation as part of your power and know that your radiance will only deepen with time. This is how you step fully into your most authentic, magnetic self.

Radiance is not something you do. It is something you are when you let go of everything that is *not* you. And when you step into it fully? You don't just change your life—you change the world.

This is the difference between force and magnetism.

When a woman is in her radiance:

- She walks into a room and people feel her presence before they even see her.

- Her energy is open, warm, and grounded, making others feel safe, seen, and inspired.

- She does not seek validation—she already knows who she is.

- She moves through the world with ease, grace, and quiet confidence, leaving an imprint on everyone she meets.

TRUE RADIANCE ISN'T FAKE

True radiance is not about how you look, what you wear, or what you say—it is about how deeply you embody yourself. This is why true radiance cannot be faked.

And when you embody it?

- People trust you without even knowing why.

- Opportunities flow to you with ease.

- Relationships deepen effortlessly.

- You move through life with a sense of peace, knowing you are exactly where you are meant to be.

This is the power of a woman who has done the inner work—who knows herself, trusts herself, and fully claims her space in the world.

There is a stark difference between performing confidence and embodying presence. Many women are taught to fake confidence—

to stand tall, speak loudly, take up space, and project an image of self-assurance. But true confidence isn't about how you appear—it's about how you feel within yourself.

Performing confidence feels like:

- Forcing yourself to be outgoing even when you don't feel comfortable.

- Over-explaining your worth because you need others to validate you.

- Controlling how you are perceived because you're worried about being "enough."

- Speaking loudly but feeling insecure inside.

- Feeling exhausted from trying to "prove" yourself.

Embodying presence feels like:

- Rooting into who you are without trying to impress.

- Speaking with clarity, not out of a need to be heard, but because you trust your voice.

- Walking into a room with quiet self-assurance knowing your energy speaks for itself.

- Listening deeply, engaging fully, and connecting from a place of authenticity.

- Feeling at ease in yourself knowing you don't have to force anything.

Presence is the essence of true confidence. It is the ability to be fully here, now, in your body, in your truth, and in your power—without needing external validation to confirm it. When you stop performing and start embodying, you no longer have to prove your worth. You no longer have to fight to be seen. You simply exist in your fullness—and that is more than enough. *That* is radiance.

BUILDING A LIFE OF RADIANCE

Let's explore the main pillars to embodying radiance:

Pillar 1: Self-Expression – Unleashing Your Authentic Voice

Self-expression is the courage to take up space, to speak your truth without dilution, and to live confidently in alignment with who you really are. It is the rejection of performance, the shedding of people-pleasing, and the radical act of choosing yourself—over and over again.

For years, I was trapped in performance. I had built a version of myself based on who I thought I was supposed to be. I played the role of Chelsea, the one who stayed in the background, the one who didn't disrupt, the one who quietly molded herself to fit the expectations of those around her. But there was another woman inside of me—one who was bold, radiant, and fully alive. I just hadn't let her out yet. And then came the moment that changed everything.

I stood there on my wedding day, staring down a path I knew wasn't mine. I had spent years saying yes when I really meant no. But that day, I did something different. I said no—and for the first time, I truly said yes to myself. That decision was the moment I chose my own voice over the noise of expectation.

And from there, my life exploded into color. I bought my own house. I moved to a new city. I made friendships that felt like home.

I started speaking my truth, not what I thought others wanted to hear. I became myself. That one moment of radical self-expression—the moment I stopped shape-shifting and started owning my own narrative—set off a ripple effect that changed everything. And this is the power of stepping into your voice. Because when you finally stop silencing yourself, you start hearing yourself clearly for the first time.

Owning your voice isn't just about big, life-altering moments—it's about the daily choices that affirm who you are. Here are some daily practices to help you strengthen and unleash your authentic self-expression:

Say the thing you truly mean.
Every day, practice speaking your truth—even in small ways. If you don't want to go to an event, say no. If you love someone, tell them. If you have an opinion, share it. Make honesty your default.

Stop apologizing for your existence.
Replace "Sorry, but ..." with "This is what I believe." Stand by your words without feeling the need to soften them to make others comfortable.

Write freely without filters.
Journal every morning with complete rawness. Let yourself write what you actually think, feel, and desire—without editing, censoring, or worrying about what someone else might think.

Express yourself creatively.
Whether through writing, speaking, movement, or art, find a medium that allows you to bring your internal world into the external one. Self-expression is not just about words; it's about creation.

Trust the version of yourself that doesn't need approval.
Before you say or do something, ask yourself: Would I still express this if I wasn't seeking validation? The more you listen to the voice inside of you—not the one shaped by external expectations—the stronger your authentic self becomes.

Practice saying no.
Every time you say no to something that doesn't align with you, you are saying yes to yourself. Let your no be a full sentence. No explanations, no justifications. Just trust that your boundaries are enough.

Speak from your body, not just your mind.
When you talk, notice where your voice is coming from. Is it anxious, rushed, seeking approval? Or is it grounded, certain, and coming from a place of truth? Let your voice flow from your whole being—not just the part of you that wants to be accepted.

Live in a way that makes you proud.
Self-expression is not just about words—it's about how you move, create, and exist in the world. Ask yourself: If I were fully, unapologetically myself, how would I show up today? Then, act accordingly.

Self-expression is not just a skill—it is an act of self-ownership. It is standing in the fullness of your truth, knowing that your voice is not too much, your presence is not too loud, and your authenticity is not something that needs to be filtered. When you own your voice, you own your life. And when you stop performing and start being— fully, freely, and without apology—you unlock the radiant woman that has always lived inside of you. This is your permission slip to take up space, to be heard, and to step into the power of your own expression.

Because when you do? The world doesn't just hear you. It *feels* you.

Pillar 2: Self-Acceptance – The Power of Embracing All of You

People can feel when someone is at war with themselves. That anxious, uncertain energy seeps into everything. But they can also feel the opposite—the grounded, magnetic presence of someone who is completely at peace with who they are. And the difference? Self-acceptance.

When you embrace yourself fully, you move through the world differently. You stop waiting for permission to exist. You don't need validation, because you already trust yourself. That is the kind of energy that draws people in. Self-acceptance isn't just about loving your best qualities—it's about embracing all of you. Your quirks. Your contradictions. Your failures. Your fears. The parts of you that still feel like a work in progress. The versions of you that made mistakes, that didn't know better, that you sometimes wish you could erase.

When you reject certain parts of yourself, you create resistance. You block your own energy. But when you integrate all of you, instead of fighting your insecurities, you acknowledge them and remind yourself that they don't define you. Instead of punishing yourself for the past, you honor it as part of your evolution. That is what true radiance looks like.

When I launched my first book, *In Search of Us*, about building women's circles, I was drowning in imposter syndrome. I had already built two successful women's groups—proof that I knew how to create spaces of connection—but my mind wouldn't let me own that truth. *Who do you think you are? What if no one reads it? What if people think you're ridiculous for writing this?* I hesitated. And in that hesitation, I felt the weight of every moment I had ever doubted myself. Every time I had dimmed my light to make others comfortable. Every time I had waited until I felt "ready" before stepping forward.

Then I realized I was waiting for permission that I didn't need. So, I walked through a door frame in my mind—one where I let go of needing to be "good enough." One where I chose to simply be. And in that moment, I stepped from Chelsea into Stella. And everything changed.

My energy lightened. My posture straightened. I exhaled fully, as if I had been holding my breath for years. I smiled—not because the fear was gone, but because I had decided it didn't get to run the show anymore. I accepted all of it—the doubts, the imposter syndrome, the nervous excitement—and still, I walked forward. Because I trusted myself.

That is what self-acceptance does. It shifts how you show up to your own life. It reminds you that even when you're scared, even when you don't have all the answers—you are still enough. Self-acceptance is not a destination. It's a daily practice—a conscious choice to meet yourself with kindness, over and over again.

Here's how you can cultivate radical self-acceptance every day:

Speak to yourself like someone you love.
Replace self-criticism with curiosity. Instead of *Why am I like this?* ask *What is this teaching me?*

Honor every version of yourself.
Thank the past versions of you for getting you here. They were doing the best they could with what they knew.

Stop waiting to be "ready."
Confidence doesn't come before action—it comes from action. Take the step now.

Trust your instincts.
You don't need permission to be who you are. You already know. Listen to yourself.

Let go of the need for approval.
Not everyone will understand you. Not everyone has to. You are not for everyone—and that's a good thing.

Hold space for your emotions instead of resisting them.
Feeling insecure? That's okay. Let it be there. It doesn't mean you're not worthy.

Own your uniqueness.
The things that make you different are your magic. Stop hiding them.

Remember: You are already whole.
You don't need to be fixed. You don't need to "improve" to be worthy. You are enough, right now.

A woman who fully accepts herself moves through the world differently. She does not shrink. She does not beg for validation. She does not hesitate to take up space. She is not waiting for someone else to crown her worthy—she already knows she is. And because of that, she radiates. And that kind of energy? It's undeniable.

Pillar 3: Self-Empowerment – Leading with Unshakable Confidence

There is a distinct energetic shift between waiting to be chosen and choosing yourself first. Most of us spend our lives seeking— seeking validation, seeking relationships, seeking opportunities, seeking approval. We hope to be noticed. We hope to be wanted. We hope that if we say the right thing, act the right way, or prove ourselves enough to someone, we will finally be chosen.

But true power doesn't come from being picked. It comes from choosing yourself first—from walking into a room without an agenda, without the need for validation, without the hunger to be seen. It's the energy of a woman who already knows her worth. She doesn't have to prove it. She doesn't have to announce it. She simply is.

This is the moment when you stop chasing and start being.

- You don't network out of desperation—you connect because you're genuinely curious.

- You don't enter relationships from a place of lack—you open yourself up from a place of wholeness.

- You don't cling to friendships that feel one-sided—you move toward the people who meet you where you are.

- You don't beg for opportunities—you create them.

When you choose yourself first, you shift from being the seeker to being the magnet. Your energy speaks before you do. You radiate a quiet confidence, an undeniable presence, a sense of fullness that requires no external validation. You are no longer trying to prove that you're enough. You know you are. And the world responds to that certainty.

Empowerment isn't about forcing outcomes or controlling situations. It's about standing—standing in your truth, standing in your values, standing in the energy of a woman who is grounded in herself. The world doesn't need more people who are performing for approval. It needs more people who are fully themselves.

There was a moment when I knew, without a doubt, that I was worth more than I was being given. It happened in my career when I realized that the work I was doing, the value I was providing, and the expertise I had built were far beyond what I was being compensated for.

So I asked for more. Not a small amount—a lot more.

I walked into the conversation with certainty. I didn't plead. I didn't over-explain. I simply stated what I knew to be true: I am worth more than this, and I would like to be compensated accordingly.

The answer was no.

Now, in the past, that no might have crushed me. It might have made me question my worth. It might have made me shrink back, accept less, and stay small. In that moment, I had a choice. I could shrink. I could accept what they told me—that I wasn't worth it. That this was all I could ever expect. That I should just be grateful.

But not this time.

This time, I didn't waver. I didn't argue. I didn't let their perception of my worth define me. I knew my value, whether they recognized it or not. So I shifted my energy. I stayed professional, I stayed composed, but I quietly made a decision: *I will not stay somewhere that does not see my worth.*

And I left.

I moved on, and in doing so, I created something far greater than what I had been asking for in that room. Because when you truly know your worth, you don't settle. You don't beg. You don't wait to be given what you deserve. You go and get it. That is self-empowerment. That is unshakable confidence.

> *Empowerment isn't something you "arrive" at—it's something you cultivate, moment by moment, choice by choice.*

Here's how to integrate self-empowerment into your daily life:

Decide Before You Enter the Room
Walk into every space already knowing your worth. Don't wait for someone else to validate it.

Detach from Outcomes
Whether it's relationships, work, or personal goals, stop clinging to how things should unfold. Do the work, show up fully, and trust that the right things will align.

Speak with Certainty
Not from a place of defensiveness, but from grounded confidence. Own your words. Own your decisions. Own your truth.

Make Decisions Based on Worth, Not Fear
When faced with a choice, ask yourself: *Am I making this decision because I truly want it? Or because I'm afraid of what will happen if I don't?* Choose from power, not scarcity.

Set—and Uphold—Boundaries
Your time, energy, and emotional well-being are precious. Honor them. Boundaries are not walls—they are acts of self-respect.

Surround Yourself with Empowered People

Energy is contagious. Be around those who also stand tall in their worth. Let their confidence remind you of your own.

Own the Space You Take Up

Literally and figuratively. Walk into rooms with presence. Speak without shrinking. Move through the world as if you belong— because you do.

Self-empowerment isn't just about what you do—it's about how you carry yourself. It's the decision, every single day, to choose yourself first. And when you do? The world doesn't just notice. It adjusts to you.

Pillar 4: Self-Respect – The Foundation of Worth and Boundaries

Self-respect is the quiet, unwavering knowing of your own worth. It is the foundation upon which confidence, boundaries, and self-trust are built. At its core, self-respect is not arrogance—it's alignment. It's not about proving anything to anyone; it's about moving through life in a way that honors your needs, desires, and standards without guilt, apology, or hesitation.

A woman who respects herself moves differently:

- She does not beg for attention, affection, or recognition. She knows she is already enough.

- She does not over-extend herself to be liked. She prioritizes her well-being.

- She does not let fear of rejection keep her in spaces that no longer align. She walks away with grace and certainty.

- She does not settle for breadcrumbs in love, friendship, or career. She waits for—and creates—what she truly deserves.

- She does not explain or justify her boundaries. She upholds them with quiet confidence.

Self-respect is about choosing yourself, not just when it's easy, but especially when it's hard. It's about standing firm in your worth when others try to diminish it, about walking away when something doesn't feel right, about trusting yourself enough to say: *This is not for me*—and knowing that something better will come.

For the longest time, I didn't know how to do that. I used to stay in relationships where I was barely tolerated, let alone cherished. I allowed myself to be breadcrumbed—the occasional sweet word or kind gesture tossed my way, just enough to keep me hanging on. And I would internalize the emptiness, thinking *What is wrong with me? Why doesn't anyone choose me? Why am I not enough?*

What I didn't realize was that I was teaching people how to treat me by the way I treated myself. I wasn't choosing myself. I wasn't standing up for myself. I wasn't even being kind to myself. I was so desperate to be loved that I kept abandoning myself just to stay in the room with partners, with friends, sometimes even with people who barely noticed I was there. And it wasn't until I hit a point of deep exhaustion—emotional, mental, spiritual—that I realized I couldn't keep living that way. Something in me broke open. Or maybe it broke free. I stopped asking why no one was loving me and started asking: *How am I loving me?* I began making different choices. I started showing up for myself the way I had always wished someone would. I spoke up. I set boundaries, shaky and uncomfortable at first, but I stopped tolerating the bare minimum. And every time I chose myself, it got a little easier. A little more natural. A little more powerful.

And the people around me started to shift, too. Some fell away—the ones who had benefited from my silence and self-abandonment. But others rose to meet me. They saw how I respected myself, and they followed suit. I had been waiting for someone to treat me like I was worthy. And all along, I had that power within me. I just had to go first.

Many of us are conditioned to believe that self-respect is selfish —that saying no, prioritizing our needs, or refusing to tolerate mistreatment makes us difficult, demanding, or unkind. But true self-respect is the opposite of selfishness. It is integrity. It is showing up for yourself in the way you show up for those you love. It is refusing to abandon yourself for the sake of being palatable to others.

When you respect yourself:

- You honor your own needs as much as you honor the needs of others.

- You stop waiting for permission to live the life you want.

- You let go of guilt for choosing yourself.

- You no longer tolerate people who drain, diminish, or disrespect you.

A woman who respects herself does not need to demand respect —she embodies it. She moves through the world in a way that commands it simply by existing in her fullness.

Daily Practices to Cultivate Self-Respect:

Set—and Uphold—Boundaries
Self-respect means drawing a line between what is acceptable and what is not. Define your boundaries clearly and hold them without hesitation or guilt.

Speak to Yourself with Kindness
Pay attention to your inner dialogue. Would you speak to a friend the way you speak to yourself? Treat yourself with the same grace and compassion you give others.

Stop Explaining Yourself
You do not owe the world justifications for your boundaries, choices, or decisions. A simple "no" is a complete sentence.

Choose Environments That Reflect Your Worth
Surround yourself with people, places, and experiences that uplift you. Do not stay where you are undervalued.

Walk Away from What No Longer Serves You
If something—whether a relationship, job, or habit—diminishes your energy and self-worth, release it. Staying in spaces that shrink you is the opposite of self-respect.

Prioritize Your Well-Being Without Guilt
Rest when you need to. Take care of your body. Honor your emotional needs. You do not have to earn rest, love, or care—you are inherently deserving of it.

Stand Firm in Your Standards
Do not lower your standards out of fear that you're asking for too much. The right people, the right opportunities, and the right experiences will meet you at your level.

Celebrate Yourself Daily
Acknowledge your wins, big or small. Validate yourself before seeking it externally. Recognize that you are already enough, exactly as you are.

Self-respect is not about proving your worth—it is about knowing it. And when you know your worth? The world rises to meet you.

Pillar 5: Community & Connection – Thriving in Authentic Relationships

Radiance does not exist in isolation—it expands when it is shared. A truly radiant woman is not just magnetic on her own; she uplifts, empowers, and inspires those around her. She doesn't hoard her light—she creates spaces where others feel seen, safe, and supported. This is the heart of true connection: a space where you can be fully yourself, without performance, without shrinking, without pretending to be anything other than who you are.

We live in a world that often glorifies independence to the point of isolation. But the truth is, we were never meant to do this alone. We *need* people. Not just one person—not just a romantic partner, a best friend, or a mentor—but a whole ecosystem of connection. Every person in our lives plays a unique role, offering different forms of support, wisdom, and companionship. Relying on one person for everything—whether a friend, partner, or family member —can create an imbalance. True community is built on many connections, each bringing something valuable to your life.

Deep, fulfilling relationships cannot be built on fitting in—they are built on belonging. And belonging only happens when you show up as your full, unapologetic self. True friendships, true love, and true belonging happen when you stop trying to be liked and start letting yourself be fully seen. Community is not just about proximity —it's about shared experiences, vulnerability, and the willingness to go deeper. The most meaningful relationships are not built on small talk but on shared stories, mutual support, and the courage to be real with one another.

A radiant woman doesn't seek approval—she seeks alignment. She doesn't chase friendships, relationships, or community; she attracts them by being who she truly is. And in doing so, she creates the kind of relationships that are not just fulfilling but deeply nourishing.

I used to think I was the only one feeling disconnected—like everyone else had their circles figured out, their people dialed in. But the more I started stepping into rooms with other women and actually talking to them—really talking to them—the more I realized we were all quietly craving the same thing: to be seen, to be heard, to be met without judgment.

When I started the women's groups, I wasn't trying to build a movement. I was just trying to create a space where we could be honest. But what happened in those rooms surprised me—not just how much people needed it but how instantly it started to heal something in them. And in me. I heard women share things they'd never said out loud before. I saw their shoulders drop, their walls soften, their eyes light up—not because someone gave them advice, but because someone witnessed them. That's when I knew this was bigger than just one group in one city.

So I started building more—more gatherings, more opportunities to connect outside of a circle and inside of life. Hikes. Music nights. Collaborations with other groups. Even my gym became a space to cultivate something deeper: not just physical strength, but emotional support, soul-level community. Because here's what I know now: true connection doesn't come from showing up as the best version of yourself. It comes from showing up as your real self —and giving others permission to do the same.

This is why spaces like women's circles, deep friendships, and intentional communities matter. They remind us that we are not alone. They provide a space to celebrate victories, navigate challenges, and be witnessed in our growth. When we allow ourselves to be open—to be seen in both our light and our struggles —we create deeper bonds. Because connection is not built on perfection. It's built on truth. Creating deep, meaningful relationships doesn't happen by accident—it's an intentional practice.

Here are ways to cultivate authentic connection in your daily life:

Show Up as Yourself
Let go of the need to impress. Be real. The right people will be drawn to your authenticity.

Create Spaces for Connection
Invite people in. Host a gathering, start a conversation, initiate plans. Don't wait for connection—create it.

Be Generous with Your Energy
Support others. Celebrate their wins. Offer kindness without expectation. Authentic connection is a two-way street.

Deepen Your Conversations
Move beyond surface-level talk. Ask real questions. Share your experiences. Be open to listening and being seen.

Don't Be Afraid to Be Vulnerable
The strongest connections are built on truth, not perfection. Let people see the real you.

Surround Yourself with the Right People

Seek out those who uplift, challenge, and inspire you. Let go of relationships that drain your energy.

Nurture Your Relationships
Connection requires effort. Reach out. Check in. Don't take the people you value for granted.

Trust the Process
Building community takes time. Keep showing up as yourself, and the right people will find you.

A radiant life is not lived in isolation—it's lived in connection. The more we allow ourselves to be seen, the deeper and more fulfilling our relationships become. And when we build a life surrounded by people who reflect our values, support our growth, and celebrate our radiance? That's when we truly thrive.

EMBODYING RADIANCE

With these five pillars—Self-Expression, Self-Acceptance, Self-Empowerment, Self-Respect, and Community & Connection—you create a life that radiates from the inside out. Self-respect ensures that you honor yourself. Community ensures that you are seen, held, and supported. And when these elements are woven together, you don't just shine—you illuminate the world around you.

Knowing these pillars is one thing. Living them is another.

This is the difference between understanding transformation and embodying it. It's easy to read about self-expression, self-acceptance, self-empowerment, self-respect, and deep connection. It's another thing entirely to live it—to integrate it into your identity so fully that it becomes second nature. True transformation isn't about constantly reminding yourself of who you are trying to be—it's about becoming her so completely that it no longer feels like effort.

A woman who has fully embodied her radiance doesn't need to seek attention—her presence speaks for itself. She doesn't need validation. She doesn't shrink, overcompensate, or contort herself to be liked. She walks into a room and takes up space without apology. Her energy is steady. She is fully in herself—not overthinking, not trying to prove anything, just being.

And people feel it.

Because true confidence is grounded, effortless, and magnetic. You can feel the difference between someone who is *performing* confidence and someone who *embodies* confidence. This isn't just about relationships or leadership or social situations—this framework applies to every part of life.

When you fully embody radiance:

- **You lead differently.** You trust yourself to make decisions and own your voice.

- **You love differently.** You don't settle. You build relationships based on truth, not need.

- **You create differently.** You stop holding yourself back from sharing your gifts.

- **You show up differently.** You move through the world with a deep sense of knowing who you are.

And most importantly, you continue evolving. Radiance is not something you achieve and then maintain—it is something you grow into more fully every day. The more you live in alignment with who you are, the more natural it becomes. Becoming the radiant woman you are meant to be is a daily practice. It's not about perfection—it's about small, consistent *toward moves* in the direction of the woman you are becoming.

Here's how you cultivate and embody radiance in your daily life:

Move Toward, Not Away
Every day, ask yourself: Am I making a choice that brings me closer to my most radiant self? If not, what is the next best move?

Live as Your Radiant Self
Embody her now. Speak like her. Stand like her. Make choices that align with her values.

Regulate Your Energy
Pay attention to how you feel in spaces, conversations, and situations. Radiance comes from self-trust, not forced positivity.

Practice Being Instead of Performing
Stop thinking about how you're being perceived. Just be.

Take Up Space
Whether it's the way you speak, sit, or express yourself—practice existing without shrinking.

Lead With Presence
Make eye contact. Pause before speaking. Let your energy fill the room before your words do.

Own Your Desires
Radiance comes from alignment. Stop apologizing for what you want.

Release the Need to Be Liked
Not everyone will understand you, and that's okay. Seek alignment, not approval.

Make Aligned Decisions
If it's not a full-body yes, don't force it. Trust your intuition.

Commit to Growth
Embodiment is a lifelong process. Stay open. Keep evolving.

LASTING TRANSFORMATION

Radiance is not a final destination. It is an ever-deepening state of being. And the more you live in full expression—the more you trust, accept, empower, and respect yourself—the more natural it becomes. This is the key to lasting transformation: You don't just think about it. You live it. *Every single day.*

When you reach this state, you don't ask for opportunities—you create them. You don't search for connection—it naturally forms around you. You don't hope to be valued—you embody worth, and the world responds in kind. This is the power of a woman who has fully stepped into herself.

I will never forget the night I led a women's group with the topic *Unpacking Self-Worth.* Up until that point, most of my gatherings had been small—five, maybe eight women. But that night, twenty-two women showed up. From the moment we began, I could feel it —this uncontainable, overflowing energy, like a wellspring rising up inside me, spilling out into the room. As each woman spoke, sharing thoughts they had once believed were theirs alone, the energy thickened with connection. *I didn't know I needed this. I'm so glad I showed up. Wait ... you feel that way too?*

It was pure expansion—a deep, embodied sense of belonging, of recognition, of shared truth. And as I looked around that room, I felt tears welling up because I knew. *I had created this.* I had brought these women together so they could feel this moment, so they could see themselves in each other. And in doing so, I had found a version of joy so profound, so full, that it felt like liquid bliss spilling through me. That night, I stopped questioning whether I was enough. I stopped wondering if my work had value. *I knew.*

This is what fulfillment is supposed to feel like. This is how radiance works—it's not something you hold inside; it's something that flows through you into the spaces you create, into the people you touch. And once you find that kind of joy, you realize it was never scarce. It was always here. It's in the way you show up, in the way you connect, in the way you choose to live in fullness, not lack. Radiance is abundance. And when you embrace it fully, it touches everything.

This is your moment. The world is waiting—not for a more polished version of you, not for the version that has it all figured out, but for the real you. The one who is ready to own her power, her presence, her radiance. So stop waiting. Stop seeking. Step in. Step into the fullness of who you are. Into the conversations that ignite you, the spaces that expand you, the life that is already yours to claim.

Let your energy speak before you do. Let your presence be a declaration. Live in your truth so fully that it creates permission for others to do the same. This is your power. Own it. Be it. And watch the world shift around you.

CHAPTER 21: LIVING YOUR RADIANT LIFE

Shining Fully and Unapologetically in Every Area of Life

RADIANCE ISN'T ABOUT being louder, brighter, more successful, or more productive. It's about being more of yourself—boldly, fully, and without apology. It's easy to say, *"Just be yourself,"* but are you actually doing that? Are you being yourself when you're dating? When you're leading? When you're uncomfortable? When you're trying to impress someone? Or are you slightly tweaking, slightly quieting, slightly shifting, just to make yourself a little more palatable?

Here's the truth: when you dim yourself to make others comfortable, you also dim the life that was meant for you. And this life—this radiant, extraordinary life—isn't going to show up if you're hiding behind who you think you should be. You're the only person you'll spend your entire life with. If you don't like who you are, if you don't feel free to be who you are, it doesn't matter what job you land, who you date, or what milestones you hit—it will never be fulfilling.

Radiance is an energy. It's a quiet kind of confidence that says, *"I know who I am, and I love her."* And that energy attracts what's meant for you. It opens every door. And you don't need to do more to earn it. You just need to return to yourself—again and again.

What follows isn't a call to become someone else but an invitation to return to yourself. To be more *you*. To live from your core. To stop waiting. To take your hands off the dimmer switch and let the world see you in your full light. So, let's begin, one last time.

SMALL STEPS

I remember the day I went to a local coffee shop with a chalkboard I'd made—just a simple sign that said something like, *"Let's talk. I'm here for conversation."* It was part of a personal challenge I'd given myself to connect more deeply, to be open, to stretch socially in ways that scared me. But when I got there, fear sat heavy on my chest. My heart raced. My palms were sweaty. The idea of actually placing the board on the table where people could see it—where they could judge me, ignore me, misunderstand me—felt unbearable.

I texted a friend.

I needed someone to coach me through it because even though it seemed small, it felt enormous. Not because of the board itself, but because of what it represented. Vulnerability. Exposure. The willingness to be seen for real. Slowly, breath by breath, my friend helped me through each step. Take the board out. Set it on the table. Turn it over. Sit with it. Put it upright and turn it so it faces the room.

I did.

I sat there for an hour. No one came over. No one struck up a conversation. But still I sat there with my coffee and my racing heart. But I wasn't ashamed. I wasn't defeated. I felt ... powerful.

Because radiance isn't just joy or confidence. It's the quiet courage to do the thing your soul is nudging you toward—even when no one claps, even when your voice shakes, even when you're alone with your coffee and your fear. That day, I didn't leave with new connections. I left with something better: a deeper connection to myself.

When was the last time you did something just because it lit you up? Not because it made sense. Not because it was productive. Not because it made you money or checked a box. But simply because it made your soul exhale and say, *"Yes. More of this."* Joy and creativity are not luxuries. They're lifelines to your radiance. They reconnect you to your essence—the part of you that isn't worried about being good enough, or doing it right, or having it all figured out. Radiant women let themselves play. Radiant women let themselves wonder. Radiant women listen to what lights them up—*and then they follow it.*

So many of us stopped playing a long time ago. We got busy. We got serious. We got responsible. And somewhere along the way, we forgot how much magic we had access to in the little things. In dancing barefoot in the kitchen. In painting badly. In taking ourselves on a solo date just to watch the clouds. And yet—it's that energy that makes us magnetic. Joy is expansive. Creativity is healing. And wonder is a portal back to our true, authentic selves.

So, let's try on a few questions to awaken joy and play again:

- What did I love doing as a kid that I haven't done in years?

- What am I curious about right now? Could I try it just once?

- Where can I be a beginner again without pressure?

Now that you've stirred those questions awake, don't just leave them in your head—let them guide you into motion. Joy, play, and creativity aren't just things we remember; they're things we reclaim by doing. You don't need a grand plan. You just need a moment of permission. So if even one answer sparked something in you, follow it—gently, curiously, like you're letting life surprise you again. Joy and creativity are not the reward for getting it all right. They are the path to getting back to who you really are. And that's what makes you radiant.

Here are a few practices to reignite your creativity and wonder:

Joy Journaling
Each night, write down three small things that brought you joy—no matter how tiny. Let your brain start to learn how to scan for beauty.

Creative Curiosity Day
Take yourself on an artist date—go to a museum, take a pottery class, visit a thrift shop, try a recipe you've never made. Let your hands move without a goal.

Play Without Purpose
Do something silly or spontaneous. Swing on a swing. Color outside the lines. Let yourself be delightfully inefficient.

ABUNDANCE VS. SCARCITY

Abundance doesn't start with having more. It starts with being more —more open, more trusting, more aligned. Scarcity whispers, *"It's not enough. I'm not enough. What if I never get what I want?"* But expansion says, *"There's so much waiting for me. I don't need to grasp or chase. I just need to align."*

Radiance and abundance go hand in hand. When you're fully yourself—unapologetically, deeply, and vibrantly—you naturally attract people, opportunities, love, and success. *Why,* you ask? Because authenticity is *rare*. Presence is magnetic. And you're no longer striving to be chosen—you're choosing *yourself*. When you cling too tightly to one vision, one person, one outcome, you narrow the field. You tell life, *"Only this thing. Only this way."* But abundance flows where openness lives. And often, the love you crave, the career you dream of, the friendships that feel like home—they come wrapped in packaging you didn't expect or couldn't even begin to imagine.

Here are some signs you're trapped in a scarcity mindset:

- You feel urgency, pressure, or fear of missing out.

- You compare yourself to others constantly.

- You fixate on what you don't have instead of what's already working.

Here's how we can practice shifting into expansion:

Practice presence.
Right now, in this moment, what do you already have that once felt like a dream?

Say yes to newness.
Try saying yes to one thing this week that feels expansive—even if it's a little outside your comfort zone.

Hold desires with an open palm.
You can want something deeply and still trust that life will deliver what's meant for you.

Try these ways to attract love, success, and opportunities effortlessly by welcoming abundance:

Own your energy.
The more authentic you are, the more life responds with aligned matches. You're not here to please—you're here to *be*.

Expand your receiving capacity.
Practice receiving compliments without deflecting. Can you accept help or support without guilt? That's abundance.

Speak life into your future.
Talk about your dreams like they're on their way. Because they are.

There is no one path to love. No one version of success. No single route to fulfillment. But there is one essential ingredient: *You.* Fully and wholly expressed. And when you're living in alignment with your truth, abundance can't help but find you.

PROTECT YOUR RADIANCE

Your radiance is not a performance. It's your essence. But that doesn't mean the world will always celebrate it. In fact, the brighter you shine, the more you may notice subtle (or not-so-subtle) cues to tone it down. It can show up as micro-corrections, backhanded compliments, silent judgments, or cultural messages that say, *"Don't be too much."* But here's the truth: You are not too much. You are just enough for the life you were born to lead. Your light just disrupts things. And that's exactly what it's supposed to do.

So let's talk about how to protect your radiance—not from a place of defensiveness, but from reverence. This is about honoring yourself even when others don't.

Know the cost of dimming.
Every time you shrink to make someone else comfortable, a piece of your truth goes quiet. You become harder to recognize— even to yourself. Dimming may seem like self-preservation, but

long-term, it erodes your sense of self. Protecting your radiance is an act of self-trust.

Stay rooted in your body.
When you feel that urge to contract—whether in a meeting, a date, or a conversation—come back to your breath. Straighten your spine. Plant your feet. Reclaim space.

Let "no" be a sacred word.
Every "no" is a boundary that reinforces your light. You don't need to explain or justify it. If something dims you, dishonors you, or drains you—it's a no. And in saying no, you make space for more yeses that align with your soul.

Surround yourself with people who reflect your brilliance.
Build relationships where your joy, your vision, your voice, and your dreams are not only welcomed—but celebrated. These are the people who won't ask you to shrink. They'll ask you to rise.

Create rituals that nourish your glow.
Whether it's morning sunlight on your face, dancing in your kitchen, journaling your dreams, or simply saying kind things to yourself in the mirror—your radiance grows where it's nurtured.

You don't need permission to be seen. You don't need to earn your space. You are not here to be small. You are here to shine.

As we close this chapter, I want you to remember one simple truth: *You are the light.* No one can take that from you. It is your birthright, your essence, your true self. You are the one who creates your life, moment by moment, choice by choice. And the more you embrace who you truly are—without apology, without hesitation— the more the world around you will reflect that truth. This is the magic of living radiantly: *the more you stand in your full brilliance, the more the universe will conspire to make space for your light to grow.*

When life feels overwhelming, when it feels like you're being pulled in every direction, or when you get distracted by doubt or fear, remember: *you are the light you've been seeking to guide you.* You don't need to search for it outside of yourself. It's always been here, inside you, waiting for you to come back home to it.

Life is an ongoing process of growth, healing, and coming back to yourself. It's not a destination, it's a journey. One filled with both breakthroughs and setbacks, ebbs and flows, highs and lows. And through it all, *you remain the constant*—radiating your unique energy, your gifts, your love, your truth. The journey is never finished. It will always be about becoming more of who you were always meant to be.

You will fall, and you will rise. You will have moments of doubt, but you'll also have moments of deep self-belief. You'll have times when you shine brighter than ever and times when you feel clouded by external pressures. But through it all, you will always return to your radiant self, because that's where your power lies. You are meant to shine, and nothing can stop that. Not the world, not other people, not your past.

The only thing standing between you and your brightest life is your choice to show up fully, unapologetically, and with grace.

As you step into each new day, remember that your light is an ongoing process, *a daily practice.* And as long as you keep choosing it, you will continue to rise, to grow, and to shine with ever-increasing brilliance.

You are the light. And this, *this is your radiant life.*

CHAPTER 22: IN CONCLUSION
The Beginning of Your Most Radiant Life

AS I FINISH writing this book, I look back at the shell of my past self, and it feels like a lifetime ago—a different era. There was a woman back there, one who was shedding her skin, a woman who didn't know how to love herself or where her life was going. Even who she was on the inside. That woman, in many ways, is dead. She doesn't exist anymore, and the people who once knew her would probably no longer recognize who she has become today.

But you know what? I don't think that's a bad thing. There was no eulogy for my past self, no grand ceremony to mark her passing. But in many ways, this book has served as her reckoning, a tribute to the girl who used to lie on her floor, drunk and tearful, wondering why the world seemed to overlook her. I remember those nights vividly—the feeling of loneliness, the desperate question: *Why doesn't anyone love me?*

And the answer, the one I could never have seen then, is so simple now. I never asked myself, *Do I love me?* If I had asked that, if I had had the courage to look inside and offer myself the love I was so desperately seeking elsewhere, I don't know what my life would look like now. Maybe I would have been ten years ahead in some way, but I can only imagine. I've come to learn that self-love is the foundation for everything else—every step, every choice, every evolution that follows is built upon those bricks.

So now, as I reflect on where I stand today, I realize that I have become the woman I once longed to be. The love I once searched for in other people, I have begun to build within myself. I am both the woman I've been searching for and the love I've been seeking. It is a constant, unfolding process. Every day, I build it anew. And so will you.

You now have your invitation—right now, at this very moment. Take all the pain, all the questions, all the hiding, all the shrinking you've done in your life. Take it all and look at it, face-to-face. And with all the courage you can muster, say to yourself:

There is another way.

I am ready.

I am ready to step out of the shadows.

I am ready to live in the light of my true self.

You don't have to have it all figured out. You don't have to be perfect. You don't even have to know where this journey will take you, but you must choose it. You must choose *you*.

Because you are the radiant woman you've been searching for. You always have been. So, step into your power, step into your light, and never look back. This is just the beginning of your most radiant life.

ACKNOWLEDGMENTS

To the wonderful women at Light Warrior Publishing, Donna, Ashley, Liberty and Missy—thank you for believing in this book and refining it with such care.

To my mentor, Stella, for guiding me through the valleys of imposter syndrome and cheering me through the climbs.

To my beta readers—Brittany, Angela, Lakshmi, Lindsey, Meghan, Io, and Jenna—your feedback, encouragement, and willingness to walk alongside me gave this book its strength and clarity.

To my women's group members, thank you for being my practice ground for confidence, authenticity, and leadership.

To Criss—the universe placed you in my path at exactly the right time. From that first podcast conversation where we said, "me too," I knew our connection was something rare. Thank you for your friendship and for gifting this book with such a magical, soul-stirring foreword.

And to every Radiant Woman in the process of becoming—thank you for allowing me to witness your light and shine mine more fully in return. This book exists because of all of you.

ALSO BY CELESTE CASE-RUCHALA

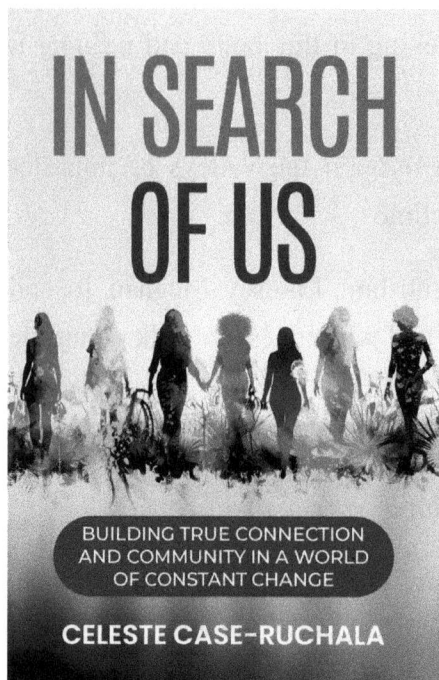

A heartfelt exploration of what it means to seek, build, and sustain meaningful relationships. Designed for women seeking a space for connection, growth, and shared wisdom.

Explore upcoming groups, workshops, and retreats.
Together, we heal louder.

ABOUT THE AUTHOR

CELESTE CASE-RUCHALA is a life coach, speaker, and the radiant voice behind *Becoming the Radiant Woman*. With a background in performance and a calling toward deep transformation, she creates spaces where women can return to their fullest expression— boldly, bravely, and without apology.

She is the founder of multiple women's groups in the Pacific Northwest, where she curates meaningful experiences for connection, growth, and self-discovery. Her work blends emotional depth with practical empowerment, helping women rediscover their voice, rebuild self-trust, and reconnect with the joy and power they've always carried.

Celeste is also the author of *In Search of Us*, a moving exploration of identity, belonging, and the desire to feel truly seen. Whether through her writing, coaching, or speaking, her mission is clear: to help women come home to themselves and live lives that feel like truth in motion.

How to Connect with Me:

Website: www.myhealingisyourhealing.com
Instagram: @myhealingyourhealing
TikTok: @myhealingisyourhealing
Podcast: *My Healing Is Your Healing* (new episodes every Monday)

Why I Wrote This Book

THERE COMES A moment when you look at your life and realize you've been living it for everyone but yourself. That moment came for me when I was supposed to be planning the happiest season of my life. Instead, I felt empty—lost in yeses I didn't mean, disconnected from the woman I once knew. That ache forced me to change.

Like many women in seasons of self-discovery, I grabbed at anything—books, podcasts, workshops—hoping for a quick fix. But what I found missing was honesty. Authenticity. Not enough people were sharing the real stories of how they healed, the messy middle, the moments of self-abandonment, and the climb back into self-trust.

I wrote this book because healing is not meant to happen in isolation. Healing is collaborative. It happens when we bear witness to each other's stories, when we see ourselves reflected in someone else's becoming, when we realize we are not alone in the struggle or the breakthrough.

My process may not be your process, but if these pages remind you that you are not broken, that you are not behind, and that you too can live as the radiant woman you were always meant to be— then this book has done what I hoped it would.